PRAISE FOR LAURA KASINOF AND DON'T BE AFRAID OF THE BULLETS

"Well written . . . essential reading for anyone wanting to understand the details of events during this historic year in Yemeni politics."

—*British-Yemeni Society Journal*

"This is a beautifully written, highly personal account of a young journalist's experience with revolution and war in Yemen. Kasinof offers a revealing portrait of the lives and work of a rising generation of young journalists at a time of urgent and perplexing changes. She weaves together their stories with a compelling account of Yemen's ambiguous revolution as witnessed by one of the few Western journalists on the ground. It is a gripping, thought-provoking read about how the news is really produced in today's turbulent Middle East."

—Marc Lynch, professor and director of the Institute for Middle East Studies, George Washington University

"A fast-paced journey through the Yemeni uprising that began in 2011, by someone who witnessed much of it firsthand. Kasinof offers a welcome corrective to the pervasive view of Yemen as an incubator of terrorism and little else, showing the humility, humor, and grace of ordinary Yemenis as they attempt to navigate fiendishly challenging circumstances."

—Sarah Phillips, the University of Sydney, author of *Yemen's Democracy Experiment and Yemen and the Politics of Permanent Crisis*

"As I was anxiously watching the political situation in Yemen unravel and become more dangerous in the years leading up to its Arab Spring, there was one reporter whom I read with interest and confidence, and that was Laura Kasinof. She clearly knew Arabic well, was familiar with the local scene, and talked to more than the 'usual suspects' when she wrote up her columns. To produce that kind of nuanced reporting required a person of tenacity and ingenuity, a true force of personality. This memoir provides us with a fascinating glimpse into both those turbulent years and the kind of fearless reporting it took to render them intelligible."

—Steven C. Caton, Khalid bin Abdullah bin Abdulrahman Al Saud Professor of Contemporary Arab Studies, Harvard University

"Laura Kasinof has written one of the most fascinating books about Yemen. It paints an excellent portrait of the country's politics and society. Just as it was essential to read Kasinof's reporting in 2011 to keep up with Yemen's revolutionary news, it is essential to read *Don't Be Afraid of the Bullets* to understand and capture the fuller and more complete picture of Yemen."

—Farea Al-Muslimi, journalist, activist, and a 2013 Foreign Policy Leading Global Thinker

DON'T BE AFRAID OF THE BULLETS

DON'T BE AFRAID OF THE BULLETS

AN ACCIDENTAL WAR CORRESPONDENT IN YEMEN

LAURA KASINOF

ARCADE PUBLISHING • NEW YORK

Memoirs by definition are written depictions of events in people's lives. They are memories. All the events in this story are as accurate and truthful as possible. Some names and places have been changed to protect the privacy of others. Mistakes, if any, are caused solely by the passage of time.

First Arcade paperback edition 2016

10 9 8 7 6 5 4 3 2 1

Names: Kasinof, Laura, author.
Title: Don't be afraid of the bullets : an accidental war correspondent in Yemen / Laura Kasinof.
Description: First Arcade paperback edition. | New York : Arcade Publishing, 2016.
Identifiers: LCCN 2015047263 (print) | LCCN 2015051041 (ebook) | ISBN 9781628726480 (pbk. : alk. paper) | ISBN 9781628724455 (hardcover : alk. paper) | ISBN 9781628726879 (ebook)
Subjects: LCSH: Kasinof, Laura. | Yemen (Republic)--Politics and government--21st century. | Protest movements--Yemen (Republic)--History--21st century. | Americans--Yemen (Republic)--Biography. | Foreign correspondents--Yemen (Republic)--Biography. | War correspondents--Yemen (Republic)--Biography. | Yemen (Republic)--History--1990---Biography. | ?San??a? (Yemen)--Biography. | ?San??a? (Yemen)--Description and travel. | ?San??a? (Yemen)--Social conditions--21st century.
Classification: LCC DS247.Y48 K38 2016 (print) | LCC DS247.Y48 (ebook) | DDC 953.305/3--dc23
LC record available at http://lccn.loc.gov/2015047263

Cover design by Brian Peterson
Cover photo credit Laura Kasinof

Printed in the United States of America

For the *shabab* from the media tent

For Ibrahim and Chris, I wish we could laugh together about these stories, and more

AUTHOR'S NOTE

After moving back to the United States from my home in Sanaa, I wondered at times if I would have been better off had I left Yemen before the turmoil of 2011—if I had not experienced the heartache or grown more cynical. I know now that this is not the case. To debate such options is a luxury, and to be able to pop around the globe and be welcomed into foreign lands is a privilege. I took this for granted when I first went to Yemen. That is to say, I feel privileged, blessed, and honored to have had the chance to live a portion of my life with Yemenis, through the good times and bad, and to have been brought into that endless delight with which Yemenis approach life. The Romans knew what they were doing when they nicknamed Yemen "Happy Arabia." I am lucky to have experienced some of that happiness myself.

I want to briefly touch on what this book is, and what it isn't.

This is not a step-by-step account of what happened in Yemen in 2011 during the height of the so-called Arab Spring and after, so it should not be read as such. I leave parts out. I stress parts that probably aren't crucial to the larger story of the uprising and presidential transition. Rather, I hope readers can learn about a place that isn't as black and white as Western rhetoric sometimes leads one to believe, and come to understand that there is a richness to Yemen that cannot be expressed in a two-minute clip on the news about al-Qaeda. I hope that those who are interested in

Yemen and the Middle East more generally learn some of what happened behind the scenes during this decisive year in the country's modern history. For those who dream of someday becoming a freelance foreign correspondent, I hope this provides one glimpse of what that world is like. Although it is, of course, far from the only glimpse.

Also, I need to stress that I am not an academic. Right now the academics in the crowd are saying, "Clearly you aren't," and will be saying that even more after they finish this book. The fact that I am not an academic means I do not use any one system for transliterating Arabic words into Latin script. I know that some of you will hold your heads in disgust at this, but I find official systems of transliteration difficult to decipher for those not familiar with the language, and I don't want that. So instead of abiding by anyone else's rules, I go by my own.

Lastly, this book has been a personal endeavor and by default will be different from my previous work as a reporter in which I strove everyday to remain neutral. Any opinions that reveal themselves in these pages are not reflective of the entity that was employing me as a freelancer during 2011, the *New York Times*, and do not appear in my reporting while I was in Yemen. That said, I hope readers find that this book supplements my reporting and vice versa.

Thank you so much for going on this journey along with me.

SAUDI ARABIA
OMAN
YEMEN
Saada
Amran
Sanaa
Marib
Shabwah
Al Hudaydah
Red Sea
al-Mukalla
Arabian Sea
Ibb
Taiz
Mokha
ERITREA
Zinjibar
Aden
Gulf of Aden
DJIBOUTI
SOMALIA
ETHIOPIA

Preface to the Paperback Edition

At a popular cafe near downtown Beirut, I met a friend who had just arrived from war-torn Yemen. At a time when smart, moderate voices in Sanaa were being snuffed out, there was certainly reason for him, a politically active journalist, to leave.

Despite what he had just been through fleeing war, my friend was in a positive mood, laughing and reminiscing. I wouldn't expect anything different from a Yemeni. They are strong as stone. I know this all too well: I spent nearly three years living in the country as a reporter during times of peace and war—but that war was not like the one currently raging, in which Arab neighbors are dropping bombs from above, in which forces from within claw one another with a new ferocity.

Abdu Rabbu Mansour Hadi's presidency was a failure, and Ali Abdullah Saleh never stopped conniving after he relinquished his role. The Houthi rebels, an Iranian-supported militia from northern Yemen, made an alliance with the ex-president and took over Sanaa in the fall of 2014. This ignited the fury of Saudi Arabia, which, along with an alliance of other Arab nations, began a war with the Houthis in March 2015. The average Yemeni has suffered the most.

It hit me, as I was talking to my friend, that he is a refugee. The word has become so loaded, the label so definitive, that I didn't want to use it.

He's not a refugee. He's my friend. But to the rest of the world he was a statistic, part of the first wave of Yemenis fleeing their country as it crumbled, brought down by conflict from the outside and from within. Yemen's unraveling was a truth about my former home—a home I loved dearly—that I had been loath to admit.

A few years ago, when the world started to realize that the wave of anti-regime protests spreading throughout the Arab world may bring more destruction than our hopeful energy was ready for, I happened to cross paths with another friend in Washington. He was an American who had spent a year teaching English in Homs, Syria.

President Bashar al-Assad's regime had begun its brutal attacks on the city relatively early in the Syrian war. I asked my friend, "Have you talked to people you know in Homs? How do you deal with all of this?"

"Honestly," he answered, "I just don't think about it. I block out that I lived there. I tried to get in touch with people at the beginning, but I didn't hear back from them, and now I don't want to think about it."

That's awful, I thought to myself. I'm better than that. I'm better than him.

But then I sat in a taxi in Beirut when news about Yemen aired over the radio, and I told the driver to turn it off. He probably thought I was crazy, but I couldn't care. I didn't want to hear about the war in Yemen in a one-minute audio clip. I didn't want to hear about it at all.

I have written before about my love for Yemen, how I enjoyed my years living in Sanaa. I even wrote this book based largely on that theme. At lectures on Yemen, Americans often seem surprised that I could have positive memories about Yemen. They are surprised at what life was like for a twenty-something American woman in a country that they were told is nothing but a messy knot of extremism. I've watched people refuse to believe me when I said that Yemenis couldn't help but ooze kindness to foreigners in their country. These Americans think I'm the delusional one, not them. "When are people over there going to stop choosing weapons over everything else?" a man once asked me during a Q&A, and he was a medical doctor.

The truth is, if you are a foreigner who has lived in Yemen, you have worried that this day would come, when the country would burst into conflict, because it always seemed possible, not because of an inherent violence in Yemenis, but because of fraught geopolitics and a clash of old traditions—many of which are beautiful—with the reality of the modern world. But I, the foreigner, lived there anyway, because in Yemen I could forget the anxieties that weighed me down in America, because I didn't have to worry about fashion or productivity. In Yemen my concerns were human relationships because those are Yemenis' concerns. I lived there because it was fun and because Yemenis became my friends. I lived there because it made sense for my career and I was able to find purpose in writing the news.

Then the nightmare came to life in 2015 and Yemen did devolve. And though it was not unexpected, I had never thought about how I would handle it when it happened.

When the war that still rages in Yemen began—when Saudi jets started bombing Sanaa—part of me wanted to forget that the city being reduced to rubble had also been my home. It ruined my day to worry about how the lives of people I once lived among were in danger. Worse, it sent my already burned-out nervous system reeling. Maybe people I know are doing the killing. What good does it do to dwell on all of that? I didn't want to watch the city I loved get bombed by a foreign force, or watch other cities I loved, Taiz and Aden, be desecrated from an internal force, the Houthis. I didn't want to be aware of just how hard it will be for the country to come back from this, not just because of the bombs but also because of retaliatory fighting and killing. Yemen is leaderless, and the Saudis and other Arabs bombing the capital view Yemenis as less than themselves, not unlike how Americans viewed Arabs at the height of the Iraq war. It's okay if they die like that. They are not our equals.

My situation while living in Yemen was easier than that of most Yemenis—I could afford the rising prices, I could leave the country whenever I chose to. But I did experience some of life as an equal to my neighbors. I felt fear when the shelling started. I felt hope when peace was near. The war affected my life, too. Now I don't feel any of the things they feel. I can only feel sadness that a beautiful place is suffering. Without living alongside Yemenis to see their strength in times of war, all I see is destruction, and I'd rather not see that.

Now, my friends are scared while I am not. I can fly to Europe without immigration questioning me, and they can't. I don't have to sit awake in my house at night knowing that at any time a Saudi or Houthi bomb might hit my house, and I'll die instantly along with my family. I don't have to worry about when a rebel militia will release my kidnapped father.

I could carry this burden. It could weigh me down. It probably does. Part of me wants to rely on the excuse that I am not Yemeni and that it is not my problem, that I need to focus on the life that is before me and not find myself floundering in the past. Part of me thinks I should sit and call my friends in Yemen every day and pay limitless attention to every detail of the war. Part of me is guilted by what I should do.

If I was truly noble, I'd go back to Yemen and report. That was the person I used to be: someone who watched too many superhero movies growing up and wanted to find the ways that I could save the day as well. But now I'm older, married, and aware that as an only child, I have a duty to my aging parents. I realize now it's not so easy to be a hero.

Shouldn't I also have a duty to Yemenis, who have gone out of their way for me time and time again? Yes, I should. This kind of guilt will eat you alive.

When I saw my friend in the Beirut coffee shop, denial was no longer possible. This thing I had tried to escape was staring me in the face—there's a war in Yemen, and that's why you, oh friend, are right here in front of me. A wall broke, or at least shifted. I felt restless faced with my futility. I felt guilty because of my ignorance.

I fought these feelings by traveling to Djibouti to record refugees' stories, but I went also because I thought it would be a way for me to stop willfully ignoring the fact that war is destroying Yemen. I still couldn't bear to look at photos of bombed buildings in the Yemeni cities Sanaa, Aden, and Taiz, let alone those of the dead bodies left in the streets. I wrote an article about Yemeni refugees who had fled to Djibouti by boat for an American magazine, but I did it all for myself.

It worked. In Djibouti, I sat on the floor all day, chewing qat with Yemenis, and heard that the home I once lived in and loved, that had taught me to be a good person, didn't exist anymore. More so, I saw the chips in the stone. As an outsider, I had idealized the integrity of Yemenis and their tribal codes. But now I saw that they are people just like me. I could no longer deny this war.

After that, when my partner, Austin, wanted to read me a part of the novel he's writing, my thoughts drifted back to Yemen. When he reminded me of why I loved him, my thoughts drifted back to Yemen, and I couldn't reconcile the two loves, the one I felt for Austin who makes me laugh and the one I felt for a place that had once made me laugh and that now makes me cry. It felt impossible to hold on to both at the same time. When living through a war, one clings to love because it is so needed. But now I'm not living through a war. I'm just watching it on television.

Soon it became old news that Yemen is overrun by violence, that children are dying, and the hospitals are understocked, and the snipers are killing, and there is not a peaceful solution so why get your hopes up? The funny thing—ha ha—is that Yemenis are getting used to the war too. But no one should have to get used to this. That's the thing about the human spirit. It's so incredibly adaptable. I almost wish it weren't.

There was a TV station in the Arab country where Austin and I were living that played nothing but images of dead Yemenis, and after Djibouti, I would sit and watch it. I wanted to feel something when I did. I felt nothing. I could watch it forever. I only switched away because I didn't want Austin to see.

Yemen is becoming just one of those wars that happen in the far-off distance of American consciousness that a few well-read, internationally minded people keep up with here and there. Look at people dying in Yemen! Look at them! Children are dying! But children are dying everywhere, children are dying in the Mediterranean on the path to Europe, and why should I expect an American to care about Yemeni children in particular?

I could list the reasons, but I think readers can find them for themselves.

There are characters in this book who have passed away. There are characters in this book who are right now imprisoned by the Saleh-Houthi regime. There are characters in this book who are now refugees. That's what life has turned into in Yemen. There are Yemenis whose names aren't mentioned in these pages, who I had the privilege of sharing life with for a few years, who are suffering from a war that no one in the international community is standing up against. Did we know it could get this bad? Can it get worse?

I hope these pages show how it all came to be this way, via the lens of one young American woman who traveled to Yemen for all the wrong reasons, to find herself writing about the country for the world's most famous newspaper, who now yearns, more than for anything else, to one day return to Sanaa, to Taiz, to Aden, to all the places I have yet to visit, to a Yemen at peace.

DON'T BE AFRAID OF THE BULLETS

CHAPTER I

I slid into a taxi for my daily commute, the road to Change Square. It was a Friday around noon, and Sanaa's dusty streets were quiet, small appliance shops shuttered, restaurants closed, everyone praying.

I leaned my head against the taxi's backseat window, watching the outside world pass by while shielding my eyes from the sun. Sleep had become more elusive with each day. I just hadn't been able to drag myself out of bed early enough this morning to gulp down an extra cup of Nescafé. Now I regretted it. I looked down at my brown leather satchel and dug through it, making sure I had remembered to bring my cell phone. I caught a glimpse of my brittle nails, chewed from worry, and scolded myself for the nervous habit. So far, 2011 had not turned out how I had expected.

My friends, young journalists like myself, had been deported from Yemen a few days prior. The same threat hung over my head. During the last few weeks, I had seen people fire guns for the first time in my life, and those guns had been aimed at other human beings. I had never planned to cover conflict. Never dreamt of being a war correspondent. I was afraid of what the future would bring, but also believed in what I was doing. I loved Yemen and had the opportunity to write about the country for one of the most important newspapers in the world. The sense of purpose trumped fear. That's also how the protesters at Change Square felt, except some of them ended up dead. That sense of purpose had betrayed them.

It was March 18, 2011. Just over a month since former Egyptian president Hosni Mubarak had conceded power after mass protests swept through his country, jolting the remaining dictators of the Arab world. Inspired, Yemenis were taking to the streets in the thousands, more every day, calling for the resignation of their president, Ali Abdullah Saleh. They set up a city of blue and green tents in a part of Sanaa that had once been a busy thoroughfare, dubbed their sit-in Change Square, and protested, slept, prayed, and danced there for days on end. Occasionally, the Square came under attack from the army when the protesters tried to expand the sit-in, taking over new street blocks on Ring Road. Tear gas, water cannons, and at times live gunfire were shot at them. A handful of the peaceful protesters had died as a result. Yet this had only strengthened the protesters' resolve and attracted more to join them at the Square.

On this morning, I arrived at the sit-in's northern edge, concerned that at the main, central artery into the Square I would have run into government soldiers who would prevent me from entering as the government was trying to quell media coverage of the growing political dissent. I passed by a row of men, protesters, standing with their hands on their hips, elbow to elbow like a human chain, guarding the entrance and searching all those who entered for weapons. It had come as a surprise to us, the few foreign journalists in Sanaa, that Yemenis had insisted on peaceful resistance and that no guns be allowed inside the Square. Weapon use is endemic here ("A man isn't a man if he leaves his house without a Kalashnikov," a northern tribesman once told me), and so is conflict, the traditional dispute-solving mechanism. Blood feuds, tribal war, these were put aside upon entering the Square.

I was patted down by a tiny woman in a black *niqab* who stood next to the male gatekeepers. She giggled when my ticklishness made me squirm. I was dressed significantly less conservatively than Yemeni women in a long trench coat–like beige jacket that hung to my knees and a scarf around my neck. Yemeni women almost exclusively wore the long black *abayas* and thin black veils that covered their faces, the niqabs.

Making my way southward on Ring Road, I walked along the curb and passed by crowds of men with their colorful prayer mats draped over their shoulders, fringes blowing slightly in the wind. The communal

Friday prayer had just been completed, during which blocks full of men and women, prayer mats lined in a neat row, listened to a sermon delivered over a loudspeaker by an imam on the Square's central stage and performed the customary prostrations afterward. They had been doing this every Friday morning since the Square began.

Now it was time to protest, and the men around me were chanting in unison against their president—"*Ya Ali,* After Mubarak!"—with the sort of determination that made it seem that there was no question their president would be the next dictator to go, their voices blending together like a choir. On one side of the street, the large, deserted campus of Sanaa University sat behind a gray wall. On the other, there was a line of small stores and a rickety gas station that stayed open to serve the needs of those living at the sit-in. All around me, rows and rows of tents, either the type that are used for camping or large green tarps propped up with poles, had taken over the street.

I noticed a group of men had gathered in a circle along the side of the road. Their focus was on a handful of bouncing young boys, each launching himself into the air on a trampoline that had been erected at the Square that morning. The boys laughed and jumped in chaos, one springing into another with no regard for safety. The men surrounding the trampoline clapped their hands, cheering, goading them on with loud yelps. They were in their own world of merriment despite being in the middle of a large antigovernment protest. The sight made me smile. It reminded me why I enjoyed working here as a reporter after all, and some of the morning's anxiety dissipated. Yemenis sought to enjoy life, despite the hardships of their present situation—and they were so good at having fun.

Aside from the trampoline, I could see most men spoke amongst one another with furrowed brows, concerned eyes. Their attention moved from one area of the Square to the next, searching for any indication that the government was about to attack. Their protest chants were angrier today, underlined with tension. I knew they were expecting soldiers and their Kalashnikov-toting thugs to show up once again. Yet they were still here, protesting. In fact, there seemed to be more people at the Square than ever before, swarms of bodies had taken over this street for a mile. Some ten thousand came out. And they weren't just university students and civil society activists anymore; tribesmen from the countryside had started to come to Sanaa to join. They dressed traditionally, in floor-length white robes called *thobes*, with blue, gray, or brown suit jackets worn over them. A curved dagger—or *janbiya*, as it is known here—tucked securely into a wooden sheath decorated with rust-colored leather and intricately detailed silverwork, and then attached to the center of the men's leather belts, worn at the waist of the thobe.

A group of such tribesmen had surrounded me, an obvious Western reporter. They shouted in my face about how corrupt Saleh's family was, and how they couldn't get jobs, and how there was no electricity in their villages. Once one started talking, another felt like he had to tell his story as well.

"Okay okay, but I won't understand any of you if you don't speak one at a time," I said in Arabic as I reached into my bag and pulled out my spiral notebook and pencil. I was accustomed to this, the zealous verbal diatribes of protesters that spilled out whenever a Western reporter was present. But I was still eager to record. I felt they were the underdog and somehow I could help them. I was not afraid of the anticipated violence. Attacks on the Square had always been localized, and I had always been able to find safety. And anyway, I had great trust that a Yemeni would never intentionally hurt a foreign woman. That went against their honor code. The only Yemenis who broke such codes were al-Qaeda, and they lived in the southern deserts, far away from the capital.

"I want you to tell President Obama that we are not terrorists. That we want democracy just like you," one of the tribesmen shouted at me.

"Yes, yes," I said, nodding my head. I looked up to see the tribesman's unkempt hair, his wrinkled suit jacket, and his black-stained teeth.

As I was taking notes, I saw one tribesman turn his head to concentrate his gaze down the street. Then another did the same, until the collective attention of the crowd turned southward. Men pointed and murmured about a large cloud of smoke billowing to the sky on the southern end of the Square, about a half mile down Ring Road. We were all confused by what this could be. A car on fire? That's what happened last week. I needed to get down there to see.

A group of white-robed medics ran past me through the crowd toward the site of the fire and I jumped in behind them as people did their best to make way. One of the medics in the front shouted "*Isaf, isaf!*" "Emergency, emergency!" as if they were an ambulance rather than a handful of volunteer doctors and nurses on foot.

After we jogged a few blocks through the crowds of tents and men, a buzzing sound made us all look to the sky. A military helicopter descended near the Square's center stage, high enough that we couldn't see inside, but low enough that there could be no doubt that its presence had to do with what was about to happen. It hovered for a second, and then continued flying westward toward the surrounding mountains as protesters shouted insults to the sky, pumping their fists.

Before I could figure out where the helicopter was headed, my focus shifted down Ring Road again, to the more residential section of the street. My ears immediately recognized the sound of gunfire. Not just the occasional bullet like in the past, but a banging that crescendoed into a blanket of noise enveloping us. I could feel its reverberations in my chest.

For the first time since the start of the protests in Yemen, bullets rained down from the sky onto the large crowd of men and children who were just rolling up their prayer rugs. Snipers opened fire from the fourth and fifth floors of nearby brick residential buildings. It was one bullet after another, as if they were trying to pick off the protesters one by one.

Despite the onslaught, dozens of protesters did not run, but stood their ground. They defiantly took their positions in the middle of the street and yelled out to the men who were aiming assault rifles at their heads. They pulled their T-shirts up over their heads and faced the snipers with bare chests. A mix of adrenaline and conviction drove them to sacrifice their lives. This was the start of the massacre that would change the course of Yemen's history.

I pressed forward toward the gunfire because I didn't know how to draw the line between my inner desire to get to the story, to see what was happening, and keeping myself safe. The street, a four-lane road, was crowded with men. There was no clear directive as to what to do, whether to run away or stand ground, yet we all knew that the government had crossed the line and entered new territory of brutality. "This is Gadaffi!" one protester yelled, referring to Libya's draconian leader.

This was around the fifth time I'd been near gunfire in the past two weeks. I had grown used to it because a person can grow used to anything. I didn't grasp the severity of what was unfolding in front of my eyes because I didn't yet understand what fellow humans, fellow Yemenis, could do to one another. Yes, there was the bang of the gun, but no one expects that he will be the unlucky soul to take a bullet. And anyway, I thought that I needed to be there to do my job.

"*Ganasa*, there are *ganasa*," I heard the protesters telling one another. There are snipers. It was a new word for me. Snipers meant that we didn't know the source of the shots being fired. Snipers meant anyone could be a target.

About six men ran past me, eyes locked straight ahead, holding the edges of a bloodied blue-and-red checkered blanket, a blanket that had been inside a tent for warmth in Sanaa's chilly nights. Now it was holding a man whose face was pale white. His hands grasped futilely at his blood-soaked T-shirt, around his stomach, as if he couldn't believe what had just befallen him. Another group of men ran past, hauling another man in a blanket. He was already dead. I could see it in his eyes. His neck hung limply. Another blanket; the man inside just stared at the sky with a dull expression. I couldn't tell where he'd been shot.

I had already started building the wall that prevented me from being debilitatingly traumatized by all this. It was the wall that allowed me to report, to suspend a part of my humanity, the part that feels. The wall came so naturally, I didn't even know I was building it at the time. I suppose it's an intuitive defense mechanism. My brain knew that my body would not flee, that it must stay and be witness to tragedy, to men dying violent deaths. I knew I wouldn't run because that's not who I believed myself to be—a person who flees.

I had come to Yemen with the desire to be tough, the need to prove myself to some nebulous judge of the universe. The harder the situation was, the more I felt that I earned the right not to feel guilty for my privileged white American upbringing. But what if, in doing so, I put my well-being in jeopardy? It wasn't possible to realize that distinction in the moment.

Some of the Yemenis around me were panicked—a boy ran through the crowd holding his arms straight out in front of him, trying to force his hands as far from his body as possible. They were stained in someone else's blood. His face was contorted in shock and horror. Most others, though, stood their ground or continued walking toward the worst of the gunfire. A young man defiantly threw his arms up into the air, bellowing to the sky curses at his president.

It was as if with each bloodied body carried through, the crowd's resolve strengthened. Young and old, rich and poor, they were standing together, facing whatever may come. A protester patted another on the back. "Look," he said, pointing to the top of a nearby building where he thought there was a sniper. "God will hold them to account," another told a group of men, strangers brought together in this moment.

Then a whizzing sound, like a racecar zooming by. I instinctively understood what that meant. I realized I didn't even know from where the bullet had come.

That's not safe. So that means I'm not safe.

My thoughts were no more complex than that.

I searched the side of the street for a hiding place, a small alley to run down or a store that would open its doors to me, a foreign woman, someone whom Yemenis were always eager to protect. I saw a couple of Yemeni journalists ducking behind a large, rust-colored metal gate to my right. One motioned for me to join and I ran to them. We hid in a small frontyard of dirt, shrubs, and pavement that led to a four-story apartment building. I leaned the backs of my shoulders on our enclave's brown brick wall and inhaled deeply.

Finding rest in my new position of safety, I felt that part of what had just taken place had actually been fun, dodging gunfire, adrenaline pumping. I didn't know how easy it could be to become addicted to adrenaline. I wish someone would have told me that from the beginning.

I giggled nervously and looked around to engage with the other men hiding with me. An older male journalist was bent over at the waist, hands on his knees, panting. He glanced up, his eyes met mine, but he was far from smiling.

I turned back to peer out through the crevice between the garden's gate and wall into the street. I saw some men retreating from the gunfire, walking—certainly not running—back toward the center of the Square, but others pressed forward. One man dressed in tribal attire with round belly spilling out over his janbiya belt walked southward toward the carnage, chanting into a megaphone, "Don't be afraid of the bullets! Don't be afraid of the bullets!"

Don't be afraid of the bullets?

These were the Yemenis I had come to know, with whom I had spent life at the Square for several weeks. Were they brave or were they crazy? I didn't know, but I admired them.

Another bullet whizzed very close by, and I pulled back against the wall with a jolt, moving away from the door.

"Be careful," said a man's voice from behind me in clear English.

I turned to him. "I know," I said, wide-eyed, smiling.

"Are you a journalist?" he asked. He was tall, attractive, Western-dressed, and spoke English in a near flawless American accent.

I told him I was, and the man took out his camera to show me a video of when the sniper fire began just as prostrations ended. He showed me that a protester standing right beside him was shot in the head and collapsed to the ground.

"See, they are aiming for people with cameras. They were aiming at me, but hit him instead," he said.

I can't remember if I asked the man why he spoke English like an American. Even if I did, his answer wouldn't have been honest, and I wouldn't find out the truth about him for many months, during which hundreds would be killed violently, including this man's brother.

For now, we were just two strangers brought together in this moment, searching for safety in a massacre.

• • •

After about an hour, I felt it was safe enough to walk up to the mosque at the center of the Square that was being used as a field hospital. The shooting had slackened off to the intermittent bullet.

The mosque's frontyard, a square, barren, dusty space, was full of frantic protesters bringing in bodies, ambulances bringing in bodies, and bodies that hadn't yet made it inside the mosque lying in the dirt yard. The scene contradicted the defiance I had witnessed on the street. It all became less exhilarating immediately. Any fun that I was having earlier evaporated in that moment.

Volunteers guarded the mosque's gates, trying their best to only allow in medics, journalists, and victims' families. Inside the large foyer area, bodies were lying on the stone floor in no particular order, blood pools everywhere, limbs hanging at weird angles. There were far fewer beds than injured. Everyone had expected the government to resort to violence, but not at this level. I learned what death smells like because the air was rank with it. My mind immediately recognized the smell though I had never encountered it before. *This is death*, it told me. *And it has a dull stench.*

I searched through the congestion for friends. Had anyone I knew been injured or killed? I only found Salah, a young, skinny protester whom I had come to know in recent weeks. Salah was a know-it-all and stubborn, but sweet enough that it didn't matter. He was trying to help the doctors and had an empty look in his eyes, just doing what was required of him. This was not the time to reflect, but the time for urgent action. Work on adrenaline, suspend empathy. I wanted to hug him, but that would have been inappropriate in conservative Yemen.

All of these people lying on the floor were fathers, sons, brothers. These men had once been alive, smiling Yemenis—because Yemenis are a happy people, despite their poverty. They came to the Square because they wanted to peacefully pursue a better future for their country. Now they were dead. And death came so quickly. A bullet is a small thing, but it can steal a life in the blink of an eye. Fifty-three died that day, and around one hundred others were shot. All displayed before me. I had to step over them to avoid getting in the way of the volunteer medics who weaved around the bodies in blood-stained smocks, cursing their president—who had turned against his own people—under their breath. They tried to save lives, sending the most severe cases to a nearby hospital, unless there was no hope. An emergency surgery center was inside what had been the mosque's administrative offices to the left of the entrance. To the right were the doors that led into the mosque's main room, where usually men lined up side by side in neat rows for prayer, but where on this day dead bodies were laid side by side on the cold, tiled floor lining the wall, bandages covering their most gruesome wounds, a Quran placed on their chests next to a piece of cardboard on which their names were scribbled with a black marker.

I knew that there was a kind of tyranny in dictatorship that, as an American, I had difficulty fully understanding. But that it could be taken to this level seemed like a crime against humanity. *Why did this have to happen?* played on repeat in my mind and, looking at the faces of the alive around me, it seemed they were thinking the same. I didn't know the victims' histories; maybe the bloodied man before me writhing on the stone floor of the mosque had been a bad man. Maybe he beat his wife and abused his children. But that doesn't matter when you're watching someone die in such a needless way. Though he is a Yemeni man and I am a young American woman, though our histories outwardly are disparate, we are connected because we are alive, breathing the same air. But he was soon not to be, and I could not fully grasp the magnitude of what that meant.

Sadness choked me standing there, like a corset drawing ever tighter. Sadness because this death seemed so futile. I felt it would suffocate me if it weren't for the realization that, if I couldn't be a doctor, at least I could be a journalist—at least I could report.

I stood in the back corner of the mosque's prayer room and tried to speak slowly during a radio interview while connected to a producer in New York. In front of me was the scene of the dead, the injured, the medics scrambling, the guttural shouts of Arabic, the sunlight peppered with dust shining in through the windows. I felt as if I were watching it through a screen. How was this real? I could picture the office in Midtown Manhattan where the producer on the other line must be sitting.

"There were several instances of snipers shooting protesters from houses that are just outside the demonstration," I said for the interview, trying to speak slowly and calmly. "There were a lot of people shot in the head today. A lot of people shot in the head and neck."

• • •

In the mosque's frontyard, on my way out of the field hospital, I ran into a friend, Hassan al-Wadhaf. Hassan was a Yemeni cameraman for a production company that works with a number of international news outlets. He and I had worked together on a project for ABC News a few months prior. Hassan was reserved, but subtly funny. I found him quite endearing, like the shy kid in class who never gets any attention but should.

A few tears were running down Hassan's cheeks. He just looked at me and shook his head. We were witnesses to tragedy together. Hassan always filmed from the line of fire. It seemed that he too believed deeply in the purpose of his work.

I passed through the front gate of the mosque and made my way back down to the south end of the Square, where the shooting had finally stopped and a few hundred men had gathered without any particular agenda except to express their outrage. I stood among them, barely balancing on that thin line between observer and participant.

A few blocks down from us, on the other side of the street, there was a unit of Central Security Forces (CSF) dressed in riot gear: dark green camouflage uniform, helmet, baton. Our ire was focused on their very existence. Blood and collapsed tents were on the street on our side of the road, and a water cannon truck and armored personnel carriers on theirs. The standoff reached its breaking point when CSF fired silver tear gas canisters into the crowd from their large barreled guns. The sound of a tear gas cannon is more of a deep thud than the bang of a rifle, and when the canisters they omit spew gray, smoky gas into the nearby air, each inhalation stings as if a thousand tiny sharp needles are poking the insides of your throat.

We all ran up Ring Road, coughing and squinting. But as soon as the air became remotely breathable again, we returned. Women who lived in the houses lining the street opened their windows and, holding black veils over their faces, dropped down slices of onion, which relieved the sting of the gas when held to the nose.

I became swept up in the protesters' rage, mine rising with theirs. I couldn't help it despite the need for a reporter's neutrality. Wasn't I allowed to be upset with a government that just shot more than one hundred unarmed protesters? I wanted to talk to all the men around me, to hear why they were angry, as if telling this to a reporter somehow offered a hint of vindication—for both of us.

"Tell me what happened today," I asked a man dressed in a long, light blue thobe, with a white *kefiya* draped over his shoulder, and a surgical mask hanging from his neck, a meager attempt at protection from tear gas.

"You know, we were praying Friday prayers, it is a sacred day for all Muslims, and then they begin to use the gunfire, firing at them directly," he replied in English, which is spoken only by the relatively few Yemenis who have enjoyed a formal education. "A lot of people praying in that corner over there," he pointed down to where a brick wall had been, "are getting killed. They killed them directly. They fired from that building," and then he pointed to the top of a nearby residential building, about six stories high. He went on and on. I couldn't get him to stop talking.

The protesters nabbed at least two of the snipers by breaking into the homes from which the deadly shooting came. I saw one of them being beaten bloody before he was dragged away and thrown in a temporary holding cell. Incensed, the protesters showed me the Ministry of the Interior ID cards they said they pulled from the sniper's pocket—proof of what few doubted any longer: that the Saleh regime was behind the day's slaughter.

After hauling off the sniper, protesters ransacked the building from which he was shooting, discovering that it was the Sanaa residence of the Governor of Mahweet, a district just to the northwest that used to be popular with the few foreign tourists who came to Yemen. They found a large bag with dozens of unused bullets in the house, as well as a blue binder apparently from the US government, which had the words STATE DEPARTMENT written in Arabic on its front along with the department's insignia. The last of the booty was a plaque noting that the Governor of Mahweet had been deemed the honorary mayor of Baton Rouge, Louisiana. The protesters held the plaque up in the air and paraded it down the street, though they had no idea what it was except that it came from America. This brought me a moment of respite, of amusement amidst the horror and anger.

Then the protesters set fire to the governor's house.

• • •

I spent a few more hours at the Square, though I didn't feel the normal passage of time. I glanced at the time on my cell phone and didn't understand how it could have become so late. For me, hours and minutes stopped existing that afternoon, because each second was so full of the extremes of life.

Back at the field hospital, news spread that the Yemeni government had just declared a state of emergency, though we didn't know what that meant. What does a state of emergency mean in a country with few state-enforced laws to begin with? The last time it was declared was during a civil war in 1994. But word got around fast once the news was broadcast on state media. In anxious voices, Yemenis passed on the information to whoever was standing around: "There's a *halat atawary* in place."

At this point, there were no other foreign journalists with me. I always preferred to work alone, not partnering with one of the few other young freelancers, but now I didn't want to take a cab back to the old city alone. Armed, pro-Saleh thugs were guarding the outer rims of the Square, and I was afraid of what their reaction would be to discovering a foreigner, one who had been among the opposition, the worst offense in their eyes. My trust was already waning. I called my fixer and friend Yasser, who worked at a local news organization, al-Masdar, which had an office nearby, and proceeded down Ring Road in its direction.

On my way to the office, I got a call from the *New York Times* correspondent who was co-writing the day's article with me. The story was already up on the website, written by others with me calling in the reporting. "So today sounds like a bad day," came the much older male voice on the line from America. I felt defensive. Did he think I couldn't handle this? I envisioned the editors of the foreign desk holding their heads in their hands in frustration at having to rely on an inexperienced twenty-five-year-old after the story in Yemen had taken such a violent and chaotic turn. I tried to clearly explain on the phone what had happened, but words spilled out of my mouth involuntarily. Was it coherent? It was difficult to care.

Along the few blocks I had to walk after leaving the territory of the Square, I saw men with AKs in their hands and angry expressions on their faces. Otherwise the residential street was eerily empty, the few small shops boarded up hours ago. I hurried to the door of the apartment building in which al-Masdar was housed and called Yasser to come downstairs and let me in.

This door had never been locked before, I thought. I glanced behind me, a stab of fear in my gut, though the gunfire had stopped hours ago.

Yasser opened the door part way to let me in, but first poked his head out to have a look at the surroundings.

"Today was bad, no?" he said as we climbed the stairs to the third floor. "Here, have some *qat*." He handed me a clear plastic bag full of the green leaves. Yasser had light brown hair, a receding hairline, and a mischievous and playful demeanor, which is why I enjoyed his companionship. We entered the office and walked across a short hallway to a side room where two other journalists, Hakim and Samir, sat atop thin cushions on the ground in the far corner.

"*Ya Laura*, today was a crime," said Hakim, the publication's main reporter, a stout and normally good-spirited middle-aged man. "Today was . . ." he moved his lips into a circle. "Ooof," he said, as if he got punched in the gut. Hakim looked at the bare wall for a second, then turned back to me. "This is Ali Abdullah Saleh."

What else could he say? Hakim went back to watching the Al Jazeera clips of the massacre on his laptop along with Samir, the publication's owner. I sat at one of the few office chairs in front of an old PC, tried to work out the Arabic keyboard, and pulled out tender leaves of the qat Yasser had given me.

Shooting to kill, as I would learn later, is an abomination to the unwritten code that governs Yemeni society. In northern Yemen tribal conflicts, the aim is rarely to kill the enemy. Men shoot their guns or RPGs above the heads of their enemies on purpose. Conflicts are there to display machismo, not destroy the opponent. Yet the Saleh regime resorted to extreme violence because of politics, because of fear their power was threatened. In the eyes of Yemenis across the country, that was what made this massacre more than just a massacre. That was also why Saleh would forever deny his involvement in the affair.

I chatted online with a fellow freelancer in Cairo because I needed to commiserate. We talked about how screwed up Arab dictators were, how I was afraid of being deported, and that I had just realized I didn't have any photo ID on me. We had a conversation that would seem cruel to a person who hadn't experienced conflict; we spoke of death in passing, because it was becoming our new normal. I was one dangerous step further down the road of bang-bang addiction. My adrenaline had spiked so high this day and danger had felt so close, yet I had survived. I could do this all over again.

Finally, around three a.m., after editing and phone interviews, tweeting and uploading, I fell asleep in a back room that was about as long as I was tall amongst boxes of old newspapers and some dirty blankets.

A few hours later, I tiptoed out of the office while the other journalists still slept, down the three flights of stairs, and found a cab on the nearly empty street that took me back to my home in the old city, almost always an oasis of tranquility, no matter if there was a war raging outside. I walked past my neighbors, who supported Ali Abdullah Saleh, waving hello, opened the heavy wooden door of my picturesque brown brick house with its white trim, and trudged up the stone steps, past intricate Arabic geometric designs engraved into its gypsum walls, a flaky white plaster. My mind felt hollow. My thoughts only extended to the bare essentials: sleep, eat, contact the foreign desk at the *New York Times*. Yet somewhere inside me, a seed of rage had been planted; a rage that, over the coming months, would at times make me hate, not a specific person, but a world that could be host to such atrocities against the innocent. I walked into my bedroom, fell down on my knees on the mattress, and sobbed.

CHAPTER 2

November 2008

Sitting at a high table inside a coffee shop in midtown Manhattan, I anxiously awaited what I hoped would be the writing on the wall, the advice to help me move from life's current rut. I wanted someone else to tell me what to do. I didn't want to have to figure it out for myself. I was waiting in one of those chain places with shiny desserts and stale croissants, nervously monitoring the door to see if Mona had arrived. New Yorkers walked in, bundled in long black or gray pea coats. It was a cold day. My palms wrapped around my coffee cup and I took a small sip so as to not scald my tongue.

A few minutes later, a woman with black hair that hung to her shoulders in tight curls walked through the door. Mona al-Tahawy gave me a big smile.

"Hi, Laura. Sorry I'm late," she said, taking a seat across from me. "How are you doing?"

"Well, how are you?"

"Good, good. Busy as always."

I had first met Mona, a prominent Egyptian American journalist-turned-activist, a year ago when I interviewed her in Cairo. It was for a story I was writing for a small English-language business magazine based in the Egyptian capital. Mona was one of the first people I had ever interviewed. I definitely didn't know what I was doing at the time. I had stumbled into journalism quite haphazardly after quitting a job as a kindergarten teacher at an international school in Cairo. Working as a copy editor for the business magazine just happened to be the first job that availed itself at the time. I had never before considered a career in journalism, but it had grown on me. I never thought I'd be one of those reporters who goes to press conferences and reports on breaking news and all those stereotypical things I saw about journalists in movies. Rather, I just liked telling stories.

I recently had run into Mona again at an Egyptian author's event at Barnes & Noble in Union Square. I saw her across the rows of folding chairs and approached her, praying she would remember me. She did. I asked her if she would be willing to meet me for a coffee. She agreed. And now here we were, a week later.

"So you're wanting to move back to Egypt?" she asked after turning down my offer to buy her a coffee.

"Yeah, or maybe Syria. Just somewhere where I can find work as a freelancer. But I'm worried that if I go to Syria, I'll get kicked out. But I kinda want to go somewhere new, you know?"

"That is a risk of working in Syria."

I explained to Mona my life predicament, thinking she would understand. My New York friends sure didn't. For them, New York was the proverbial city on the hill, the pinnacle of all professional aspirations, the best place a smart, hip, young person could live out their twenties.

For me, it was claustrophobic. New York represented a monotonous commute to the office, only to party on weekends with other young adults who were obsessed with making it in the finance, entertainment, or fashion industries. Then back to the grind on Monday.

I had withdrawn from a graduate program at the New School, a liberal arts university in Manhattan, that past September after being struck with the feeling that, for my life right at that moment, grad school was a waste of time. I was working two temporary jobs I knew wouldn't be going anywhere. I hid the fact I had left the master's program from as many people as possible because it made me feel like a failure, like I was someone who couldn't follow through on her commitments.

"I'm just trying to figure out if it makes sense to go back and freelance," I said to Mona. I missed reporting, I told her. I missed the way it made me feel tied to the larger world. I missed the process of looking for leads, and then once I found one, putting the pieces together to create a news story.

"Listen," she said. "Are you single?"

"Yes."

"If it doesn't work out, do you have a place to come home to?"

"Yes." I imagined living in my old bedroom at my parents' house. I'm an only child. Of course my mom and dad would let me move back in with them.

"Okay, so you're young, single, and have few commitments. There's a financial crisis here, and freelancing abroad is a much better way to get into journalism than here in New York, especially if you speak the language. If you want to be abroad, and you want to be a journalist, then I'd say do it."

"Yes, I do want to."

I was so relieved to be hearing this advice from a successful professional journalist. Mona had worked for Reuters. Reuters! I considered that an unattainable dream. I had written two stories for American publications while living in Cairo the past year, but that was such a far cry from a staff job at Reuters.

The truth was that I didn't want to figure out how to live life in New York. Going abroad could put that on hold. The social anxiety that bogged me down in America had practically disappeared when I was living in Egypt. There were bigger things to worry about there: safety, sexual harassment, debilitating air pollution, where to meet with guys because my landlord wouldn't allow someone from the opposite gender in our apartment of unmarried women. When I negotiated life successfully in Cairo, it made me feel all the better for it. I could thrive in Africa's largest city. A place many Americans would be afraid of going. *That must mean I'm tough and special,* I thought. I missed feeling special. I wasn't special in New York. I was indistinguishable from every other twenty-something living in Brooklyn. It would take until the new year, though, for me to make my move.

• • •

It was January 2009, and Barack Obama would be inaugurated as the first African American president of the United States of America two days after my arrival in Washington, DC. I had traveled down to the capital for the inauguration and, this night, was attending a house party with friends whom I'd met as an undergraduate studying abroad at the American University in Cairo. We all were Arabic nerds. Some of us worked for the government or international banks, others were academics. What brought us together was that we were fascinated with a part of the world that was often vilified in American culture—and this made us feel somehow braver, tougher, better than our peers. While we studied abroad in Cairo, militants in Sinai detonated a bomb in a beach resort that most of us had visited over spring break. We had watched riot police amass on a downtown Cairo street corner ready to attack a political demonstration of opposition supporters. The sense of adventure was addictive. Especially to me, which was yet another reason I felt called to move back.

"Laura! Hey!" My friend TJ greeted me with a hug as I walked through the door of his apartment.

"So glad you could make it. You're living in New York now?"

"Well, I'm just finishing up work for this author. I'm sort of figuring out stuff right now. I think I might move back to Egypt to work as a journalist."

I wanted to pretend my life was going just as well as I imagined everyone else's was.

"Sweet, that's awesome! Jeez, I miss it. You gotta look up Umm Ahmed when you get back there," he said of his old doorkeeper in a dilapidated, 1960s apartment building in Cairo's posh Zamalek neighborhood. Zamalek was on an island in the Nile. That's right: we used to live on an island in the Nile. Now I lived on Long Island.

"That's so cool that you're getting into journalism," TJ added. "I read some of the stuff you wrote in Cairo."

"Really?" I blushed. TJ recognized that I wrote about important issues. My friends in New York didn't.

"Yeah, that one about the Iraqi refugees. What was it again . . . ?"

"The refugees who were denied resettlement by the US government even though the reason they were refugees to begin with was because they were targeted for working for America in Iraq."

"Yeah, that's so messed up. God, I miss it."

A few hours later, I was chatting with Kyle, a friend who had gone to New York University with me and also studied in Cairo. We survived an Advanced Arabic class as seniors by studying countless hours in NYU's library while we retold each other stories of our Cairo escapades. Kyle was cool and collected, with well-kept brown hair. He was a good-looking straight man at NYU. A rarity, it seemed. In college, I had felt proud that he wanted to hang out with me.

Kyle told me he had recently spent a few months studying language in Yemen and Damascus after quitting some corporate job in Boston. I told him about my desire to move back to the region.

"It just makes more sense to work as a journalist overseas, you know?" I said.

"Dude, totally." He took a sip of his beer.

"I just don't know where I should move. I don't really want to move back to Cairo. Syria seems like the only other choice. There are too many freelancers already in Beirut."

"Dude," Kyle said, "go to Yemen."

I can still picture myself that night, standing in a living room that seemed impossibly big to someone who lived in New York. I can see all the people around me, chatting away, drinking beer, unaware that someone else's life in that room just changed course. I can still hear Kyle's words, clearly echoing in my head.

While thinking over the various locales in the Middle East where I could move, it had never occurred to me to try Yemen, though I had a few friends who had traveled or studied Arabic there. Kyle had nothing but praise for the country and its over-the-top hospitality. Another friend who had studied there, Emilie, said the same thing. She had bought a lighter in Yemen that projected an image of Saddam Hussein from a little light bulb on its bottom end. We used to bring it out at parties at the apartment where we lived in Cairo. Sadaam in his green uniform with a scowl and mustache would be surrounded in a halo of light.

I thought Yemen sounded like a great idea.

• • •

Six weeks later, I was on a plane to Sanaa. It never crossed my mind that, as a twenty-three-year-old woman, this move might have been a strange decision. I knew two Americans who were living in Sanaa; what else did I need?

I hadn't read anything about Yemen until this point. I didn't even know who the country's president was. It never crossed my mind either that was both stupid and completely irresponsible. I was going to try to represent this country to the Western world, and I didn't care to do any research about it prior to arrival. I was just happy to be moving away from my life in New York because to a great extent that's what this was about, escape.

My flight stopped in Cairo and I stayed for a few days to see friends. In the midst of all the excitement of catching up and telling everyone about the new adventure that lay ahead, an American friend recommended that I meet her Yemeni coworker, Atiaf al-Wazir. Atiaf had been raised in northern Virginia and hailed from one of the most prominent of northern Yemen's families. There's a photo of her grandfather at Sanaa's Military Museum right before he is to be beheaded, punishment for trying to stage a coup in 1948 against North Yemen's ruling imam. Though, I knew nothing about Yemeni coups during our encounter.

Atiaf and I planned to meet at Costa Coffee on Mohammed Mahmoud Street in downtown Cairo. It was busy, full of girls chatting away in bright *hijabs* and overdone makeup at tables that were annoyingly small, a Celine Dion song playing a little too loudly over their chatter. Atiaf sat amidst the crowd with long, thick, black hair and an angular profile indicative of her Yemeni roots. She looked like she was in her late twenties.

Atiaf began to explain Yemen to me. In a small notebook, she listed names with her pen that meant nothing to me at the time: President Saleh, his allies in the military, his opponents. She explained that Saleh liked to sell himself as a democratic leader, though he assuredly was not. I leaned over and looked at the names she listed in the notebook: JMP, Islah, Ahmar, Ali Mohsin. I became exhausted trying to sort through it all.

Yemen was desperately poor—the poorest country in the Arab world, Atiaf said—and its population chronically undereducated. Saleh did little to address these issues and instead stayed busy consolidating his family's power and growing rich off Yemen's limited resources, both of which were not easy tasks in a country of powerful tribal leaders, the sheikhs. I liked the idea that there were "sheikhs" in Yemen. It sounded so exotic. *If I can thrive in this faraway land, then that definitely would be braver than my peers, right?*

Atiaf told me that Saleh made friends out of enemies by providing them with financial perks or high positions within his government. He jailed or assassinated the rest, or sent them off to work in foreign embassies so they wouldn't be a nuisance to him in Sanaa. He was a very smart leader in some ways, but stupid in others. He underestimated his own people. He capitalized on their ignorance or their apathy toward politics to push forward his agenda, but that wasn't a strategy that could last him forever. At some point it would have to break.

Atiaf was incredibly kind and helpful, but I was distracted by thoughts of meeting friends at the grungy former communist bar in downtown Cairo later that night. Atiaf told me she was getting married soon to a Frenchman whom she had met in Cairo. *That all sounded nice,* I thought. *I wish I could meet a charming Frenchman abroad, but for now I'm moving to Yemen.*

• • •

My flight to Sanaa arrived very early in the morning a few days later. I descended the portable staircase rolled up to our plane's front door and stepped onto the tarmac. Sanaa's crisp air cooled my cheeks—the city is nearly 7,500 feet above sea level. Aside from our plane and another recently landed Turkish Airlines jet across the runway, the world around me was dark and still. Alarmingly so. I could make out the shadows of looming mountains in the distance.

Sanaa International Airport may be the airport of the nation's capital, but to me it resembled a sardine can. It was small, musty, and leaky around the edges. I stepped into the gloomy passport control hall, a square open room with plastic window-enclosed booths lining the front. Yemeni men shoved to line up behind the two booths manned by men in uniform. A group of poorly dressed Ethiopian women huddled in a back corner, waiting for their next move. The stern image of President Ali Abdullah Saleh was everywhere, on the walls and the wooden beam in the middle of the room. Wherever I stood it seemed that at least one pair of Saleh's eyes were noting my every move.

I walked up to a side window labeled VISAS in both English and Arabic to get an entry sticker, and then stepped across to one of the booths to get my passport stamped by a skinny man with a mustache. I appeared to be the only Westerner in the hall, apart from a blond European-looking man who seemed to be my age and didn't look too concerned with the world around him. His presence put me at ease. If he wasn't worried, then I didn't have to be worried. I looked to this stranger for guidance. Though he, as an apparent outsider, was not the person on whom I should be relying in Yemen.

Just past passport control, I waited in another line that led into a second room where an officer checked to see that I had indeed gone through the passport control that was less than ten feet away. Then I stepped up to an X-ray machine where I nervously placed my carry-on bag. There was a bottle of whiskey inside. I had been told this wouldn't be a problem by friends who had lived in Yemen, but I didn't trust their assurances. The two officers sitting behind the machine's monitor told me to open up my book bag after it had been scanned. I didn't say anything and did as told, stone-faced. A stern officer reached inside and pulled out my iPhone.

"What is this?" he asked in heavily accented English.

"My phone."

They attempted to ascertain the true nature of the object for a few minutes, ignoring the liter of whiskey.

It was then that a man approached me and introduced himself as Mohammed. He said that he was from the Arabic school where I would be studying. He was tall, long-faced, and slumped at the shoulders.

"Don't worry, don't worry," Mohammed said in Arabic after security guards took my passport into a small side office. We waited for the next twenty minutes in front of the room's solo conveyor belt that wound in a tight U-shape before depositing unclaimed suitcases on the floor. I wondered how Mohammed would have communicated with me had I not come with Arabic skills already. I wondered why the officials took my passport. I looked across the baggage claim area to the closed duty-free shop where shelves of Marlboro cigarettes and European chocolate sat untouched.

The whole scenario came across as gravely serious, yet void of any set order. The security officers responded to me just because they felt they should probably do something about a young American woman entering their country without a clear reason, but they weren't sure of exactly what that something was.

While waiting, I debated whether I should wrap the scarf I had brought in my carry-on over my head. The few other woman around me were veiled in all black and I felt uncomfortable. I half flung an end of the scarf around my hair, but then felt anxious with what the men around me must be thinking of my sad attempt at modesty.

The questions began to mount: where are our bags, where is my passport, and do I look like a whore? I had yet to learn that such concerns should be abandoned in Yemen. That the more I tried to be the one driving my own life, the more frustrated I would become. My life was not my own in Yemen. My life would move forward by some odd mix of chaos and fatalism that can only make sense in this very pious yet law-flaunting environment.

After thirty minutes, Mohammed and I exited the airport with all my things and got into a dented white car parked in a small parking lot. That's when my naivety truly came into its own. Despite it being the wee hours of the morning, I expected to see people out on the streets, as was typical in Cairo. I expected to see some signs of a capital city. Instead, all I saw were darkened buildings, closed store fronts, and the occasional man squatting along the side of the road for no clear reason, whose gaze would follow our car as we passed. Then we reached a long stretch of road where, outside my window, an open field of darkness expanded as far as I could see. The silence of the night would be interrupted occasionally when we passed through security checkpoints where soldiers shined flashlights into our car and mumbled something to Mohammed. Militants had (unsuccessfully) attacked a delegation of South Koreans just weeks before on the way to the airport. I wondered if we were on that same road and then why I would do something that put my life at such risk.

After about another twenty minutes we drove through what appeared to me more of a commercial district—there were bright yellow Arabic billboards advertising some cell phone provider and another boasting a smiling, dancing water drop. All the shops were small, one-room affairs, with just one or two floors of apartments or offices above them. Signs were almost exclusively in Arabic, except the few that had misspelled English like AL-SABAHI FOR BEST FORTNITURE.

We then descended into a road that appeared to run through some sort of gully. Mohammed drove faster here and I felt the tires slip slightly as we went around a bend. I now knew where we were. This was the only thing I recognized about Yemen. Rising to the sides above the road were the homes of the ancient walled city of Sanaa, a UNESCO World Heritage site that has been inhabited for more than two thousand years. They were tall and narrow, pressed together side by side, and many were slightly off-kilter, leaning in one direction or another. White gypsum lined the windows and edges of the homes' brown bricks like frosting. Before I traveled to Yemen, I found images of the old city of Sanaa strikingly beautiful, but in the shadows of night, their unique architecture only reinforced my feeling that I was far out of my comfort zone now.

We approached the location where I was going to be meeting Heather, one of the two people I knew living in Yemen at the time. I had met her a year earlier when she came through Cairo for a few days. Heather had moved to Yemen on a Fulbright scholarship, but after the American embassy in Sanaa was attacked by al-Qaeda in September 2008, the Fulbright program was canceled in the country. Heather, a Midwesterner, stayed in Sanaa and married her Arabic teacher, Abdullah. She adored Yemeni culture and found rest in Sanaa's slow pace. She and Abdullah offered to put me up when I first arrived, and Abdullah taught at the Arabic school where I was registered to take lessons.

The two of them were standing down on the edge of the *saila,* a beltway-like road that encircles the most ancient quarter of Sanaa, waiting for Mohammed and me. Illuminated by a light shining from the white dome of a nearby mosque, Heather was wearing a long black abaya, the type that conservative Muslim women wear. It hung down to her toes and her auburn hair was concealed in a pink headscarf. She smiled warmly.

Why is Heather dressed like that? I was instantly worried. I knew I was going to have to dress more conservatively in Yemen than I had in Egypt, but didn't think it would have to be like that. And more importantly, why on God's green earth does that Yemeni man have what appears to be a dagger stuck into his belt? I could see its hilt sticking up above his belly. *Does he use that on a regular basis?*

Abdullah stood there, dressed as any Yemeni would when expecting a guest. A finely pressed long white thobe, his curved janbiya tucked into his green belt, a tightly wrapped turban sitting atop his head. Abdullah presented himself as the authentic Arab man, yet that certainly was of no comfort to me.

Egypt is Westernized. Jordan is Westernized. Lebanon, for God's sake, is the Paris of the Middle East. But Yemen, oh Yemen, she dances to the rhythm of her own drum, with many parts still untainted by influence from the Western world. I hadn't thought that through before I arrived. I expected to see something I recognized, that I could frame with my past experience. Yet so far, Yemen was like walking into a world that I previously didn't know existed. A world that I was soon to learn was still full of guns and daggers, of arranged marriages and antiquated caste systems. But also a world of honor codes, filled with the utmost hospitality toward outsiders that rivaled that of the good Samaritan of Biblical lore.

Heather, Abdullah, and I walked down a narrow, silent cobblestone alley that ran between the tight rows of brown brick houses with white chalky trim outlining their windows. The pat of our footsteps were the only sounds in the night. The wooden doors to the houses were only about five feet tall. A streetlight from the main road around the corner cast a fading glow, but otherwise the way before us was dark and dusty. I gazed up at the houses' windows, randomly sized and placed, that led into the unknown world of Yemeni domestic life.

Heather and Abdullah stopped in front of one of the tiny entryways.

"This is it," Heather said softly.

I remained silent. We ducked to enter the building and climbed three flights of narrow stairs. Abdullah used a flashlight on his phone to light our path to the door of an apartment. Heather asked me to leave my shoes by the door before we entered.

"Well, here we are. It's small, but it's home."

She showed me the bathroom, a tiny tiled room with a Turkish-style squat toilet. The showerhead was practically placed above the white porcelain lining the hole in the ground. Next to the bathroom was a square, carpeted room with colorful cushions lining its wall.

"This is the *mafraj*," Heather explained. "It's where the chewing happens and, really, all of life. Every Yemeni home has one."

"Chewing qat, right?" I asked, pronouncing the first letter of the word as a deep, guttural "k" sound, according to its Arabic spelling.

Heather laughed. "Yeah, chewing qat." She pronounced the first letter like it was a "g," according to a Sanaani accent. "You'll do it soon enough."

"Abdullah and my room is down there, and then there's the kitchen," she pointed down the hall. "And here's your room."

Heather opened the door to a tiny spare room that was only adorned by a thin mattress on the floor, surrounded by plain white walls. I took my suitcase inside.

After saying our goodnights, I lay down and pulled the white sheet Heather had folded neatly on the mattress's edge over me, but couldn't fall asleep. I rolled over to my side and stared out into the darkness through the window. I tried to calm my thoughts, telling myself that all of this would sort itself out in the daylight.

Just then, violent screaming pierced the silence, echoing inside the apartment like a battle cry.

Allahu akbaru. Allahu akbaru. Ashahadu an la ela ila allaaaaaaah.

It was about five a.m., time for the early morning call to prayer. But this wasn't any call to prayer I was familiar with.

Everything in this country implied violence. Their dress, the call to prayer, the need for military checkpoints on the way into the city from the airport. I wondered why my friends loved it here so much.

I curled up in a fetal position and tried to forget where I was. I tried to push away the self-defeating thought that I never should have come to this country in the first place.

• • •

A few hours later, I set off into Sanaa with Abdullah, whose enthusiastic resolve to make me fall in love with Yemen made me feel slightly less worried. He had a round face, a happy-go-lucky smile, and a warm, charismatic demeanor.

"Are you hungry?" Abdullah asked me before stepping out the apartment's doorway. He had swapped his thobe and janbiya of last night for a button-up dress shirt and slacks.

"Yes," I told him.

He nodded. "Okay, *tamam.*"

I was wearing the most conservative clothes I had packed, a long tunic bought at a Himalayan shop in New York over linen pants, hoping that Heather was honest in her assurances that this was acceptable dress.

On our way to the Arabic school, we first passed the ancient stone mosque from which the night's screaming had emanated. It was a Zaydi mosque, place of worship for a division of Shi'a Islam that primarily exists in northern Yemen; many of its adherents in Sanaa live in the old city. The Zaydi call to prayer is much angrier sounding and less melodic than that of Sunni Islam, which I had come to know in Cairo and my travels in the Middle East—something else I now wished I had been aware of prior to my arrival.

We crossed a gray stone pedestrian bridge that arced over the low road that Mohammed had used to enter the old city the night before, the saila. Now it was jammed with traffic. The driver of a crusty white minibus leaned his torso out the window and hollered to the stalled cars in front of him. I supposed it was Arabic, but it didn't sound like any dialect of the language I knew. I was kind of unsure how it could have been anything but a sequence of prolonged grunts.

We followed a cobblestone street through the old city that at some points was wide enough for two cars to pass comfortably, and at others so narrow that a taxi scraped its rear view mirrors trying to squeeze through. Motorcycles roared by us. Tiny side streets cut out from this central road to the right and left. Down one I saw two short women chatting rapidly, one dressed only in an all black abaya and niqab and the other with her head draped in a red sheet decorated with blue, yellow, and white diamond and zig-zag patterns.

Doors that were as tall as my shoulders led into the old city's gingerbread house–like homes. On their third, fourth, and fifth stories glistened the red, green, and blue of stained–glass windows, like gumdrops, made of triangular geometric designs, laid out in semicircles or rectangles with a rounded top. The stained glass was set above each plain window as if dictated by some strict code of architecture. A few souvenir shops were just opening their doors to the day, selling silver jewelry or pottery or cheaply made janbiyas.

My attention turned to the men we passed along the way. Most of them appeared to dress the same way as Abdullah had last night, with the curved daggers tucked into their belts. *How anti-American is this place?* Would they stab me with their daggers? How can I tell if someone is al-Qaeda when they all dress like this? Even the way Abdullah spoke Arabic, in a choppy rhythm in which he dropped the last letter of a word, was far from comforting. I was beginning to wonder if there was any use in my trying to make this place a home. I sped up my pace through the alley and tried to keep as far away as possible from the dagger-bearing men when they passed. So soon after feeling that I was out of my comfort zone I had relied on stereotypes. I was scared of that which was different from me, though the fear was founded only on unfair prejudice.

Five minutes later, we arrived at a breakfast restaurant cut into a stone wall, just down a path from the Arabic school, and surrounded by small shops selling flimsy plastic cleaning supplies. Another American Arabic language student, Erik, was waiting for us at the restaurant. He and I quickly discovered that we graduated from NYU only one year apart. This familiarity instantly calmed me. I wanted to be surrounded by things I knew, that looked like me, with which I could identify. I had never been like this before when overseas. Then again, I had never been so scared.

We sat at a long silver metal table and were promptly served eggs and mashed fava beans in cast-iron pots, along with chunks of soft, white bread. There didn't appear to be any other food options. Breakfast conversation began with Erik and Abdullah teaching me how to eat in the proper Yemeni style, using my hands to scoop out the beans and eggs with the bread, but then descended into the kind of silence you get when three people consume food as fast as possible. On the wall hung a cheap plastic poster of two young girls cloaked in white holding their hands in prayer position in front of the *Kaaba* in Mecca. The glitter, lipstick, and pop music of Cairo's coffee shop scene felt far away.

"So you're here to study Arabic?" Erik asked me after breakfast in a gruff, I-smoke-a-pack-of-cigarettes-a-day voice. His beard reminded me of Brooklyn, or possibly conservative Islam, I wasn't sure which.

"Yeah, and hopefully also to do some freelance journalism. That's what I did last year in Cairo."

"Oh, that's cool," he said. "It's good to have a hobby around here, because otherwise you just end up doing nothing but chew qat."

I laughed.

"No, it's true. Life in Yemen can be pretty boring. Seriously, everyone chews qat. You'll see. How long do you think you'll stay?"

"I dunno. Maybe a few months," I said, because I didn't want him to think I was already having misgivings about this place. "I'd like to write some articles here and then use them to try to get a staff job in Cairo or something."

"Yeah, a few months is good," Erik said, "but you'll be surprised. This place really sucks you in."

CHAPTER 3

January 1, 2011

This was the worst.

I was standing outside in a little brown-and-white dress at an elevated subway stop in faraway south Brooklyn. Emilie and I had fallen asleep on the train after our New Year's Eve celebrations. It was around four in the morning, freezing, and there was no return train in sight.

"I can't believe we just did that," I moaned.

"Yeah, well, I guess we'll just have to wait now," Emilie said.

"I am not waiting for another train. It could take like thirty minutes."

"Brr, I'm cold." Emilie wrapped her arms around herself.

I looked over the railing's edge, but there wasn't a cab in sight on the dark Brooklyn street below. I looked a little farther to the line of shop fronts; most were boarded up for the night, but one was open, lights beaming from the front windows onto the bare street.

And that's when it hit me.

"Emilie, I'm not waiting outside. Let's go down to that bodega. There will be Yemenis there," I said to my friend, a former roommate from when I had lived in Cairo. We were visiting New York for New Year's and meant to stay at another friend's apartment in the Crown Heights neighborhood of Brooklyn after leaving a small house party in

Greenwich Village. Both of us had lived in New York in the past, but now Emilie was living in Sudan as an aid worker, and I was still in Yemen, writing an occasional story here and there for Western publications and only occasionally feeling as if I was an actual journalist.

Emilie—petite, blonde, and Iowan, who once survived a Baghdad hotel bombing—was never one to turn down a dare, so of course she didn't hesitate at my suggestion.

Because we were in Brooklyn, I knew it was a fair assumption that the bodega would be run by Yemenis. Most are in this part of New York. Yemeni men bring to New York their sons, nephews—and whoever else from their villages they can convince the US state department visa division is a relative—to work in their quintessentially New York twenty-four-hour shops. Once I met a taxi driver in Sanaa who told me he had been shot while working in a bodega in Harlem. He spoke English with unmistakable New Yorker vowels.

I suspect most New Yorkers don't think about their local Yemenis behind the cash register too much. But for me, after having lived in Sanaa for a stint in 2009, and again for a few months in 2010, buying a soda on the way to the subway had become a more complicated affair. Do I tell them I live in Yemen? Will they think that I'm working for the US government and coming to question their immigration status—because why else could I know so much about the country from which they come? That happened to me more than once.

I always felt self-conscious walking into Yemeni-run bodegas in New York when I wasn't dressed according to Yemeni standards of modesty, wearing a sleeveless summer sundress, for example—or also when I was buying beer. If I was doing either of those two things, I never mentioned that I lived in Yemen to the shopkeepers. I imagined they would be picturing me in my sundress, carrying a six-pack, standing in the middle of a busy square in Sanaa, shaming myself and all the dagger-bearing men who stopped to gawk, open-mouthed, with green bits of qat spilling out between their teeth. I couldn't let them think I was so culturally insensitive.

I was intensely concerned about the judgment of Yemenis while living in Sanaa as well, always trying to walk that thin line between what

I could get away with as an American and what was culturally inappropriate. I couldn't let go of this, though we were in New York. Surely Yemenis here weren't thinking any of these things, but they had a keen understanding of the different social norms that applied in the United States and Yemen. But because I knew how crazy it would seem in their country for a woman to be walking around in public with her bare elbows and knees exposed to the world, buying a six-pack, I still feared their judgment.

This is why I felt a little wary this early morning when, slightly intoxicated and wearing our New Year's Eve dresses, Emilie and I were going to implore the help of Yemenis in south Brooklyn. It wasn't that I was concerned that the men would try to take advantage of us in any way, but rather that they would be judging my behavior. The decorum of a place rubs off on you. Yemen turned priorities on their heads. But Yemen also taught me unorthodox problem-solving skills.

• • •

About two months prior to that New Year's Eve night, while I was in Sanaa, I was trying to transport myself from a taxi to inside the large outer gate of the American Embassy as fast as possible. I was going to the embassy for a late morning interview, and standing in the open street in front of the first line of security—a spacious intersection ripe for al-Qaeda target practice—always stressed me out. The precedents for this concern were the few times that al-Qaeda had tried to attack the embassy; the last two incidents had taken place in 2008, when militants rammed explosive-laden vehicles into the embassy's front gates, killing a bunch of Yemeni security personnel, and when they lobbed mortars at the embassy from a nearby building, but hit an all-girls school instead, killing a security guard. The chances that something like that would happen while I was standing outside were slim. Still, the occasional press statement from al-Qaeda in Yemen about killing Americans made standing on the street in front of the US embassy in Sanaa not my favorite morning activity—and so, hurried and flustered upon getting out of the taxi, I forgot my cell phone in the car's backseat.

Once I realized my mistake, which was shortly thereafter because the Ethiopian receptionist at the embassy's second round of security wanted to confiscate my phone, I immediately used a security guard's cell to call my number. It rang two times and then was switched off, the driver obviously taking advantage of the prize left for him, which was atypical of the behavior I had witnessed in Yemen.

Two days after the incident, and after I bought a new phone and SIM card with the same number, the phone thief, perhaps suffering from his bad conscience, called me.

"I'll give you your phone back if you give me two hundred dollars," he said.

"No way. I'll give you some money, but not that much, if you bring my phone back."

"No, two hundred dollars."

"Why don't you just come to where you picked me up, across from Qublat al-Mahdi Mosque in the old city, and we'll talk."

"Okay, I'm coming now."

Before the taxi driver showed up, I told the story of my phone to every male neighbor I could find: the shy man from Thula who ran the dry cleaners next door, the two fun-seeking adolescents who ran the literal hole-in-the-wall of a shop that served as Sanaa's version of a New York bodega. I needed backup, I decided. There were a few other men who had been passing the afternoon chewing qat sitting on a low brick wall who listened to the story as well.

"I left my phone in a taxi. I realized it right away, and called the number. But the driver had stolen it. Then he called me two days ago and said he would give it back to me for two hundred dollars. He is coming right now to this spot," I relayed.

"*Ayb*! Shame! Shame!" they all responded. "You're a foreigner. Yemeni culture respects foreigners. Shame!"

Perfect, I thought.

The thief pulled up in our quarter of the old city from the saila. He got out of his car along with a friend. The driver stood in front of me in a long white thobe, arms folded across his chest. The sun beat down on us. I walked up to meet him.

"So, where's the money?" he asked.

"That is my phone. I will give you two thousand riyals for bringing it back," I said, about ten dollars, "but that's it."

"No, I will give it to you for one hundred dollars," he said.

That's when I knew what to do. Loudly, I yelled. "This man has my phone! This man has my phone!"

My band of loyal supporters, the group of neighbors, came running down from their shops, yelling how ashamed the taxi driver should be of himself. One of them grabbed the driver's thobe at the base of his neck. The driver reached into this front pocket and revealed my black cell phone. I took out two one-thousand riyal bills from my wallet and tried to hand them to the driver in exchange for my phone when one of the boys from the shop signaled that I better stop what I was doing right there.

"You are not giving him that money," he commanded and grabbed my phone from the man's hand, then handed it to me.

"*Yalla*, goodbye," they all told the driver, and he and his friend walked back to their car, deflated.

• • •

Emilie and I walked inside the bodega to find a group of about five men, most of them quite drunk. Two were behind the counter, the others lingering among aisles of toiletries. They were bantering in clipped Arabic that was unmistakably Yemeni.

"*Salaam aleikum.* Are you guys Yemenis? I live in Sanaa," I said in Arabic.

"Ah, you live in Sanaa. My God. We are from al-Dhala'a."

Al-Dhala'a is a governorate in what was once the independent state of South Yemen. Its population was known for opposition to the Saleh regime and national unity, as well as for its liberal ways. These guys had probably spent little time in Sanaa up in the northern part of the country. They probably hated Sanaa. But of course they would help Emilie and me nonetheless.

The normal line of questions I've answered countless times followed: How is Yemen? Do you like Yemeni food? Do you chew qat? They were in a jovial mood and I explained to them our predicament.

The most sober of the five placed the shop's phone on the glass countertop beside the register. "I know a car company," he told us in a voice that signaled he was about to save the day and dialed a number. No one answered on the other side. He tried again after five minutes. Still no one answered. I had a distressed look on my face.

"Don't be worried, don't be worried," one of the Yemenis said, a phrase which I would hear many times the coming year. "We'll take you home."

"You have a car?"

"Yeah, yeah, of course."

The younger, more sober one ran outside with the keys and minutes later pulled up to the curbside in a beat-up blue minivan that looked as if it had been a rescue from the impound lot.

• • •

My first memorable encounter with New York Yemenis happened on an airplane. I had just boarded in Dubai, bound for Sanaa in the summer of 2009, and I was very much questioning my life choices for flying back to Yemen after a short visit to the States. I was twenty-three, and for some reason was sacrificing a life as a spunky, single young professional in New York for life in a country where the primary daily activity was chewing foul-tasting leaves. *I chose this life*, I lectured myself, yet I was still feeling some regret.

It was a wide-body Emirates airline plane, and I was sitting in the middle aisle amongst a group of about half a dozen adolescent Yemenis, obviously from New York. They were dressed as if they had just come from Bed-Stuy, appropriating urban culture, and chatted pretakeoff in New York accents, with Arabic words peppering their conversation. I was trying not to laugh or act like I was paying attention, so I just buried my nose in a novel.

A chubby boy sitting to my right sporting a black Yankees baseball cap glanced up at his friend and said, as if it were the most normal thing in the world, "Yo man, you're like a brotha from another motha."

I couldn't hold it in any longer and giggles poured out of me. The group of young men glared at the strange American girl bound for Sanaa. I had to say something.

"You guys are from New York, right? From Brooklyn?"

"Yeah," said the one beside me.

"I used to live in Park Slope."

"Yo dawg, did you hear that? This girl, she from Brooklyn," he told his friends. "Girl, what you doin' goin' to Yemen for?"

"Well, I'm a journalist and studying Arabic . . . I like Yemen. . . ." I stumbled on my words trying to figure out how to explain my life.

"Yo, you been to Ibb?" asked one of them, standing in the middle of the aisle despite the attendants' directives to take our seats, because Yemenis never seem to act like rules apply to them on airplanes.

"No, I haven't been there," I said. Ibb is the governorate just south of Sanaa from where, as I later learned, most Yemenis in New York come. There are ancient villages with stone houses in the central Yemeni highlands where nearly everyone is an American citizen. New York is one of the main Yemen immigrant hubs in the United States, as are Dearborn, Michigan, and Oakland, California. North Carolina is becoming popular, too. From there, Yemenis illegally ship cartons of cigarettes up to New York City to be sold in Yemeni-run bodegas at a much higher-taxed price.

"Here's my brother's number. You come to Ibb, you give him a call," the guy with the black Yankees cap told me, scribbling a Yemeni cell number on a torn piece of notebook paper. I only first went to Ibb over a year later, but by that time this number was long lost.

• • •

Emilie and I climbed into the blue minivan with two of the men from the bodega. One of the back windows was permanently stuck halfway down, causing us all to shiver from the cold draft. The most sober one of the bunch was driving, but a very intoxicated, stout man sat in the front passenger seat.

I sat in the middle of the backseat behind them, leaning forward in eager conversation. Emilie leaned against the side window. We quickly realized that the two of them had no idea how to get to Crown Heights.

"You like south Yemeni music?" the fat, drunk one asked.

"I like Yemeni music, but I can't tell the difference between northern and southern music. It all sounds the same to me."

I knew that comment was going to get them stirred up.

"Oh whoa, there are major differences between the two. How can you say that? *Ya Allah*!" The drunk one picked a black cassette up off the crusty floor, inserted it into the tape deck, and cranked the volume. "You know, the northerners, they screwed us over. We were so much better before unification. They are tribesmen . . ."

I had heard the spiel many times before. North and South Yemen had unified in 1990, and the animosity between the two populations was worse than an Egyptian soccer rivalry. Yet for some reason I felt the need to goad on the Southerner's laments, because they reminded me that Yemen was my home, because I loved attaching myself to the political intricacies of this far off place.

"Prove you're a journalist," the drunk one said, as Emilie and I shivered in the backseat, hoping we were at the very least driving north.

"I am, I am!" I retorted. Though admittedly, he had hit a nerve. I often felt self-conscious about the fact that I was a young woman who probably didn't appear very foreign correspondent–like. Was I even a foreign correspondent? I hadn't ever planned to be a journalist, hadn't dreamed of it since I was young, hadn't studied it in college, didn't have any persistent desire to unearth the truth for the world to see. This made all my endeavors seem less legitimate to me. I was just having an adventure in the Middle East, and writing articles here and there was part of it. But really, what was I doing with my twenties? It must have seemed so bizarre to these men that this young American woman would choose to live in conservative, impoverished Yemen.

I blurted out, "Look I'm a journalist. Here is Tariq al-Fadhli's phone number!"

I held out my cell phone and the short fat one grabbed it to see the highlighted name: TARIQ, it read, as I was too afraid to have the entire name of a southern separatist movement leader known for being a buddy of Osama bin Laden's back in his Afghanistan *mujahid* days of the '80s in my phone.

"*Ya Allah*, you know Tariq al-Fadhli?"

"I've only spoken to him on the phone," I said confidently, hoping this impressed them enough to believe my tale, though it may have made them think I was some drunk, over-sharing CIA officer.

"This is ridiculous," Emilie chimed in from her spot by the window.

• • •

After another forty-five minutes of listening to all the reasons why northern Yemeni tribesmen are lesser humans than south Yemenis, we finally reached my friend's apartment building in Crown Heights. Before stepping out of the van, I reached into my wallet and pulled out a twenty-dollar bill for the driver.

As I handed the money to him, the driver stared at me, aghast. "*Ayb*, shame! You lived in Yemen, you should know better than to shame us by trying to give us money."

I smiled. They were right. We said our *shokrans*, waved goodbye forever, and I was happy with how this new year, 2011, had begun.

CHAPTER 4

A few weeks later, I was standing on the second floor of what used to be a Yemeni family's home, crouching low to peer through the small rectangle cut out of the mud-brick wall before me—what used to be a Yemeni family's window. The floor beneath me was a mix of dust and stone, and I was slightly concerned that it might give way since this crumbling house was hundreds of years old, but I shrugged my worries off and gave them to Allah, because what else could one do in Yemen?

Through the window I could see two Yemeni teenagers pivoting on their hands upon the roof of another crumbling, uninhabited house, about twenty feet across from me. The pair landed on their backs and spun in the dust, caking dirt all over the backs of their blue jeans. The city of Sanaa, white, brown and also covered in dust, stretched out into the valley behind them. All around us barren, brown mountains rose up to the sky.

Adam Sjöberg stood nearby on another rooftop, video camera to eye, shooting from an angle that captured the two boys' moves, and the ancient village surrounding them.

Adam was a friend of a friend from New York. The same age as me, he was traveling around the world making a documentary about the influence of hip-hop, and particularly break dancing, in unlikely places. Through a mutual acquaintance, who apparently had heard me once blathering on about Yemeni rap artists, Adam had learned there were break-dancers in

Sanaa and said that he wanted to travel to the country to tell their stories as part of his film. In Yemen, where life is guided by antiquated social norms dictating what is acceptable and what will shame your family, there weren't many activities for young people that pushed the boundaries of tradition. The break-dancers were definitely an anomaly.

Helping Adam for the two weeks he was in town was the reason I had traveled back to Yemen after the New Year. The idea for his film jived perfectly with the story I wanted to tell, a story I had been prevented from telling because all editors had been interested in for the almost two years I had, by this point, been reporting from Yemen was al-Qaeda and an intermittent war in the far north of the country. Yet the Yemen that I saw living in Sanaa was far removed from such violence. The life I lived in Sanaa had completely sucked me in, just as Erik had predicted nearly two years prior.

It's funny, the relationship you have with a place. It's like an intimate friend or significant other. Yemen had a personality that had shaped me. Yemen had taught me to not take anything too seriously, to hold life gently, to be open to what new surprise may turn the corner and slap me in the face. It had taught me that rules were suggested guidelines, but that that idea also led to systemic societal ills. Yemen had made me feel like I could handle anything life threw my way. It had taught me to fully embrace my friendly, goofy, curious self, because that's what Yemenis were and that's why I loved them. And furthermore, living there made me feel special, because, as a young, Western girl in a conservative Muslim society, special was exactly what I was.

All of this did not change the fact, though, that Yemen and I had to break up. I had to go back to the States and do what I had felt pressure to do once I understood the idea of adult expectations: I had to go home and get a job. The type of person who runs away to a faraway country forever is not the model citizen that my productivity-driven American upbringing had taught me to emulate. It would be hard to give up a country that had become my adopted home and won me over, but it had to happen.

When Adam told me he wanted to film the boys break dancing in Bait Baous, a half-abandoned village of tall mud-brick homes, I had been concerned. I was always worrying about how to toe the line between what was appropriate in Yemen and what would be considered offensive, and I was afraid that break dancing was more of the latter. The people in Bait Baous are very much village people. Their home was set upon a high, rocky outcrop that jutted over Sanaa's far southern rim. They lived by a different clock and were not accustomed to Sanaa's hustle and bustle, though sprawl from the capital's wealthy district of large villas has crept up to the edge of their mountain.

But the villagers, or at least the ones who came out of their homes, had welcomed us and were intrigued by the boys' acrobatics set to the foreign hip-hop beat. Older men came out to greet us and then stood watching the spectacle unfold on one of the dirt paths that wound its way through the village. They folded their arms across their chests, resting their palms on the hilts of their janbiyas, with smiles on their faces.

"This is for a movie," I explained to them. And they just nodded, intently observing. One of the village men even joined our circle of break-dancers, sticking out in his thobe when compared to the break-dancers' jeans and sweatpants. The man clapped his hands to the hip-hop music so Adam gave him the boombox to hold. He proudly hoisted it on his shoulder and nodded his head to the music.

Meanwhile, the village's children ran around us like mad animals. They were as excited as if the circus had just come to town, and begged Adam to film them. I chased a boy and girl down a dirt path, through a low underpass beneath one house. I grabbed the little girl by the arms and swung her around while she giggled with delight.

In the end, it was the perfect location to shoot, as we could climb all over Bait Baous's abandoned homes. Some of the boys climbed dangerously high, about four stories up, springing from roof to roof. One of the younger break-dancers, called Kimo, popped and locked endlessly around the village's crumbling wall. I stood back and watched, one hand on my hip, in a long blue sweater that hung down to my knees like a tunic, realizing that the boys were not going to listen to me when I told them not to climb so precariously high. I thought about how different this was from anything I had done in Yemen—I was participating in a Yemeni social outing that didn't involve qat consumption or political discussion (though normally these two went hand-in-hand). I realized there was a lot to this place that I had yet to even tap in to.

I was watching Yemeni teenagers be teenagers, as they would be anywhere else. They were not restrained by tradition, or by what much of the outside world thought them to be—terrorists. It was a glimmer of hope in a country whose story was underscored by one crisis or another: terrorism, poverty, lack of water, national drug addiction, rebellion in the South, rebellion in the North, and I could go on. These young men wanted to break out of that mold, wanted to dictate their own futures. It seemed like a good note on which I could end my time in Yemen.

• • •

Yet the consistency of life in Yemen was changing. It would just take me a few weeks to actually believe it.

About a mile away from my apartment building in the old city, past the dreary tourist police office, over the low-lying saila, through the old Ottoman district of tiny alleyways and government ministries, and beside the walls of Sanaa University's old campus, a woman who had long been a thorn in the side of the Saleh regime decided to up the ante.

Tawakkol Karman was thirty-two years old and one of the country's best-known antigovernment activists. She led antigovernment demonstrations every day with her band of loyal followers in front of Sanaa University. This in itself was nothing new. She had been staging protests against the regime for nearly a decade, taking up *cause célèbre* purposes, like press freedom or the protection of a marginalized population in Ibb who suffered under a sheikh who ran things as if he were the local version of Kim Jong-il.

But the protests that were gaining momentum in early 2011 were different in kind. Following the success of the revolution in Tunisia on January 14, each day Tawakkol, her hair wrapped in a brightly colored hijab, yelled into a megaphone among other activists, mostly young people. There were around thirty of them at first, though this number quickly grew to around one hundred. They carried banners and stood on the street, always in the same spot, for an hour each morning. Many but not all the protesters belonged to Tawakkol's political party, al-Islah, Yemen's Islamist party that is related to the Muslim Brotherhood of Egypt. The group chanted for the downfall of Saleh's government, not for reforms, not early elections, just that the man in power step down. The protest was brushed aside by nearly everybody, including me. Tawakkol was simply being Tawakkol, not somebody to give much consideration.

In some ways the activist was a rarity in Yemen—a powerful, outspoken woman who commanded respect from her band of loyal male supporters. She came from a family of educated Islamists who hated men of loose morals like Saleh, and she was well known for having defiantly removed her niqab, the face veil, at a rally three years prior.

On the other hand, she reminded me of nearly every Yemeni woman I had met. Behind the veils and black abayas, I found Yemeni women to be force of will and source of strength. Maybe it was because they had to develop in such a way to survive in male-dominated Yemeni society. Or maybe it was that life in Yemen was full of daily difficulties, with power outages, water shortages, and tribal conflict, and it made them tough. Women also get the benefit of having a protected role in traditional Yemeni society: don't insult women, don't hurt them, they're off limits if they're not your wife or sister. That's at least what I thought until the months of 2011 unfolded.

When I visited the small, Tawakkol-led protest one afternoon, I started feeling a tinge of jealousy for my journalist friends in Egypt who traveled to Tunisia to cover the revolution there. Things would never change in Yemen, I thought. And anyway, I didn't really want change. Chaos in Yemen would be violent. Every man here has an assault rifle, at the very least, and plenty of people in Sanaa had a stockpile of weapons that could do more damage than a gun. I didn't really think through what that all meant. I didn't let my mind go that far. Maybe it was because Yemen forced me to live in the present and abandon anxiety about the future, but more likely it was because my mind couldn't comprehend what conflict and violence were actually like.

And in any case, I would be moving back to America soon.

• • •

In the early morning of January 23, men working at the behest of the Saleh regime broke into Tawakkol's house, arrested her, and took her to an undisclosed location—though the unofficial nature of it all made Tawakkol's capture slightly more like a kidnapping than an arrest. Tawakkol's demonstrations were small and marginal, but Saleh must have wanted to display his authority—or he was just irritated by her yelling. That's the way the president worked.

Tawakkol's sudden arrest wasn't only a jab at the opposition, but also an affront to Yemeni culture, which dictates that women are immune from this sort of behavior. Editorials appeared in the local press the next day declaring, "shame on those who kidnapped Tawakkol in the middle of the night. Have you lost your mind to behave like this?" and calling Tawakkol "perhaps the bravest Yemeni citizen."

The following day, a demonstration formed in front of the general prosecutor's office, a dull-looking government monstrosity that probably didn't prosecute anything. I arrived at the protest site shortly thereafter, unsure of where I was, as it was not in a part of Sanaa I had ever visited. We stood on a road near the first armored division military base that sat perched up on a hill in the northwest corridor of Sanaa, commanded by one Ali Mohsin, whose name I had heard occasionally. I was to be writing an article for the *Christian Science Monitor* about this protest, which was only making news because it came after the Tunisian revolution and the Western media was focused on the political movement of the Arab world. I was just happy to write an article that wasn't about al-Qaeda.

A swarm of men and a pocket of women dressed in black, maybe a little less than one thousand of them, were standing in front of the building's towering main gates and making a lot of noise. They waved photos of Tawakkol and yelled out against the government. "All of Yemen loves her!" one man cried from the crowd. "This is a black shame!" the others asserted. A small band of riot police stood beside the crowd of protesters in their dark green camouflage uniforms, batons in hand, and bored looks on their faces, like they knew this wasn't going to amount to anything

I observed the crowd from the edge. They were charged up for a political cause, chanting and yelling as if their lives depended on it because a woman had given them hope by daring to publicly denounce Saleh. In the United States, I had always found protests particularly compelling—as long as I believed in their causes. This protest for Tawakkol was no different. I didn't know if it was the fervor and anger in the air, or the slightly larger numbers than those who had been protesting previously, or perhaps the presence of riot police that added a perceived threat, but it felt like something exciting was happening. Like this was a spark about to light a fuse.

But no, no, there were still so few people protesting, I assured myself. Wishing for revolution in Yemen was futile—and stupid. I should just enjoy this unique opportunity to cover an antigovernment protest.

Stepping away from the protest after an hour or so, I jumped into one of Sanaa's yellow-and-white cabs, completely invigorated as if I had just come from a good workout. But I was also concerned that my cab driver would question my being at the demonstration. What if he was pro-Saleh? I explained to him that I was a journalist.

"The president only graduated from the sixth grade," the driver told me.

"I've always questioned how he can be president of a country if he doesn't speak English," I replied, happy that he was on the side of the opposition.

"Doesn't speak English! He doesn't even know how to read or write. All he knows is how to sign his name. People bring him the papers, he signs them, and it's done."

I laughed at his comment, because this was still all a game, a way for me to have fun. And it was funny, wasn't it? A president who was completely uneducated. The driver was making it a joking matter, when in reality the fact that his president was uneducated affected the quality of his life, his children's education, and how many times his house runs out of water or tribes have shootouts on the same streets his cab drives down. But when all else fails, Yemenis knew to laugh, and to draw others into the joke as well.

CHAPTER 5

Tawakkol was released from prison a few hours after the initial protest in front of the general prosecutor's office. Using the momentum of the anti-Saleh fervor her arrest had incited, the Joint Meetings Party (JMP), the opposition coalition of political parties that Atiaf had told me about two years ago on that afternoon in Cairo, called for an anti-Saleh demonstration to be held the following Thursday. The JMP was an unlikely group of Islamists, socialists, pan-Arabists, and other small groups. They banded together because it was the only way they could have any strength against Saleh.

Elsewhere in the Arab world, Egyptians took to the streets en masse, kicking off their unlikely revolution, and this lit another fire under the Yemeni opposition supporters. Some ten thousand or so had showed up on this day to protest on the streets of Sanaa in the area surrounding Sanaa University.

Walking among the crowd at the demonstration, I nervously scanned those around me for guns but didn't see any. Rather, there were pink ribbons. The symbol of the Jasmine Revolution in Tunisia was tied around the heads of many protesters. The mood was celebratory, not angry, and I relaxed some.

The center of the demonstration converged at the intersection of Justice Street and Ring Road, right before Justice Street ran into the main gates of Sanaa University, a sandy-colored double archway that spanned the two-lane road. Beside the campus' entrance stood a large concrete sign shaped like a shield, the chipped paint of the bottom half was an aquamarine green and the top was yellow with SANAA UNIVERSITY printed in Arabic script running across its center. Men were crammed into every nook, on top of streetlights, on top of the Sanaa University sign, squatting on a six-inch ledge and getting comfortable in the Yemeni way. ("Yemenis can get comfortable anywhere," Abdullah, my original Yemeni friend, told me once, bending his knees and crouching in a posture that most Americans couldn't dream of reaching.)

At the two roads' intersection was a small cylindrical structure where the traffic police stood—these men are a necessity because Yemeni drivers wouldn't just obey a traffic light—but for now it had been overtaken by protesters shouting anti-Saleh slogans into megaphones.

Despite the JMP being dominated by the Islamist party, al-Islah, these men and women felt relatively liberal to me—no long beards or ankle-height thobes (because that's how the prophet Mohammed wore his). The majority seemed to be working class, non-tribal people from central Yemen, cities like Taiz and Ibb. They walked in clusters down the middle of the street, men and a few women, too, carrying homemade, cardboard signs that read NO TO CORRUPTION, NO TO INHERITANCE, making reference to the generally accepted idea that Saleh was going to hand power to his son Ahmed Saleh. Another read, WHERE IS THE GAS? WHERE IS THE OIL? as Saleh and his cronies lined their pockets with the revenues generated from Yemen's limited oil and natural gas reserves. They complained of systemic problems under Saleh's leaderships. "Ministers live in castles and have many cars," one man said, "while I couldn't pay the bribe I needed to get a job," only about twenty dollars. I saw that the crowd was slowly making its way to a dusty alley on a residential street a few blocks from the university. I followed them there and found JMP leaders on a stage lecturing into microphones about Saleh's faults and how, if they had their way, they would veer Yemen away from its current path toward chaos.

The people who ran the JMP were exclusively old men, mostly from Taiz or Aden, cities south of Sanaa. I knew some of them, had chewed qat with them in months past while trying to get information for stories before the uprising. In America, I was a nobody, but in Yemen I knew opposition political leaders and they knew me. I waved hello excitedly, yet awkwardly, to the old men while they sat on silver metal chairs beside the stage, waiting for their chance to speak to the audience of demonstrators. They gave me a "yes, we see you Laura" nod.

I stood for a while in front of the stage, notebook in hand, trying to translate the speeches. I already had enough material to write a story, but I couldn't bring myself to leave because I wanted to be a part of this, whatever this was. I wanted to be a part of something bigger than myself, and I would play an important role in it all—as a journalist! I was certainly having second thoughts about leaving Yemen so quickly after all. I had never imagined that Yemenis would come out to protest in these numbers, yet here they were.

Though when I looked around at the crowd of men behind me, I reluctantly had to admit to myself that the demonstration was nothing more than a constrained political rally. The only thing that made it feel exciting was that it was happening in the wake of Egypt's unrest. The JMP were just using the momentum from Egypt to put pressure on Saleh to implement parts of their agenda, like restarting a national dialogue and delaying parliamentary elections so that voter registration could be reformed. Such was a tactical move—Saleh was wedged firmly in power with his family in control of security forces and his close allies in control of the rest. Upsetting that whole system was going to be difficult, if not impossible. The JMP would not call for revolution like the Egyptians or that small band of insignificant protesters who stood with Tawakkol. Instead they were calling for reform.

After an hour or so, the rally fizzled out and the demonstrators took off to eat lunch. As I walked out with them, trying to reach an area of the street where the road wasn't blocked off so I could find a taxi, I saw a group of soldiers sitting on the sidelines. They were leaning on their guns and, despite working for Saleh's government, reading through a pile of JMP informational pamphlets.

• • •

Erik and Robert, two friends from when I lived in Yemen in 2009, were crashing at my old city apartment when they first returned to the country in early 2011. Robert was tall with floppy brown hair and was quite the English academic. He was doing PhD research in Sanaa. Erik, my fellow NYU alum who I met on my first day in Yemen, just wanted to spend some time here before he went to law school in Boston the following fall, maybe write a few news stories on the side. Erik had short brown hair and angular features. He was from Maine and had a bit of a poetic outdoorsman to his soul, but also the quick-witted savvy of a hip kid who has spent time living in New York. On those January evenings, we used to gather at the second floor apartment below ours, which was shared by two American teachers, Adam Baron (who would become a journalist in the not so distant future) and Bernard, to watch the spectacle of Egypt unfold on Al Jazeera. Past the wooden room divider adorned with a Kenyan sarong with Obama's face printed on it was the tiny, square TV room into which we all crowded to follow the events that would soon change our lives as well. Sometimes Asil, a British Sudanese twenty-something who worked for a local NGO, came up from her apartment on the ground floor of our building to watch as well.

We followed Al Jazeera's English channel, our sacred messenger, with caged enthusiasm. Erik had just flown into Sanaa from Cairo, and I had lived in Egypt on three different occasions: during a study abroad program, after college, and during early 2010, so the events were particularly gripping. We had many friends in Cairo living the mayhem.

For years, Egyptian president Hosni Mubarak cut away at political and social freedoms, yet the ramifications were few. Egyptians are too complacent, observers said. Then all at once, Egypt's mammoth population decided it had had enough. The pent-up fury that came from living in an overpopulated country where the rich got richer and the poor lived in squalor was unleashed in unison, creating a scene that was full of both rage and hope for a better future.

Tunisia's revolution didn't strike the same chord, because it was Tunisia, far away and so French. Egypt was the core of the Middle East. Its population soaring and home to Arab popular culture, film, and

TV. Egypt was being shaken in a way that we never thought possible. It affected us, filled us with hopeful energy because we had spent a bit of our lives there too.

But in no way did any of us think this would happen in Yemen. The JMP rally was scheduled and methodical—another one was planned a week after the first. The people with Tawakkol were few and far between.

We were watching thousands upon thousands of protesters converge on the TV, but then when we looked outside onto the Sanaa street, all we saw was a man with a dagger squatting along the side of the road chewing qat, police officers crammed into the flatbed of a pickup truck chewing qat, and a crazy man shouting what appeared to be a religious diatribe but you couldn't understand his mumbled words because his cheeks were so full of qat. This was life in Sanaa, moving at its own slow, uninterrupted pace. Where were the enraged young people? I had no idea.

• • •

I spent the next few days emailing every contact I had at the *New York Times* after noticing that a correspondent in Beirut had covered the first JMP rally from afar. I had done some work for the *Times* as a reporting assistant in its Cairo bureau during 2010 and figured there was a chance its foreign desk would let me report for the paper from Yemen as long as no staff correspondent was here.

On the day before the JMP had scheduled their second rally, Saleh stood before parliament and made what may have sounded like concessions to one unseasoned in the wily ways of Yemen's president, but given that he almost certainly had no intention of actually fulfilling his promises, his speech was more like a first official nod to the fact that there was a small undercurrent of dissent affecting Yemen and that that dissent was somehow connected to what was happening across the Arab world. Saleh declared he would freeze a proposed constitutional amendment that abolished presidential term limits and vowed neither he nor his son would run for president again once his term was up in 2013. "No extension, no inheritance, no resetting the clock," he said.

This was a very Salehesque move. The president's speech signaled to his supporters that he was not hard-nosed like the rest of those haughty Arab leaders. Rather, he was a humble man who did things in the interest of the nation. He had played this card over and over again in his presidency to win support among the masses.

After the speech, I was sitting in my office, in front of a plain, dark brown wooden desk, staring at the blank white wall, trying to put together story ideas in my head that I could pitch to new publications. Then my phone rang.

"Hi, I'm at the *Times*'s bureau in Beirut," the female voice on the other line said. "I heard that you were available to do some work for us."

"Yes, I am," I said as confidently as possible.

"Can you go out and get some street reactions to Saleh's speech? Do Yemenis think he's serious? Email me your notes."

"Yes, of course." *Sound professional, Kasinof.*

"Great, thanks. I need them as soon as possible."

"Of course. Bye."

All the hard work scrambling for stories in a forgotten country, the endless hours of studying Arabic, the odd life choices that left me living in a conservative Muslim society during my twenties—it all had finally paid off. Suddenly the experience in and of itself was no longer worth it, but this opportunity was, because I could prove to friends and family in America that moving to the Middle East hadn't just been about escaping responsibility. Now I didn't have to think about what I would do if I left Yemen, because how could I leave Yemen now? It was so easy to put my heart into something when that something was the *New York Times.* I was getting a chance to report for an institution, for something that mattered in the grand scheme of the world, about a country that I loved most dearly. And it wasn't even about al-Qaeda or terrorism or war. It was about pro-democracy protesters. At the beginning, the excitement masked the pressure. But dealing with that pressure is what became most difficult.

• • •

I walked the narrow, cobblestone alleyways of the old city looking for somebody I could interview. Tiny women in their long black abayas set off with me. Each would nod a hello as we passed one another, two women from different worlds with disparate futures acknowledging our mutual presence.

The key to a successful man-on-the-street interview is to find someone who is standing still and doesn't appear too busy. It wasn't qat time so a lot of Yemenis were going somewhere. There were a few hours in the morning when people got chores accomplished before settling down in a mafraj somewhere for a good chew. The pharmacist, he looks preoccupied. The guy with the coke bottle glasses at that one shop, I think he works for political security so I shouldn't try to interview him. Sami and Samir from Haraz at the other shop, they don't like politics. The guy who sells silver jewelry and always yells hello in English, he's too annoying. I made my way to the saila past Talha mosque, with its large sandy white dome and the steps on which elderly men with canes always sat for hours on end simply to socialize and observe.

I walked quickly, spurred on by my new assignment, past the square garden where plants no longer grow and sparse weeds cover the unplowed brown land, and ran almost headfirst into Ahmed, a friendly-faced man who runs a laundromat. I used to live in this section of the old city, though now I lived in another. I knew Ahmed from that time because that's just what happens when you live in the old city of Sanaa—you meet your neighbors.

"*Salaam, ya Laura*," he said. His eyes grew wide and he shook my hand. "How are you doing?"

"Praise be God," I told him, the common response to that question. "I am interviewing people about what they think of Saleh's speech. You know that I'm a journalist, right?"

Ahmed nodded. I asked if I could interview him and he said of course.

We entered his small laundromat. On a rod above us hung black and navy suit jackets that Yemeni men wore over their thobes.

Ahmed pulled up a chair for me to sit on and brought another for himself. We sat across from one another, leaning forward. His stubble faded into his leathery dark skin. His features were sharp and he had an intelligent look to his face signaled most of all by his eyes, always alert, which actually seemed to glisten in the sun when he spoke.

I asked Ahmed about Saleh and he told me the man was a liar and that if he was announcing anything that seemed like a concession, it was merely a ploy he hoped would somehow benefit him. He waved his hand in the air to show that we should ignore the leader. This is how our president works, he told me.

Arabic is such a full body language in which people speak their soul with their arm movements, the way their upper bodies lean forward, as Ahmed was doing, to drive home a point. I appreciated these efforts to put one's all into his words and enjoyed trying to adopt it as my own.

I asked Ahmed what he thought of the antigovernment protests and he told me that, God willing, they would bring change.

Change—the word itself brought hope. Did anyone ever think that things could change for the worse? I didn't ask Ahmed because that's not what we were asking in those early days.

Ahmed asked me if I wanted a tea. I told him I had to work. It's so silly, I know, one should have time to relax and have tea in Yemen, but I have to. "Of course," he said, nodding. "*Masalama*, Laura, goodbye."

• • •

Herds of tribesmen who supported Saleh's rule entered Sanaa in droves that night. Like a swarm of termites, they took over the main square of central Sanaa, Midan al-Tahrir, the same name of the square that was the heart of the protests in Cairo, so it was a very symbolic move. Rumor had it they were armed. If this was Saleh's follow-up to his concession speech, it was clear how insincere he had been. The tribesmen erected a cluster of large green tents, in which they would come to live for months on end during 2011, receiving free qat, lunch, and sometimes money as well. I knew refined gentlemen who, as members of the General People's Congress (GPC), Yemen's ruling party, worked for the Saleh government. They drank only the finest whiskey and read intelligent books. Then there was this type of Saleh supporter: men whose qat wads spill uncontrollably out of their mouths any time they make a grunt, who are incapable of speaking in inside voices, and who rarely bathe. Men who only support Saleh because their sheikh told them to.

Later that same evening, I walked the short distance from my apartment through the vegetable market of Bab al-Sabah down to Midan al-Tahrir. Busy streets lined with shops of cheap electronics, shoes, or scarves formed a rectangle around a macadam pedestrian area. There was a small walled area of bleak vegetation and ledges for sitting next to the newspaper stands.

The *midan* was packed with the most unruly tribesmen I had ever come across. Poorly combed hair, aggressive attitudes. They were standing around doing little, yet even this they did in a chaotic way. They stomped instead of walked. Some sat in Toyota Hilux pickup trucks with assault rifles placed to their sides. Others milled about the square, Kalashnikovs slung loosely over their shoulders.

The public display of weapons was illegal within Sanaa city limits. It was one law that the government actually had enforced, but now there was definitely no one telling these men to put their guns away. Laws in Yemen were like that. They worked only at the convenience of the regime.

What if the JMP rally the next day tried to march to Midan al-Tahrir? The fear wasn't enough to stop me from reporting; it just heightened my level of vigilance. I was constantly aware that armed violence could break out between the two sides at any moment, constantly aware that I was not safe. You never know who has a gun now. Perpetual vigilance is something I grew accustomed to, something that didn't leave me once I left Yemen. It didn't mean that at times I didn't find the threat of violence invigorating, adventurous, and even fun. But this was the point when I became acutely aware of my surroundings at all times. So many around the world have to live in this sort of environment where their safety is constantly under threat. I wonder if they just shrug it off or if they live in a constant state of anxiety. I certainly tended toward the latter.

• • •

On the edge of Sanaa, behind a high concrete wall, sits the mammoth, white, and soulless Ministry of Information. It's a new building, much nicer than many other ministries, as it's one in which a foreigner may roam. Government money invested into the veneer of competency when everything else is crumbling.

I was going to the ministry to push for a visa for a *New York Times* correspondent. A real *New York Times* correspondent. Protests had been growing bigger and bigger in Yemen over the course of the last three weeks. Though there hadn't been any major violence yet between the pro-Saleh tribesmen of Tahrir Square and the protesters in front of Sanaa University—just a few fist fights here and there at the worst—the foreign desk definitely didn't want to have only me, a young freelancer, in the country, and I didn't want to be covering the story alone either. Covering Yemen alone for the *New York Times* during a time of political chaos that may lead to violence? No way. There was no way I'd be able to do that. I was ready to grovel at the ministry for the other correspondent's visa.

On the inside, the Ministry of Information felt hollow. Men in oversized suits shuffled across shiny floors from office to office promoting government propaganda. I climbed stairs that wound through the center of the building and entered the one office devoted to foreign media coverage of Yemen.

Ahmed al-Lahabi, the division's director, looked up from his desk. Other men were sitting around drinking tea or making copies of stamped papers.

"Ah Laura," he said. "Who do you write for again?"

"As you know, for the *Christian Science Monitor.*" I paused a second. "But I've been doing some reporting for the *New York Times* as well."

Lahabi gave me a scolding look. His squatness was amplified when he sat behind a desk. I never had a journalist visa in Yemen. I always had a student visa, which stipulated that I not work in Yemen. This didn't matter when I was writing for other publications, but now I was afraid Lahabi was going to make it an issue, an issue that could lead to my deportation.

"We have a photo of you next to a sign that says 'fall fall Ali Saleh.' Do you want to have the same fate as Heather and Adam?" Lahabi threatened.

He was referring to two American journalists with whom I had also lived in 2009. They had been deported in May 2010 after sneaking off to an area of the country they weren't supposed to be in to interview southern separatist leaders.

"Fine, give me a journalist visa then," I retorted. "I am here to play by the rules. I am trying to play by the rules."

Lahabi shrugged.

I asked him about the visa for the *New York Times* correspondent. "We want to do things officially," I told him.

"We have your request," Lahabi said, though his tone made it clear it was a lost cause.

A young French woman, who was trying to start her career in journalism in Yemen as well, sat on a side chair, waiting patiently. She was wearing a sleeveless fur vest, her full arms exposed. I didn't know if she was culturally stupid, intentionally trying to win over the men at the ministry with bare skin, or just French. I rolled my eyes, but then used my own subversive tactic:

"Listen, you can't kick me out because you can't kick out the actress," I said in Arabic with the tip of my head, and the raise of the eyebrows, that was the Yemeni version of warning that I meant business. Lahabi gave me a smirk back from his desk. This wasn't a hollow threat. He and his men knew I was the star of a Yemeni soap opera two years back and they partially loved me for it. It would be bad press to throw me out of the country. Or at least that's what I was counting on. I was trying to strike a balance, to play by semi-official rules by applying for a visa for another *Times* correspondent, but also play the Yemeni way as well.

"Ah, that's right. You were the actress with Ganaf!" one of Lahabi's sidekicks piped up. I just smiled. My future, for now, would be the *New York Times* in Yemen.

CHAPTER 6

August 2009

My phone rang.

"Ah hello, Abdullah."

"My friend is an actor. They need a foreign guy and girl for filming a program tomorrow. Will you and Robert do it?"

"Sure. Why not?" It sounded innocent enough.

• • •

And so one fine summer morning, the day after Abdullah had called me about his friend's request, Robert, at that time a fellow Arabic student, and I showed up with Abdullah to Bait Baous. We were supposed to perform in a local TV program about which we knew nothing. In an open, dusty space below the village's cluster of mud-brick houses a film crew lingered, along with a variety of actors, some carrying drums, others assault rifles. Abdullah wasn't too certain about what we should do, so we just sat on some rocks under the shade of a tall leafy tree while he went to find his friend among the gun-toting actors. Village boys and girls who were watching the spectacle came over to the rocks to poke at us, the strange foreigners. They may have been the same children I would see running around the village a year and a half later when I came here to film the break-dancers with Adam.

After about five minutes, a tall, well-dressed man with graying hair approached us.

"Ah, you are Robert and Laura. Welcome, welcome. I am Mohammed. I am the director. Please sit down. We will be with you soon."

"He's Iraqi," Abdullah said after rejoining us. "He is working with the Yemeni government to make this show. The subject is kidnapping, against kidnapping, you know?"

"Wait. What?" I asked.

"We're going to be kidnapped on national TV?" Robert asked.

"Yes," we were told.

The kidnapping of foreigners was a problem in Yemen, though it rarely ended poorly for the captives. If a tribe wanted to bribe the government in some way, to get Uncle Mohammed out of prison for example, then foreigners were good bargaining chips. While they were in captivity, foreigners said they were always treated kindly, given lots of food and qat. Still, kidnapping boded poorly for Yemen's reputation, and it certainly dissuaded money-generating tourism.

One of the actors came up to us. He was tall and stocky for a Yemeni. His black hair was shaved very short, and on top of it he wore a long, scraggly wig with pieces of its fake hair sticking out in different directions. He and the other actors were meant to look like tribesmen from Marib, a province to the east of Sanaa, because Maribis are most often accused of kidnapping and unruly behavior. And apparently also lacked barbers.

"Welcome. Thank you so much for being here. I'm Fahd," he said. This was Ganaf, the main character and star of the show.

"You look like Muammar Gaddafi," I told Fahd, and we instantly became friends.

Soon, it was time for Robert and my scene. The director approached us. "Alright, here's the thing," he explained. "You two are in Yemen for your honeymoon. You are watching these musicians perform at a wedding, and that's when the kidnappers come up to you. But then there will not just be one set of kidnappers, but two. They will fight over who gets to kidnap you. I need you to act really scared."

"Do you think this is going to take more than a day?" Robert asked me.

"Yeah, I guess so," I replied.

After the first takes, the director scolded Robert and me for not looking frightened enough when approached by our kidnappers. I just looked over to the ragtag bunch of Yemeni actors in their black wigs trying to pretend they were tribesmen from Marib who lived in the desert, slept in tents, ate camel meat for lunch, and only adhered to tribal law, when really they were city folk who drank tea at street-side cafés on a Saturday afternoon.

"Why don't you yell 'Oh my God!'" the director suggested to me. "And put your hands on your cheeks like this." He demonstrated a quite affected scared look.

I did as I was told, but we had to do another take because I was laughing too hard as soon as my lines exited my mouth. And another one after that. Once the director discovered that I spoke decent Arabic, my lines would alternate between English and Arabic for many episodes to come.

After filming, the director told us to come back the next day to shoot another scene, and the next day, and the one after that, too. Production wasn't finished after Ramadan started, so we filmed in the middle of the night when everyone's bellies were full. The actors chewed qat right until it was their time to be on camera, and then reluctantly had to spit out the green wad of leaves. We tried to film in a cramped cave in the mountains, where we were being held as captives, but it rained that night and the film equipment got wet and wouldn't function. Instead, as the rain poured down, we all sat cross-legged on the dirt ground, elbow to elbow, with the glimmer of moon and glare of cell phones as our only light. The actors sang Arab melodies in deep voices about the queens who used to rule Yemen thousands of years ago.

After that, the Iraqi director decided that we should film the cave scenes in the basement of a house in Sanaa. There was a scene during which Robert and I argued about whose idea it was to come to Yemen on our honeymoon in the first place. I raised my voice at Robert and kind of pushed him to the side while Ganaf gawked at us in disbelief. This was supposed to be entertaining because a tribesman would never let his wife yell at him like that, or so tradition goes, but I've seen plenty of Arab women do plenty of yelling inside the home.

Others were being held hostage with Robert and me: "The Chinese" character, who in reality was a Vietnamese man who was raised in Sanaa, and Sami, a young Yemeni boy. "The Chinese" didn't want to leave captivity because they fed him lots of *fahsa*, meat stew he thoroughly enjoyed. (All of the actors never used his real name, even when filming stopped.) Sami would be the son of a wealthy Yemeni family kidnapped for ransom, a practice that, though not common, sometimes occurred. Meanwhile, Sami lectured Ganaf about why kidnapping foreigners was a shame to Yemeni culture. He waved his finger at the much older Ganaf and told him he should be ashamed of himself.

Then, the much-adored Sami fell ill to diabetes. He curled up on the floor of the basement under some dirty blankets and was on the verge of death. The other actors put white chalk on Sami's cheeks to make him look more sick. I happened to be a doctor and told the kidnappers that to help Sami we needed "a syringe." They ran off to the other side of the room and, lo and behold, came back moments later with the prized needle. I stuck Sami in the arm, his head hanging limply alongside his small, weak body, and—imagine this—I saved his life.

That's when Ganaf saw that foreigners weren't so bad after all. He began to heed Sami's lecture that kidnapping foreigners was shameful and a crime. So Ganaf decided to help us sneak out of our hiding place. We filmed the grand escape scene in the brown, dry mountains around Sanaa. Robert, Ganaf, and I ran across the rocks before we were ambushed by his fellow tribesmen. They pointed their rifles directly at us. Ganaf was shot. He fell to the ground grasping at his ketchup-stained chest in quite over-exaggerated horror. But Robert and I managed to escape.

• • •

"The problem isn't Islam. It's Arab dictators, they are only concerned about their own money. Islam is peaceful. The accident of September 11, *ya Laura*, that wasn't Islam."

Fahd was driving Robert and me in his large black SUV to shoot our final scene at a hospital in Hadda about three weeks after the first filming started. During the days upon days of sitting around with him on set, I had grown to appreciate Fahd. He was full of passion, drive, and energy, and he so wanted us to understand. He had been imprisoned for publicly insulting Saleh on stage in 2008, so that meant he was probably the first Yemeni activist I'd ever met. I learned that Fahd was an Islahi, an Islamist, someone who was supposed to be against the ideals that I, as a liberal American woman, held. But Fahd never made me feel this way.

"*Ya Laura*, in America, would they think I, as a Yemeni, am a terrorist?" he asked me during our drive.

"People are not just one thing," I told him. "Some people in America would be able to understand, but some people in America would not. See, Arabs differentiate between government and people because in the Arab world people don't choose their government. But in America we do. So people are not so good at distinguishing. If a government is bad then the people must be bad as well."

Fahd drew in a big breath and stared straight ahead. He paused for a moment, seemingly thinking this through. Then he turned to me once more.

"You will see in Taiz, we are very civilized," he said. "Have you been to Taiz *ya Laura*?"

"No, but I really want to go."

"I will drive you to Taiz myself! In this car. When do you want to go? We will go after Ramadan is over."

"*Inshallah*, God willing," I said. We never did go to Taiz together, not exactly anyway, but when I went there by myself to report on the spreading protests in 2011, it would be the next time I saw him after this day.

Inside the hospital, Ganaf, who was supposed to be recovering from a bullet wound from our grand escape, lay in bed, covers pulled up to his chest. He didn't wear his long wig anymore, a kidnapper reformed. Robert and I stood by his bedside, loyally looking after our kidnapper-turned-savior. Robert, sick of filming by this point, said only the minimum of what was required of him, and stood as stiff as a board while he stared at Ganaf. The director, far from happy at such amateur acting, especially when compared to the kidnappers who said their lines with the gusto of Broadway stars, was going to make us go through take after take. So I tried to make up for Robert, and let affection for Ganaf's heroism gush out of me.

"Oh Ganaf, you saved us!" I exclaimed, leaning over the bed, but not touching his arm, because such male to female contact would be frowned upon.

"Ganaf, we love you," Robert said, only because he was told to or else we couldn't move on. His lips hardly opened.

Ganaf explained once again, this time for the camera, that Islam was a religion of peace that does not want to hurt foreigners. He talked to us like a school principal. It was obviously a message that was supposed to resonate with the wider audience who would be watching the grainy serial on their home televisions a few days later.

Next, the rest of our kidnappers entered. Robert and I cowered in fear by the side of the bed.

Ganaf told us not to be afraid. Then he told the kidnappers that they should apologize to us. The smallest of them, whose long hair from the black wig kept falling over his eyes, balked at this, but finally they all obliged.

"What can I say? I am sorry. Sorry," he came forward and said in Arabic.

"He is. You said. Sorry," Ganaf said in English to Robert and me.

"I understand him, but I don't understand my translator," I replied in Arabic. Viewers at home would then hear a Loony Tunes-like sound effect, like *boooing*, just so they knew this was a joke.

Then came the moment when I endeared myself to households across Yemen.

"There are good and bad people all over the world," I said to the group in a singsong voice, the sort of tone you hear in a child's TV show. "And I can see that Yemenis are a good people."

The kidnappers standing around Ganaf's feet at the end of the bed nodded in agreement.

"*Hathy hely*," Ganaf said after my declaration, which is a very localized Taizi dialect phrase that can be loosely translated to, "well, isn't that something?" It was thrown in for humor. All Yemenis knew Fahd was from Taiz, but he was supposed to be speaking in Ganaf's Marib accent, in which this phrase would never be used.

"*Hathy hely*," I repeated with a smile.

"Cut," the director stepped in. "You're not saying it right. *Hathy hely. Hathy hely*. No cut, let's do it again."

"*Hathy hely.*"

"Nope, again."

"*Hathy hely.*"

"That'll have to do," the director said. Fahd winked at me.

• • •

Two months later

I banged shut the door of a taxi as Erik paid for our ride. A dark green striped scarf was wrapped around my hair and an abaya covered the T-shirt and jeans I was wearing underneath. I slipped on large square sunglasses, wishing that my face would disappear behind them if the abaya I was wearing wasn't enough concealment. We entered an exhibition hall to visit Sanaa's annual International Book Fair, hoping to ingest a bit of culture in our qat chew–driven lives. Through the aisles of religious texts from Saudi Arabia, where big-bellied men stood behind booths of Qurans, we searched for the small Arabic literature section.

"Ah! You're the actress!" came the first shout drawing attention to Erik and me. More took notice of our presence. My disguise was futile. "*Enty hag Ganaf!*" they said in disbelief and elation, those staccato three words I heard on repeat every time I ventured outside in Sanaa, literally meaning "I am belonging to Ganaf."

Yemenis didn't remember the name of the show (*Hammy Hammek*), nor the name of my character (which, not so creatively, was Laura. Although that wasn't as bad as "the Chinese"). They just called the show by the name of its star. And I was whittled down to "the actress, *al-momathala.*"

Erik rolled his eyes. This happened whenever we went out together into Sanaa. At first it was a fun way to start a conversation with the random passerby. Then it became overwhelming. The Yemeni paparazzi were always there, only they were harmless; they just wanted to show admiration and perhaps exchange a few words, but for now they were surrounding us, forestalling enjoyment.

I looked at Erik with "Well, what am I supposed to do?" eyes. I didn't know this all was going to happen. Abdullah made it sound like I was going to only be in one show, not ten. He never told me that this show would be wildly popular, airing every day of the holy month. After families broke their fasts, they gathered around the TV and watched *Hammy Hammek*. It just happened that one day I walked out of our house and everyone recognized me. Robert left Yemen for England, so it was only me who got to experience the results of our fame.

The typical old-city crowd had grown used to seeing the actress *hag ganaf* around the block, eating fava beans for dinner at a local haunt or buying water bottles from the corner shop. The book fair, however, was new territory, crowded and not a place I should have dared try to keep a low profile.

There was a part of the attention that I loved, though. The baggage of being an American woman in Yemen wasn't my defining characteristic anymore—being from a place of loose social morals and invasive politics. Being the actress trumped all that. I felt that I now had my own identity in Yemen, and that identity was beloved because Yemenis were excited that outsiders would star in their TV show. I felt like I belonged here in Sanaa, an important factor drawing me back to the country a year later.

On the drive home from the book fair, we passed the main intersection where Sixieth Street leads to Hadda Street, where Sanaa becomes more wealthy. Our driver stopped the car at the intersection and waited for the traffic policeman to signal from his cylindrical booth. An animated street beggar began washing the front windshield of our taxi with a dirty rag. He looked inside as our driver scolded him.

"*Enty al-Momathala*! *Enty al-Momathala*! You're the actress!" he yelled in jubilation. He danced in circles on the street with his rags. I looked over at Erik and saw him crack a smile at the spectacle.

CHAPTER 7

February 2011

The Yemeni government never gave a real *New York Times* correspondent a visa. They really weren't giving many foreign journalists visas during those early months of 2011, or the months after that. So I continued to do work for the paper as a freelancer, the greatest opportunity ever it seemed, but also unnerving to the extent that it was difficult to just sit back and be satisfied with the accomplishment. My editors were militant that the words I was writing were true—that's how they are with freelancers. That obsession for accuracy bled over to me. As did my obsession for proving to them that they would not be disappointed with relying on me.

Aden was going to be my way of proving to them I was up to the job. Life had to be more riotous in Aden, more story worthy. It almost always was. I figured my editors would like riotous. I also hoped in Aden I would find the spirit of the Arab Spring that I so desperately wanted to be a part of, and that I was disappointed to be missing in Cairo.

Aden sits along Yemen's southwest coast. It's a natural deep water port that used to be one of the busiest in the world until South Yemenis kicked the occupying British out of what was formally an independent state, separate from northern Yemen, where Sanaa was the capital. A ragtag Marxist-Leninist government took over until the late 1960s, supported by the USSR, although South Yemen was more of a Soviet backwater plagued by infighting than anything else. Then, the year before the Soviet Union collapsed, South Yemen and North Yemen merged to form the country that exists now. But the union has been far from happy—especially for southerners. And Aden, with its underused port, unemployed youth, and cracking infrastructure, was most representative of that decline.

This afternoon, I was sitting in an open-air restaurant by the sea after flying to the city from Sanaa. I was eating fish alongside a man of mixed Arab Indian descent. He spoke flawless English with an accent reminiscent of his former home in Sheffield, England. While we talked, my gaze fell on the small painted fishing boats, hypnotically rocking back and forth with the waves of the Gulf of Aden. Behind them was Crater, a neighborhood of crammed streets and lively markets set inside an ancient volcanic core. The weather was balmy, very balmy, the sort of balmy that would be intolerable had this not been a winter month.

Society was already rife with dissent in the South. It's where peaceful street protesters had been fatally attacked by government soldiers during the years prior. Yet southerners weren't demonstrating for reform or to oust Saleh from power like the protesters in Sanaa. Theirs had been protests demanding secession. Demanding a return to an independent South Yemen. I believed that the wave of dissent sweeping across the Arab world would further galvanize people here in Aden because they had longer experience in opposition to Saleh—and because they were less tribal, had a more active civil society, and a more educated population, at least as far as the older generation was concerned. Surely southerners would give me the excitement that I believed I would have seen had I been in my old home of Cairo.

The drive into Aden from the airport was framed by the blue expanse of sea to the south and, to the north, desolate, charred mountains—the remnants of an extinct volcano—reached down to the road's edge. I was struck by how this city was far different from Sanaa. Aden truly felt like a different country. The hot, humid weather down at sea level, the darker-skinned population, a mix of Arab, East African, Indian, and whoever else ended up at this once bustling port, a former British protectorate during the time of empires. Driving was more organized, janbiyas more absent. Aden's seedy port-city atmosphere permeated its alleyways among crumbling British colonial–style buildings with their wooden lattice verandas and drab Soviet-style apartment complexes built during the decades-long period of communist rule. Saudis—in Aden for a cheap vacation—populated its seaside discos, such as the dimly lit Sailor's Club, where men threw American one-dollar bills at Yemeni, Russian, and Somali prostitutes performing on stage. Aden's culture felt more laid-back than Sanaa's. Here, adolescent girls and boys walked side by side in Aden Mall and smoked shisha together by the sea. It wasn't so long ago that a brewery existed in Aden, run by Germans. But Islamic militants burned it down in the mid-1990s, goaded on by leadership in Sanaa.

"We Adenis don't just want the return of South Yemen," explained Bilal, my lunch companion this afternoon, a local journalist whom I had just met for the first time. "We want Aden to be its own, independent city-state."

I picked out a morsel of the juicy white fish flesh with my hands, dipped an end into a small bowl of spicy tomato sauce, and listened intently to Bilal's dream. I felt slight disappointment that there didn't seem to be a grand, united revolt among all southerners against Saleh. I hoped Bilal was an anomaly in his view for the future of southern Yemen.

"Everything was much better when the British were here," Bilal continued. Like most native Adenis, he clung fondly to the city's colonial past.

I too romanticized Aden, but more so as a city of faded glory. Truly, though, it was a city of contradictions: Aden is where the only churches in Yemen publicly bear the cross, yet it has also been the site of some of the country's worst anti-Western terrorist attacks. It was the capital of the only Marxist state in the conservative Arab world in the '70s and '80s; Carlos the Jackal and other leftist militants trained for guerrilla warfare in camps just east of Aden. It's the same area where Muslim fundamentalists aligned with al-Qaeda organize now. The city is home to a large number of *mujahideen* who fought the Soviets in Afghanistan and also some of Yemen's only functioning bars: a red-tinted Chinese restaurant set in a busy shopping center that feels like a relic of colonial Hong Kong served some of the cheapest beer in Yemen.

A group of European-looking foreigners, probably aid workers involved with services for Somali refugees, entered the restaurant as we stood up to leave. Bilal paid for the meal, despite my insisting. The cashier, standing in front of a large fiery grill, smiled at me.

"Where are you from?" he asked in English.

"*Amrika*," I responded, the Arabic pronunciation for my home country. I was slightly worried there might be anti-American sentiment here. After all, Aden was also the site of al-Qaeda's 2000 USS *Cole* bombing.

But the cashier's face lit up, eyebrows raised. He gave me a thumbs up. "Very good," he said in English. "Five stars." He raised his other four fingers to show me just how many stars I was worth as an American.

I followed Bilal out of the restaurant and stepped onto the street, a short isthmus. Across from us were Somali-looking fishermen peddling the day's catch: snapper, grouper, shrimp, all laid out on dirty blue-and-brown tile. Above them on a peak of rocks sat Sira Fortress, a military post built around the tenth century. Now just to its right perched a mansion by the sea belonging to Sanaa's most powerful tribal sheikh. It was a beautiful locale, sure, but its existence was also a reminder to Aden's residents about who exactly was in charge.

• • •

"Did you learn that from the *dahbashis*?" a smug Adeni journalist, a friend of Bilal's, asked me at a qat chew the next day.

I quickly pulled my hand down from my face. I had instinctively been chewing on a nail, a bad habit I have when I'm stressed. *Dahbashi* was the pejorative term southern Yemenis used to describe northerners. It comes from a popular television show in which a character whose last name was Dahbashi played the fool.

Mildly embarrassed, I attempted to win favor in return: "Yes, I noticed that here in Aden everyone throws their leftover qat in trash cans. In Sanaa, they just throw it on the floor."

The remark set off a round of smiles, chuckles, and I told you so's. The mafraj was full of men, some journalists, others who worked in commerce, all Bilal's friends. We sat on cushions on a cold tile floor instead of a warm carpeted room like in the North. A tiny TV sat on the ground in a corner of the room, airing Al Jazeera.

South Yemenis had originally welcomed the effort to join with its northern neighbor since its perennially dysfunctional government had left the country impoverished and in shambles by 1990. Southerners soon regretted the unity agreement, though, after they felt marginalized and violated by the Saleh government, who excluded southerners from rule in many ways and took advantage of the South's natural resources, such as oil. A civil war broke out between the two sides in 1994 that left the northerners as victors, securing unification, and enraging southerners all the more.

Revolt was in the air again in Aden. A new movement for secession, known as al-Herak, held protests in cities throughout the South several years prior. Everyone hated Saleh, so it seemed. Adenis were forever telling me about police brutality against southerners and the time police killed a young boy named Khaled Darwish. Everyone was inspired by the mass protests in Egypt, but nothing was organized or defined. It was hard to figure out when and where protests were being held. Bilal's friends were either Adenis from way back who thought their city shouldn't be involved with the rest of the uncivilized south, or favored a return to the old South Yemeni state, or supported a federalist model for the entire country. They could argue with themselves for hours and never reach a conclusion.

Two female activists from al-Herak came over to Bilal's apartment for an interview with me. I got up from the mafraj to meet them. We entered a small square side room and closed the door behind us so the girls could remove their niqabs. I was eager to speak with youth activists from the separatist movement, hoping that maybe I could learn how revolts across the Arab world were going to stir up things here in the South. I then imagined Aden's fervor of mass protests sweeping across the North like fire, spurring other Yemenis to revolt against Saleh's government.

I asked the two young women if al-Herak was planning on mass street protests after what was happening in Egypt. One of the women, Zahra, raised her hand in the air, signaling that my question was not the appropriate one to be asking.

"We are not in the opposition. We are calling for our own state," she said to me. "Whether Ali Saleh changes is not important to us. Unity has been canceled since the war of 1994."

"Okay, I get that, but are you interested in joining with the other protesters in Sanaa and in Taiz?"

"We call them colonists," Zahra answered.

We weren't really getting anywhere.

Arab women can be touchier than I am accustomed to, and Zahra grabbed me when she spoke and urged me to listen to her words. She spoke quickly, passionately, yet disjointedly. So much so, I didn't know if I could trust her, like her sanity was in question.

"*Inshallah*, God willing, it will happen in Yemen too!" she said of the idea of revolution, pointing her finger at me as if teaching me a lesson. The idea of joining up with northern activists for a nationwide anti-Saleh protest may have disgusted Zahra, but she still couldn't help getting swept up in the revolutionary spirit that was giving hope to young people throughout the Arab world.

The girls urged me to come to a street protest with them the next day. I felt like grabbing them and saying this is what I was trying to ask the whole time, but refrained. I still didn't know if this would be an al-Herak protest, a Saleh must fall protest, or what, and they left before ever letting me know. Classifying what was happening here, putting it into my nice little box of explanation, was apparently way more important to me, the outsider, than to these activists. I was hoping things would become clearer tomorrow, but tomorrow would only yield more unknowns.

• • •

After the qat chew, as the setting sun cast its glow over Aden's velvety-blue sea, as the fishermen dragged the bows of their blue-and-yellow painted boats onto the sandy beach, as the heat began to lift and flirtatious youth began to gather at Aden Mall, and as the sunset call to prayer echoed through the mosques, bustling street markets, and Queen Victoria park, Bilal and I took off across the city for his nightly errands. We stopped first at the office of a local Adeni newspaper on the second floor of a white-washed shopping strip. Inside, we met a cast of characters, naturally all staunch believers in an independent South Yemen, including a group of a half-dozen or so young men from outside the city. They were there to drop off a video of an al-Herak protest. When they heard there was an American journalist in the office, they desperately wanted to speak with me.

We sat on the carpeted floor together because there was only one desk in the room. They were dark, tall, and thin, yet muscular. I found them quite attractive. They came from Zinjibar, a city east of Aden and home to a southern tribal clan whose most infamous son, Tariq al-Fadhli, had fought with Osama bin Laden in Afghanistan. He was also known to have a penchant for whiskey and political drama. Islamic militants, al-Qaeda, whatever you wanted to call them (because the last thing fundamentalist militants in Yemen are is a unified entity) were known to be active in the area around Zinjibar as well.

I figured these young activists from Abyan province were the closest thing to al-Qaeda in Yemen I had ever met, at least knowingly. The potential danger and scandal of that excited me. So did their good looks. I wrote down their words passionately.

"America is a democracy, but when it comes to the Arab world, America supports oppressors. America protects these countries until they blow up," said one of them, Wagdy. He clearly wanted not just to speak about the start of the Arab Spring, but also to lecture me about my home country, as if I was his conduit for all he had ever wanted to say to the American government.

It wasn't difficult to see how American foreign policy in the Arab world could have provoked them in such a way. The tyranny of Saleh's government would have been most apparent to these young southerners, yet they also saw the American government pouring millions of dollars into the country to support the regime. And it had been the same with Mubarak in Egypt, and with the duplicitous government of Saudi Arabia. America had started an unnecessary war in the Arab world. America fully supported the government of Israel when all these men were seeing in their media were images of dying Palestinian children. And then, worst of all, American drones and missiles struck targets in the exact region where these young men lived, meant to take out al-Qaeda operatives, but inadvertently killing innocent civilians in the process, including women and children.

Wagdy looked at me gravely, wanting to drive his message home: "If al-Qaeda is against the oppression, I am with them. If America is against the oppression, I am with them."

I wondered if these young men would end up joining al-Qaeda. And what that even meant: fighting with a cohort of rebels that the Yemeni government labeled al-Qaeda? Or actively committing themselves to fighting the West? They had kind faces, yet there was a restlessness among them, the restlessness of young men left with few options for their future. It was difficult to see them as the faces of a new global terrorism with which America is at an endless, ill-defined war. Yet that's exactly what these men were just by nature of where they were born; they could become targets of a drone strike by accident. They could be killed outside Zinjibar and then would just turn into an empty label appearing in a wire story across American newspapers: "An al-Qaeda militant was killed in Yemen."

• • •

A Yemeni journalist friend in Sanaa gave me contact information for an Adeni who he said was a leader in al-Herak. I phoned the man, who was called Ali, to set up a time when we could meet that night, though Bilal warned me that he had never heard of Ali the al-Herak leader and dismissed him completely. The two belonged to different divisions within al-Herak that supported different visions for South Yemen's future. They supported different top leaders, and if there was anyone the handful of top al-Herak leaders hated more than Ali Abdullah Saleh, it was each other.

Ali was tall, educated, and middle-aged. He told me that his grandfather was an American citizen. We ate a dinner of fried chicken at a brightly lit fast food restaurant by the sea on the eastern edge of Aden and afterward strolled along the beach. Little boys played in the waves and couples sat in white plastic chairs smoking shisha on the sand, enjoying the cool evening air.

"You know how women used to dress in the South?" Ali asked me as we found a seat on some chairs far from the ears of anyone else.

I told Ali that indeed I had seen photos of women in Aden in the '70s, wearing skirts and short-sleeve blouses, their hair in cute updos. Ali blamed the monumental shift in culture on the Saleh government, and then, by default, extended that blame to all northerners.

It was an easy thing to do. Saleh had encouraged, if not directly participated in, the spread of conservative Islam in the South, not because he was a particularly religious man, but because he wanted to stamp out socialism as a threat to his authority. He worked with Saudi Arabia to establish Salafi schools throughout southern Yemen. The country opened its doors to former mujahideen who had fought the Soviets in Afghanistan and gave them a place to live in Aden, a proposal also supported by Osama bin Laden. Aden had become drastically more conservative over the past few decades. While fewer women wore full face veils here than in Sanaa, the days of miniskirts and whiskey on the beach were long gone.

Ali shooed away a man who came by asking us if we wanted to buy a water pipe. He nervously glanced over his shoulder to see if anyone was listening to him. "We are trying to build our country like it was 1967," he said, 1967 being the year the British left and the incompetent Marxist government took over.

"We are a more civilized culture," he added.

I found that in Ali, and many others I met in Aden, the prejudice and hatred for the northerners was pervasive. An educated Adeni man once told me that northern and southern Yemenis are two different races because they descend from different sons of Noah. ("It's in the Torah!" he cried.) Sometimes this irked me, as I could see the southerners' point, but northern tribesmen have an ancient and at times beautiful culture all their own.

It seemed near impossible to imagine a scenario in which the Yemeni state would function with any sort of competency when such a large portion of its population felt completely excluded from the republic. And it was because the country was so divided that the southerners' ire was barely felt in the high, dry valley of the capital.

The exclusionary state building of Saleh's rule that fueled southern anger also had much to do with why a poor *qabili*, a northern tribesman, didn't have electricity in his village. I wished the two sides could unite under their shared grievances, rise up, and change their country for the better, but it was as though their hatred blinded them to what they had in common.

I thought of small-town conservative types in Texas compared to Upper East Side elitists, San Francisco artists and Western Pennsylvania coal miners, and how they exist in the same America. The southern Yemenis' hatred of their northern fellow countrymen ran deeper than any prejudices I saw in my own country. This wasn't just hatred caused by cultural disparities, because north and south speak Arabic in a different accent, but because of feelings of utter violation. Southerners were killed on their streets by an army of northern soldiers at al-Herak protests over the past few years. They were excluded from official positions, though they were well educated, unless they had ingratiated themselves with Ali Abdullah Saleh himself so that their allegiance couldn't be in question.

I supposed a lot of countries function like this, a portion of its population advantaged at the expense of another. It didn't seem to be a recipe for stability.

• • •

Zahra yanked open our car door and jumped in beside me in the backseat, texting and talking at the same time to three people at once. It was February 11, and multiple protests were set to be taking off down the streets in different neighborhoods of Aden. Their exact locations were unknown to all but a few protest leaders who would make phone calls to gather others at the last minute. Zahra was on her cell phone trying to figure out where our car, with Bilal in the front, should drive. I was keyed up for some action and my eyes scanned the shop fronts of this Adeni neighborhood where men sat on chairs and sold qat for the day.

Suddenly, as if just recognizing my presence, Zahra stared at me as though I had committed a deplorable crime.

"*Ya Allah*! You need to be wearing a niqab! What about the police!"

I was already wearing an abaya and a headscarf, but Zahra wanted me to cover my face because she was sure the police would arrest a foreigner trailing an al-Herak protest. I didn't know what to think. Police didn't arrest foreigners at protests in Sanaa—not yet anyway—but things were different in Aden. Zahra had already been arrested twice, so I figured she had a reason to be paranoid.

Zahra reached into her purse and pulled out an extra niqab, which I thought was a funny thing to carry around in one's purse (because wouldn't you notice if you had left the house without wearing one?). She roughly slid it over my head and tied the face veil in the back a little too tight for comfort. Bilal drove on and we soon found a gathering of young people. There weren't many of them, a few dozen maybe, carrying the flag of the former People's Democratic Republic of Yemen, a red, white, and black striped flag, similar to Yemen's, but a baby blue triangle stuck out of its short end and a five-pointed red star sat in the triangle's middle. The younger protesters wore shirts and black slacks. The older men, whose leathery skin from a life of salt and sun creased in large wrinkles on their hands and faces, were dressed in dark red, plaid-patterned *mawaz* wrapped like skirts around their waists and button-up dress shirts. They walked down the street in a loosely structured line chanting about freedom for the South. Zahra kept insisting that more would join and that I should watch closely because the police would shoot at them, but I mustn't be afraid! Sure enough, somewhere nearby we heard the sound of live gunfire. It was far enough away for plenty of room for safety, but close enough to be thrilling.

Then Bilal got a call.

"*Wallahy*, really?" His face froze in a look of disbelief.

"What, what?!" the rest of us asked.

Bilal hung up and turned to face us in the backseat.

Mubarak had stepped down.

The news spread rapidly through the alleyways of Aden, past the Soviet-style apartment complexes and former British barracks. People sang out the news: the Egyptian people had toppled the regime of Mubarak! One of most important countries in the Arab world had just had a revolution. The thing that we thought could never happen—it had happened. People on the street shouted louder, walked faster, skipped and spun in circles. Men and women at home leaned out their small square windows and cheered the protest. Everywhere around me there was celebration and there was joy. No one in my vicinity could stop smiling.

For me, the news was a shock to the system before it transformed into exhilaration. Like the future had just started down a path that I never before knew was an option. Yes, the protests in Egypt had seemed to indicate that Mubarak's abdication was imminent, but I didn't dare imagine that would happen until life smacked me in the face with it. Dictators meant that life would follow a certain pattern—namely that populations would continue feeling disconnected from their political system. That pattern had just been disrupted. Mubarak's downfall meant anything was possible for the region.

Yemen would change as a result, and thus my life would change. This much I knew to be true. What that change would look like I had no idea, but an unknown future is an exciting future. I didn't come to Yemen for predictability.

I sat in the Mansoura district of Aden hiding behind the blackness of a niqab, far from friends, from anyone to hug or call. I tried to relish and breathe in the excitement moving through the streets like an infectious disease striking us all. I told myself that this was going to be one of the moments about which we foreigners who lived in the Middle East would always ask "where were you when Mubarak stepped down?" Then gunfire again cut through the sticky air, reminding me that Yemen's jubilation was tainted by its current reality. Security forces were firing at a group of al-Herak protesters a few blocks away. Still, the boys marching along beside our car only chanted all the louder.

"Now we need to make a better revolution!" I heard one of them tell his friend.

I secretly wanted it, too. I wanted us all to feel what my friends felt in Egypt at this moment.

CHAPTER 8

Mubarak's presidency had been the linchpin. For Libya, for Syria, for Bahrain—and for Yemen.

When I returned from Aden to the capital, gangs of Saleh-loving thugs were beating up activists during the ever-growing protests in front of Sanaa University. Protesters and thugs lobbed stones at each other over the wide Sixtieth Street. The thugs, the *balateja*, which means "to bully" in Arabic, stood on a high overpass so they had a good angle. Soldiers stood among them, shooting their assault rifles into the sky. Protesters in retaliation set tires aflame in the middle of Rabat Street.

I was suddenly swept up in the thrill and political fervor that signaled the height of the Arab Spring. It was just what I had wanted. Dodging falling stones felt like a game, while recording quotes from impassioned protesters gave me reason for having such fun to begin with. Journalism and living in the Middle East had until now always been about having such adventures for me, and the Arab Spring sure kicked it up a notch. One day I hid in a bakery to take cover from a throng of angered balateja chasing protesters down the road. I giggled with the baker while he removed round bread loaves from a large brick oven. We rolled our eyes at the idiocy of the thugs.

There were disconcerting moments, of course, like the time I saw a snarling *baltajy* near the edge of a protest with a broken hubcap in his grip. But, as long as no one was dying, I didn't feel too guilty for having fun. Also, these moments and the shot of adrenaline they provided only heightened my excitement because there was risk involved. Risk made me feel like I was some greater version of human because I was willing to put my safety on the line for the sake of reporting.

The JMP leaders didn't want anything to do with the new street protests. They stood back while the kids were pelted with rocks. One of the smartest of the JMP old men's club, Socialist party leader Yassin Saeed Noman, told me one afternoon: "If the people on the streets take the lead, we will say thank you for that," but that the protesters "should deal wisely with this big moment."

It was the old guard versus the new among the protesters, as well. The young generation saw the Egyptian revolution and wanted to take to the streets, beating their chests, sacrificing their lives. The JMP leadership saw the establishment as they knew it changing, but knew they were themselves part of that establishment. Nor were they hasty. They also knew Saleh could be capable of no good.

So did the protesters, but they didn't seem to care. Instead their numbers grew by the day. "If they kill me, okay, but we will still be peaceful," Jalal Bakry, a humble student, told me one afternoon.

Saleh announced more empty concessions, but nothing that the JMP wanted. He announced that income taxes would be lowered, though few paid taxes in Yemen anyway. He announced that the government would hire more civil servants, though everyone knew it would never happen.

Then one evening during a protest at the front gates of Sanaa University, the sky already dark, balateja roared in. A gang of them surrounded a young protester I had been standing next to. They yanked at him, dragged him, beat him hard in the middle of Ring Road. It was their anger that was most alarming.

"Stop!" I cried, pulling the arm of a tribesman. I thought they were going to kill him. Was it wrong to step in?

The tribesman pushed me back. "They are dogs," he said to me.

I took a few backward steps and then looked across to the street when I heard the screeching of tires. Tawakkol's car raced past us to exit the scene, swerving left and right, trying to dislodge the two balateja standing on its back rim. Others chased the car down the street, throwing glass bottles at the escaping activist. They crashed open on her back window before the car sped out of range.

• • •

On the southern edge of Sanaa is Hadda, the diplomatic quarter, with coffee shops, pizza joints, and Western-style grocery stores. Huge houses hide behind tall metal gates. Somali beggars hold out their palms to passing cars on the main thoroughfare as ragtag children playfully weave in and out of traffic touting water bottles. Yellow and black painted slabs of concrete bar many of the side streets, protecting the homes of sheikhs, European embassies, or United Nations offices. The neighborhood resembles Saudi Arabia more than the rest of Yemen aside from the blue, red, and green stained-glass windows of Sanaani architecture glistening throughout.

On the very edge of Hadda, a row of columns marks the entrance to one of the neighborhood's largest homes: a square, white, multi-tiered building that takes up an entire street block. It's not just a mansion, it's a castle.

When I visited on February 14, outside there were dozens of armed guards, standing, sitting, patrolling in Toyota Hilux pickup trucks. Inside, just to the right of the gold-trimmed entrance, two large square mafrajs opened into an airy reception area, expansive Persian rugs covering its marble floors. In the center, a few steps led up to a table raised above the ground. I sat at it on red cushions, drinking overly sweetened black tea and waiting for Hamid al-Ahmar, who is not just a sheikh, but, as Yemenis call him, he is the sheikh of sheikhs.

"The people, they love Hamid because he truly cares about the average Yemeni. He thinks about them. He wants Yemen to be good," explained Fawzy, Hamid's obedient, middle-aged public relations assistant, while we waited.

"What does he do for them?" I asked.

"Ah, he has so many programs. He is rich, of course he is rich, but he is generous. Do you see the Salehs being generous?" Fawzy asked me.

"No," I said.

Hamid is one of at least seventeen children, the first son of his father's second wife, and at this time was thirty-nine years old. His family were the kingmakers—the leaders of Hashid, the most powerful tribal confederation in northern Yemen and the one to which Ali Abdullah Saleh belonged. Saleh would not have been able to rule without at least some of the al-Ahmars' good graces. Hamid had few good graces left to give, but his brothers had not yet completely cut ties with Saleh and the larger ruling party, the GPC.

To keep the al-Ahmars appeased, Saleh provided the family with financial perks and political appointments. It was the patronage system Saleh used to rule the country, and the al-Ahmars sat squarely on the top rung. They worked with Saleh openly, covertly, militarily, and in business. It was rumored that Hamid didn't have to pay taxes on all his business earnings. He was a reputed billionaire, one of the richest men in Yemen.

Yet Hamid was also one of Saleh's nemeses. Many believed he wanted to be president. He had a growing rivalry with the president's first son, Ahmed, someone who used to be a friend, but desire for power had gotten in the way. Hamid was in a comfortable position to publicly throw punches at the president. He had told another journalist, notably an older male one, that if Saleh "travels abroad he always carries Viagra in his pocket."

At the end of the day, though, the Ahmar and Saleh families were cut from the same cloth: they were uneducated northern tribesmen who lived in big houses in Sanaa. And despite Fawzy's platitudes, the number of Yemenis who hated Hamid rivaled those who hated Saleh. Still, Saleh wasn't from a sheikh's family, and that could not be underestimated in this traditional society. He had to co-opt the support of sheikhs so that, for one, he would have the might of their tribesmen at his disposal (these were the balateja). Hamid already had his armed militia, tribesmen whose loyalty to their sheikh was unwavering.

As soon as the protests had started in early 2011, many Yemenis said Hamid was financially backing them, or, if the accuser was really pro-Saleh, that all the protesters were just minions of Hamid's grand plan for power. The latter was far from the truth—the young activists I knew were against everything Hamid represented, but when a memo released by Wikileaks revealed that Hamid had told the American embassy in 2009 that they had better not be surprised if protests broke out in Yemen calling for Saleh's ousting, it only strengthened the GPC's accusations about Hamid and the demonstrators.

Hamid entered the grand reception room this afternoon with two bodyguards in tow. I stood up to greet the sheikh, but no handshake was permitted; Hamid was a staunch Islahi. Not that all Islahis were the same. Some of them shook my hands, but Hamid didn't. This was also because of his sheikh status; he shouldn't do anything that wasn't of utmost character when it came to women—except that I heard from women gossiping at qat chews that he had married probably about forty times, cycling through his many wives.

We moved into the right mafraj for the interview and sat atop high red cushions as sturdy as brick blocks. Golden fringe decorated the mafraj's arm rests, each placed equidistant around the red cushions. Hamid's thobe was bright white and pressed. His face, round and juvenile. He wore no weapon, but his ornate janbiya was a foot and a half long, the largest I had ever seen, and placed brazenly at the center of his belt. Most janbiya hilts are made of water buffalo horn imported from India, but the most expensive, such as Hamid's, are probably made from the horns of East Africa's critically endangered black rhinoceros.

"What happened in Egypt made the blood flow in our bodies. If you have blocked veins and suddenly the blood would be pumped into them, this is what happened," Hamid told me. His rather boyish voice was muffled by the qat wad in his left cheek.

"It made our nations braver, and our rulers weaker. It makes the bad people in our country feel that they can't act in the same way."

"Okay, that's great. But you personally, are you excited about what's happening?"

"I would be ashamed of myself if I was doing all this only because I was aiming to be in a position in Yemen," he said. I smiled. He knew what I was getting at. I was pressing him on the common assumption that he wanted a leadership role in the government, maybe even president.

"My aim is to see my country go in the right direction. My aim is to see Yemen stable. We are fighting for democracy and freedom in our country.

"We know the Americans and Europeans, they are more worried about Yemen than they were about Egypt. They would like to give a chance to this regime and to the president to fulfill what he announced. That he will implement real democracy."

"Do you think he will?" I asked Hamid.

"If so, he would have done it already!"

Hamid's tone grew more whiney, as if he were a schoolgirl complaining that it wasn't fair the other girl got to be class president.

Many Yemenis hated Hamid because they found him conceited and Ahmed Saleh much more humble. They thought Hamid represented an old order of sheikhs and power that kept Yemen stumbling around in its past. To still others, particularly Yemenis from the capital, the al-Ahmar brothers represented a time when northern tribes came down to sack the old city of Sanaa, around the middle of the twentieth century, the power of collective memory driving their hatred. The purpose of memory remained crucial in such an ancient place as this

"I can assure you that the Yemeni tribe today is more willing to fight for civil society. They are paying a very big price for the absence of law with their poverty," Hamid continued. "The government is attacking them from time to time. They want to see law implemented in Yemen."

Hamid knew what to say to a journalist. He had no interest in rule of law. But I left the interview liking him, won over by his niceties and faux forward thinking because I had been surrounded by anti-Saleh rhetoric over the past weeks. Maybe Hamid was a good alternative to Saleh? He was at least dignified. Much more so than those snarling balateja.

I had no idea, truly, who Hamid was. I didn't fully understand that he had an entire army at his disposal.

• • •

It was a bright morning in late February. Today's demonstration had gathered in front of Sanaa University, taking shape around the big intersection of Justice Street and Ring Road. There were around one thousand protesters. The balateja weren't far away, a few blocks east, down Justice Street, coming closer and closer. Rocks started flying between the two sides. Then shoes arced through the air, smacking the pavement. Then glass bottles crashed onto the street. "Be peaceful! Be peaceful!" some of the activists cried to their fellow protesters, but they didn't listen. They kept throwing whatever they could find at the balateja. I stood on a concrete step along a shop's wall, watching. Eventually the balateja were pushed back blocks down Justice Street.

The protesters celebrated. A party broke out on the street. They sang and danced and clapped their hands. "*Ya Ali*, after Mubarak!" They waved a poster of a face I had never seen before, that of Ibrahim al-Hamdi, a president of Yemen in the 1970s whose assassination many believe was orchestrated by Saleh. Hamdi was their memory of a better past onto which they clung so fervently.

"Today is progress," said Zacharia, a particularly scrawny twenty-four-year-old, coming up to me, speaking English. "Before, they beat us. Today, we beat them." Zacharia worked at his uncle's textile shop, but was soon bound for China for his studies.

The boy gazed down Justice Street to where the balateja had been. "But, you know, I think that they'll get the security forces and come back," he said.

Zacharia had an uncontrollable desire to be helpful oozing out of his pores to such an extent that he grew annoying. He followed me closely and attentively, running a strand of prayer beads in his left hand as he walked.

"It's days like this that won't do anything. We need to be more organized," Zacharia lamented. "Our leaders, the socialists, and the Islamists, they need to organize.

"In Yemen it will take eight to nine months for revolution," the young activist said, professorially, and I didn't question it because I wanted him to stop talking.

Zacharia followed me over to where a crowd was surrounding two boys dressed in the forest green–colored uniform of Yemeni public schools. One boy was shy, but the other, Shihab, was doing all the talking. He said he was fifteen, but, as tall as my waist, he looked like he was ten. Such were children in Yemen though. Such were the effects of perpetually poor nutrition.

Zacharia explained to me that the boys were here because their teacher had told them they had to go to the pro-Saleh rally in Tahrir Square, but they came here instead.

"What, really? The teacher told them they had to go to Tahrir?" I asked.

"It's a government school," Zacharia shrugged.

I knelt down to talk to the boy.

"The teacher said that I have to leave to go support the president," he told me. "He said, 'don't go to the university.' I don't accept it. Here, I am with the people." He spoke defiantly, his tone setting into the staccato rhythm of poetic Arabic.

It was then I heard a buzz of voices growing louder from down Justice Street. In the distance, I could see the balateja had returned, just as Zacharia had predicted. The group of scraggly tribesmen marched right toward us. At the sight of this, dozens of protesters stormed down the street to face the thugs.

Bang. Bang.

I jumped, as I always did, startled at the sound of gunfire. But then I relaxed because I had learned that the army only shoots into the air.

Only this time was different.

There was shouting. *Something is wrong.* I could tell something was wrong because the voices sounded more desperate. Down the street I could see protesters walking toward us carrying an injured man in their arms. Those who weren't actively supporting the man raised their arms to the sky, chanting that Saleh must step down. It was almost like they were torn between being enraged that a fellow protester was shot and excited that they had a reason to hate Saleh all the more. I ran up to the group and found the injured man sitting up in the hammock of arms. He had been shot in the leg. The blood had soaked through his black pants and covered his tennis shoes. I thought for a second that I should try and ask him questions for an interview, but decided against it. I didn't know how to deal with shot people; I had never seen one before.

Then came the sound of more live ammunition. The crowd of protesters grew angrier. Some yelled "Don't be scared!" as the balateja moved closer, but their directive was completely lost on me. I looked around for a hiding spot and saw an electronics shop on the corner with its door ajar. I darted inside, along with a few other men, leaving Zacharia behind. I walked past the glass countertops displaying cell phones and climbed up the stairs into the second floor, an Internet café. The bang of the gun was so close. My body flinched with each shot, but I assured myself that I was safe inside.

"Don't be worried, don't be worried," the other men said to me in the shop, snickering at my startled reaction to the sound of gunfire. I reciprocated with a smile and went over to the large glass window that looked out onto the street so I could see what was happening.

Directly in front of my viewpoint stood two men, balateja, Kalashnikovs in their hands, barrels pointed straight ahead. Their faces were twisted in hatred, their eyes set with determination, trying to pick off their targets with each shot. I looked to the right. Standing a few blocks down was a group of young protesters, yelling, raising their hands, being defiant.

It was the first time I had ever actually seen someone shoot a gun in my entire life, and it was into a crowd of people. Yet the shooters' faces revealed they did not see other human beings in front of them. They saw vermin.

These were Yemenis, the people who took me in, made me laugh, who taught me what kindness to a stranger really meant. I wondered how they could do this to one another because of something like a peaceful protest.

What these young protesters represented to the balateja was much different from what they actually were. They represented a part of a nefarious whole. They represented the JMP. They represented the political and tribal enemies of Saleh. But the world wasn't so black and white. Just because the activists were against Saleh didn't mean they were adherent followers of Hamid al-Ahmar. Some of the protesters were of the most humble backgrounds, like Zacharia, who thought they had a chance at bringing hope to their homeland.

More balateja charged into the intersection, easily taking control of it. The remaining protesters scattered onto side streets and ran away. I came down from the computer shop and saw the balateja waving their daggers over their heads, dancing, gloating victoriously. They chanted, "With our blood and souls, we sacrifice for Ali!"

No one was killed that day, and only about half a dozen injured by bullets. Killing hadn't been the point. Not yet. This had been more of a warning.

CHAPTER 9

Periodically on the rocky roads outside of Yemen's major cities, tollbooth-style checkpoints are set up to monitor all passing vehicles. The soldiers manning the checkpoints ensure that traveling foreigners present a tourist police–stamped permission slip, otherwise they have to turn back to the capital or the nearest city. That is, of course, if foreigners fail to pretend to be Yemenis and thus pass through the checkpoint without issue, or pay off the soldiers to guarantee safe passage.

This rule was for our safety, but I found such bureaucracy frustrating when other government-enforced rule of law seemed so absent. I loathed the process of going to the tourist police to beg for permission to leave the capital by road. I didn't realize prior to living in Yemen how claustrophobic limited freedom of movement can be, being unable to just wake up and drive somewhere without permission from a higher authority.

Reports had reached me that the anti-Saleh protests were larger in Taiz, Yemen's third largest city, than in the capital, so I wanted to travel there to find out for myself.

Innocent protesters were being shot. I thought coverage of their movement deserved everything I had. Also, I would be the first Western journalist to travel to Taiz and write about the protest there. The desire to impress others with my reporting ingenuity pushed me forward, too.

I happened to live across from the tourist police in Sanaa's old city. It was a smelly, dank office with stained green carpet. It was because of this that I was exceedingly stressed about having to go there this February morning. There was no way they didn't know I was a journalist. They had to know I went to the Square every day to report on the demonstrations. All my other neighbors knew. If the tourist police stepped outside to the local shop and bought a soda, they could ask, "Hey what's up with that Laura girl?" and my neighbors would say, "She's nice and all, but she's a *sahefeya*, a journalist." Otherwise known as someone you do not give permission to leave Sanaa.

I stepped across the threshold of the office's open door, walked down the narrow hallway and into a small, bare room with plain white walls. I tried to look calm.

"*Salaam aleikum*," I said to the four policemen sitting around a desk, sipping tea.

They looked up at me and responded with the customary "*waleikum salaam*." Short, lots of mustaches, dark blue uniforms, the bane of my existence. They weren't chewing qat yet because it was still morning. The middle-aged, stern officer sitting behind the large desk projected an air of self-confidence far greater than his rank.

"I want to go to Taiz," I said. "I am going to fly there in an airplane, but I heard that there is a checkpoint between the airport and the city and I need a permission slip for that checkpoint."

Before they had a chance to ask about the reason for my wanting to travel to the lovely ancient city nestled in Yemen's central highlands, home to the beautiful mountain Jebl Sabr as well as a very large antigovernment demonstration, I started to explain.

"My best friend here in Sanaa, a Yemeni girl, she's from Taiz. But she is going to go study at a university in Canada and she really wants to show me her family house in Taiz before she leaves Yemen. This is her last chance, so I have to go to Taiz this weekend. I heard there is a big demonstration in the city, but I am very scared of the demonstrations. I will not go near it. Protesters bring chaos!"

I stopped and looked at the cocky officer behind the desk with a pleading expression. He spoke about twenty words of incomprehensible English but thought he was an all-star for it.

"Sit down," he said motioning to the decaying office chair in front of him. "You student?"

"Yes, I study Arabic."

"How is the Yemen?"

"I love Yemen."

He paused in consideration and then finally reached for his phone to call the Ministry of the Interior to ask for my permission. I tried not to look nervous and just smiled and accepted an offer of tea.

No one answered at the Ministry of the Interior. The officer tried again five minutes later, but still there was no answer. After another five minutes, still no answer.

The ministry must be too busy organizing balateja salaries, I thought.

We sat for a while, the police officers and I making small talk. Then they asked me what I thought of the protest movement and what I thought about President Saleh.

"Yemen doesn't need chaos. Yemen is not Tunis and it's not Egypt," I said, using a line Saleh had employed in a recent speech.

A plump officer sitting cattycornered from me became ruffled at my attempts at brownnosing. He interrupted emphatically, "No. Saleh must leave. *Irhal! Irhal!* Leave!" He pumped his fist in the air and flashed me that mischievous, slightly playful Yemeni grin that signals life isn't to be taken too seriously—it's the same look taxi drivers gave me when they swing their heads around to ask me in the backseat the all-important question: "Do you chew?" The same look I got from Yemeni officials when they suggested I could land an interview with Saleh because of his penchant for Western women.

Still I was taken aback. Here I was, sitting in an eight-by-ten room in a police office, and an officer in front of me was chanting protester slogans with a grin on his face.

"Oh, ignore him," the other officers told me. "He's from Dhala'a. He's a Heraki, a southern separatist."

"*Irhal! Irhal!*" the plump one chanted.

I just laughed loudly and tried to stall some more, all the while hoping that someone would pick up at the Ministry.

"Okay, okay," they said after more time passed. "You can go to Taiz. But you need to talk to our director before we give you the permission slip."

I followed one of the officers up the stairs to the upper rooms of the tourist police wondering if this was the way real foreign correspondents did their jobs.

Sitting down at the desk of the director, I repeated my story about my friend moving to Canada. It wasn't 100 percent fiction: in Taiz, I was going to be staying at the house of a Yemeni friend who was already living in Canada. Her mother and father, the al-Guneids, had offered to put me up.

"Yes we will give you permission," the director, slightly more put together than the ragtag bunch downstairs, said with a smile. I reciprocated, trying my best to be demure.

He added, "Make sure you keep hold of this slip the entire time you are in Taiz. If you don't have it, the police there will think that you are a journalist, and we don't want any journalists in Taiz."

"Of course," I said to him. "*Shokran.* I am very excited to see Taiz."

I left the building trying not to let it show on my face how smug I was feeling. I did it. I tricked them. I was going to be the first Western journalist to visit Taiz.

When I got on the plane the next day, a *Washington Post* reporter was sitting across from me.

• • •

The al-Guneid family home was a stately residence perched on the steep incline of a terraced mountain that rose up from the east side of Taiz. Outside its doors was a small swimming pool set in a quaint, tiered garden of exotic trees. Paintings—the work of Yemeni artists—adorned the walls of the salon and dining room on the ground floor, which connected to a large, well-kept mafraj.

Out of the house's colorful stained-glass windows was an amazing view of the ancient city, with its beautiful stone architecture, that spread out over the crevices of the central Yemeni highlands. Taiz is a city in the mountains, with its wealthy citizens literally set above the commotion of shops, markets, and factories in the valley below. Vegetation is more plentiful than in Sanaa or Aden thanks to the frequency of rainfall, and small trees of bougainvillea, fig, and hibiscus dot the landscape. Low-lying clouds hung over the city on the morning of my arrival, imbuing the surroundings with a mystical calm.

Months later, when I would visit Taiz again while war was raging in the city, the view from the house would also be stunning. Dr. Guneid would point out to me all the positions from which the government was lobbing artillery shells down into rebel-controlled neighborhoods.

It was ironic that Taiz would experience such fighting. Here the people weren't gun-toting, long-haired tribesmen—the type who didn't seem capable of speaking with inside voices and who populated the pro-Saleh rallies in Sanaa. Rather, Taizis were known as being *motalim*, educated, just as Fahd, the actor, had told me. They weren't military commanders, but instead served as leaders in commerce and trade or worked as doctors and university professors.

Agriculture had thrived across the fertile hills of central Yemen while the arid north was perpetually drought-stricken. Yemenis from this region settled in cities and became more industrialized, thus decreasing the role of the tribe in their livelihood. As well, Taiz has been open to the outside world to a much greater extent than the fortified villages of Yemen's north. It was near the border with South Yemen, and many of Taiz's residents traveled to Aden for work or education during the time of the British Empire.

Shortly after my arrival at the al-Guneid residence, I was served a large lunch of roasted goat, rice, fresh salads, and honey-saturated dessert. I sat at a table with the family and ate, as opposed to the traditional Yemeni way of eating on the floor. During spoonfuls of meat and rice, I tried to take in all that I could from the loquacious Dr. Abdulkader al-Guneid. He attempted to educate me about the city's complex history of opposition politics.

"Taizis, they don't like him. He is a tribesman. You know what I mean, Laura?" he said of President Saleh. Dr. Guneid spoke in English, enunciating his speech meticulously and drawing out words for effect.

He explained that Taiz was the heartland of the JMP. Many of the opposition parties that made up this coalition were born in Taiz in the 1960s. Anti-regime sentiment in the city increased as the years of Saleh's reign wore on. While Taizis were educated, they felt they always came second in line to a northern tribesman, even if that tribesman was illiterate.

"The protesters have done something spectacular. You see what I'm saying? They made a sit-in in the center of the city so the government truly feels them. Saleh feels what is happening in Taiz, and he hates it."

"I know the protesters in Sanaa copied the protesters in Taiz with making the sit-in," I said.

"We are very crafty."

Dr. Guneid's gold metal–rimmed frames slipped down his nose when he talked, which gave his words an extra feeling of admonishment.

"Laura, your articles are very good, and you understand Yemen, but they are boring," he said, while serving himself some rice.

"Okay," I replied.

After lunch came what always comes after lunch. Dr. Guneid had been kind enough to organize a qat chew with a number of Taiz's political elite for my visit. Though by profession a doctor, Dr. Guneid's passion was politics, and his influence behind the scenes in local affairs was obvious. He was also an enthusiastic fan of Twitter.

We reclined on maroon-colored floor cushions in the mafraj. As usual, I was the only woman. The men sat cross-legged or rested their left elbow on stiff, rectangular cushions as tradition dictates. We picked the best green leaves out of the day's qat pile and tossed the rest to the floor as we chatted. Conversation was dynamic, if sometimes circuitous.

"The snowball from the avalanche is rolling down and it's getting bigger and bigger. It has its own path," said Sultan al-Samie, a liberal-leaning member of parliament, about the country's political situation.

"If you are faced with a big rock you need to move, then at first you will just concentrate on how to move that rock. We expect to have spiders and scorpions below that rock, but it won't be as bad as the rock itself," said Mohammed al-Sabri, a skinny, weasely-looking leader in the opposition Nasserite party.

I was assured, by pretty metaphors mainly, and in between long gulps of water since chewing qat makes you very thirsty, that because Yemen had a somewhat functioning and established opposition, there wouldn't be a power vacuum when Saleh left office. These men from the JMP would finally be able to start saving Yemen, first by initiating a national dialogue among the various political factions about the country's future. Some would support turning Yemen into a federalist state, while all would agree that authority needed to be taken away from the Saleh clan. The JMP just needed that pesky Saleh out of the picture, and with the Arab Spring, they saw an unexpected opening for that to happen.

And anyway, there was no going back now.

"The only thing he can do is agree to an interim period where there would be no ruling party and his sons would not be in control, an interim government for six months, to prepare for peaceful elections," said Abdelkarim Shaiban, a parliament member from al-Islah. They were all adamant that this was the best scenario for which Saleh could hope. It was as if they were staring into a crystal ball only available for JMP leaders. I didn't see that the on-the-ground situation in Yemen merited such confidence yet. The protests didn't draw out nearly as many numbers as in Egypt, and even in the face of widespread dissent, Saleh sat comfortably in his position, guarded by family and tribal allies.

Dr. Guneid stood up to close the curtains on the mafraj's tall western-facing windows. It was becoming dark outside and such was customary during the chew. By this time, a few hours on, we all were feeling qat's mild narcotic effects. We had passed through the stage of chatter, when qat makes you want to engage with those around you, and were in the high's stage of contemplation, or *hodoo*. This was when I would concoct farfetched ideas and plans in my head that seemed brilliant until I woke up the next morning (I believe this is the way Yemeni politics worked, as well); or my mind would focus sharply on some mundane, distracting fact, like the career of a high school classmate. Meanwhile, my heart raced, my palms sweated, and I stared off into the distance or just intently at some blank point on the wall across from me.

I told the men I wanted to go down to Freedom Square to meet with some of the local protest leaders. The men advised me that I should wear a niqab, especially because the secret police were quite active in Taiz. There were a few minutes of awkward discussion among the room of older men about whether the long black cloak and face veil were truly necessary while I stood in the middle feeling self-conscious in my American outfit.

The quietest of all the men at the chew, Hamoud al-Mikhlafi, volunteered to drive me down to the Square because his home was in that direction. Hamoud was bearded with speckled gray hair and a contemplative expression that somehow suggested he could be taken more seriously than the other men in the room.

I borrowed one of Dr. Guneid's wife's niqabs, once again suited up, just like I had done in Aden, and went outside to meet Hamoud. We zigged and zagged in his SUV down a steep street of hairpin turns to the valley below, the center of the city.

"This is your first time at the Square?" he asked in Arabic. His voice was quiet and mellow.

"Yes. I've been to Change Square in Sanaa many times, but this is the first time in Taiz."

Hamoud moved his chin up, a reverse nod, a sign of acknowledgment. He seemed shy, demure even.

After a few moments, he added, "A grenade was thrown at the Square last week. One of the youth died, God be merciful toward him. This is because of the governor."

"You think the governor of Taiz was behind it?" I asked.

Hamoud smiled and nodded his head toward me. "Yes, that devil."

We arrived at the Square's edge and I thanked Hamoud for the ride. I figured he was just another player in the cast of characters I had met that afternoon.

But I would see Hamoud again, and at that time he would not be able to drive through central Taiz without bodyguards at his side.

• • •

Boshra al-Maqtari dressed less conservatively than most other Yemeni women, wearing a long coat over blue jeans rather than the black abaya. She was tiny in stature, but fiery in spirit, and talked a mile a minute, her voice rising with her passion. Yet whenever Boshra paused from some diatribe about the need for revolution, she looked at me with pleading in her brown eyes, desperate for me to see her side.

"This is a racist regime. If people are from the South or Taiz, they are being discriminated against," Boshra told me. "The tribes have become the rule of law. Saleh brought us back one hundred years!"

Ten or so activists and I gathered at Boshra's apartment an hour after Hamoud drove me to the Square. We piled into a tiny sitting area, men and women together, something I never experienced in conservative Sanaa. I was in a chair, but most others were on the carpeted floor or standing, and all the men were dressed in Western clothes, not the thobe of northern Yemenis. I was struck by how much these young adults, who were around my age, reminded me of my friends back in the United States. Sometimes when Boshra talked to me, she hooked her arm around mine in friendship, young woman to young woman, as if we were anywhere else in the world.

I scribbled in my notebook to try to keep up with the chatter coming at me from all sides. A woman in a niqab, the only one in the room wearing one, leaned on my shoulder from her position on the couch next to me. One person would feed off another's energy. It was hot, and we were all sweating.

"I have a master's degree, and my boss only has a first degree," said Fahim al-Monifi, a lawyer and activist. "A lot of people come out who are feeling this difficulty."

Boshra, who tied a Yemeni flag around her neck like a scarf, attributed the Arab Spring to three things: Al Jazeera, for broadcasting protests to all the corners of the Arab world and creating an alternative to state-run media; Facebook, for allowing Arab activists to organize themselves online; and Wikileaks, for telling the truth about Arab dictators to the world.

"They said before that we were becoming like Somalia and Afghanistan," Boshra explained, alluding to the terms in which Western commentators had regularly referred to the bleak state of affairs in Yemen under Saleh. "Now they will say that we are becoming like Taiz," she continued. It was this sort of attitude that caused many from outside the city to despise the Taizis for their feeling of superiority when compared to the rest of the country.

But these activists didn't care. They were riding high.

"We feel that the revolution will start here, but the results will be felt in Sanaa," Fahim said.

"We've learned that nothing is impossible," said another activist, Shinaz al-Akhali.

"We, the Arab people. The fear is behind us," Boshra added.

When I asked whether they were scared of being attacked, another chimed in: "The fear of violence is only in Sanaa." I nodded my head and believed her.

• • •

The next morning, I could have been just another Yemeni woman in a sea of black niqabs. Sectioned off in the female area at Friday prayers in Freedom Square, I was gazing out at the endless rows of men, spilling down the street into the center of the city. They sat on their brightly colored prayer mats, cross-legged, listening to an imam deliver a sermon about striving for freedom against dictatorship. The idea of peaceful revolt against the regime as a religious duty was alive and thriving in Taiz, just as it was in Sanaa.

Many men had traveled by road into the city from their tiny villages, clusters of ancient stone houses strewn across the craggy mountains of the nearby countryside. Dozens of the men sat on roofs of nearby buildings to cram into the space available. The ground at the Square was on an incline, and when I gazed eastward up it, it was hard to see where the rows of men stopped and the nearby mountains began. Sandbags lined the outer rim of the demonstration along with a civilian-run protester checkpoint to make sure no one was entering with any weapons, just as the protesters did in Sanaa. A few government soldiers milled about as well.

The women, myself included, sat on steps that led up to a warehouse on the south flank of the sit-in, segregated from the men. I half tried to understand the imam's speech while also trying to figure out the number of protesters who had showed up that day, wishing I had been trained in the science of calculating the size of a crowd.

It was the Friday of the Martyr, named for the man who had been killed the week before by the grenade. In the months to come, each Friday of protest in Taiz and Sanaa would be given a name: the Friday of No Return, the Friday of Justice, the Friday of Peaceful Resistance. Protesters would recall each Friday's title as if the name was something sacred and added legitimacy to their struggle.

I had never done this, gone and listened to a whole Friday sermon, pretending to be just another of the faithful in the crowd. In Sanaa, I always timed my arrival at Friday demonstrations to fall just as prayers were ending. But here I was, in a niqab, all alone, in a city in central Yemen, a country which most Americans cannot even identify on a map. I was trying to convey what was happening before me to the readership of the *New York Times.*

What am I doing? I thought, not for the first time. *This is crazy. What path did my life take to lead me to this point?* I was taking part in a moment that was so significant for the people around me, who were doing this out of hope for a better life for themselves and their children, but I was just a twenty-five-year-old from small-town Pennsylvania. The pressure of the moment settled squarely on my shoulders.

I felt I was not worthy of carrying this load. How did I get picked for this? I suddenly became aware of how far away I was from everyone I cared about. I could disappear here—I was in a niqab, after all. To be unknown and unrecognizable behind a veil felt both empowering and isolating.

The imam finished, the men did their prostrations—an extra one for the man who had been killed—and the crowd broke out into thunderous chanting, pumping their fists in the air and yelling against Saleh, the leader who had relegated them to a second-class city, who had created a system that favored tribalism over their civil society. I scribbled notes. I walked around and took photos. I tried to capture what I was witnessing, unsure whether I should reveal myself as a foreigner by lifting my veil so it would seem more normal that a woman was weaving in and out of a packed crowd of men.

Then I heard a familiar voice.

On a stage, right next to the steps where I had just been sitting, stood Fahd al-Qarni, my TV co-star. He was telling jokes to a captive audience of dozens of skinny, working-class Taizis who cheered him on. They laughed as he comically paced the stage, fully animated as always, with a microphone in hand, poking fun at Saleh.

I was shocked. Not because I was seeing Fahd on stage—he was a star in his home city so this wasn't all that surprising—but because for the past couple of weeks, I had been so consumed by the importance of reporting each day's events as they unfolded that I had started to forget there had been a life before this crisis. Now the symbol of my past life in Yemen, a life before the uprising, before the *New York Times*, and before the gunfire, was staring me in the face. Fahd had been a major part of what made Yemen significant for me in 2009. Now there he was, supporting and encouraging the protesters of the Taiz sit-in. And I was standing in front of him in a black niqab.

I squeezed through the crowd, lifting my niqab above my face without hesitation so that the men wouldn't be upset by a woman shoving past them—once again, as a foreign woman I was exempt from society's rules. I held my camera at shoulder height so they could see I was a journalist. I heard murmurs about the presence of a foreign journalist at Freedom Square as I shoved. The Yemeni protesters were supporting the presence of foreign journalists covering their uprising. They understood that the more positive outside attention they received the more it could only help their cause. I finally made it to the edge of the stage and saw that Fahd had stepped off. He exited into one of the rooms of the long one-story building that flanked Freedom Square's south side. I didn't know what I would have done if he had still been performing when I reached him. Would I have yelled, "Hey Fahd! It's me!" from the crowd?

Men were standing as guards outside the room Fahd had gone into. When I approached them they looked vaguely surprised that a Western journalist was here at Freedom Square.

"Hi, *salaam aleikum*," I said. "I need to talk to Fahd. He knows me. I was in *Hammy Hammek* too." I tore away the black scarf wrapping my hair, exposing my whole head.

"I mean, I'm also a journalist," I quickly added. "This is a surprise! This is a surprise!" I said literally, unsure of how to convey my exact emotions at the moment in Arabic to these protesters.

Their eyebrows rose and their faces lightened. They looked as if they couldn't believe it. But, then again, I was having trouble believing this was my life too.

"Yes. Yes, I know you!" one of the guards said. "*Hathy hely*!"

"Can I just see Fahd?" I asked and they led me back through a room where a volunteer doctor in a white smock stood beside an operating table, stitching up a protester. The guard told me the protester had been beaten up by the local balateja on his way to the Square this morning. I nodded in response so he knew that I understood the balateja were indeed a threat to their movement.

Then, past stacks of cardboard boxes containing bandages, syringes, and other medical supplies, I found Fahd sitting on a pile of rugs that lay on the dirt floor. Here was a person with whom I had spent dozens upon dozens of hours filled with fun and companionship. He was checking his cell phone and had the impatient look of someone who was about to leave.

My greeting happened the only way it possibly could have, with stuttering, few words, and large smiles. I had this burning desire to tell him everything—how I was exhausted, felt pressured, disturbed, but also motivated—but I knew that now wasn't the time. Here I was at Freedom Square on a Friday afternoon in Taiz when he had assumed I was back in America. I never called him to tell him I was still in Yemen or to ask him to drive me down to Taiz, yet we met here nonetheless. The uprising caused our paths to converge yet again.

I fumbled for something to talk about so that we didn't just stand there gaping at one another. So I interviewed Fahd. He spoke with eloquence about the future that he wanted for Yemen with the tone of a man adept at being on stage. I remembered when he used to tell me similar things a year and a half ago. I had known so little about Yemeni politics then. I had known who Saleh was, and I had met the foreign minister once, but that was about it. Now I knew the names of opposition leaders and felt comfortable calling them up on the phone. Now I was writing for the *New York Times* and Fahd was entertaining a crowd of thousands of Yemeni demonstrators chanting against their president without fear. Life did produce surprises. I longed to freeze this moment in time. I didn't want to have to step outside and continue to take notes and write an article and fly to Sanaa the next morning where protesters were being shot. I wanted to pretend I was just in a Yemeni TV show again, without all this responsibility. But the future would pull us both forward and, at this point, there was no hope at stopping it because there never really is.

CHAPTER 10

Haley and Portia sat beside me. Two strikingly beautiful young women—Haley, strawberry blonde, thin, and Californian and Portia, luscious brown hair, dimpled, and a Londoner. They both wore big sunglasses, notebooks in their laps. Haley leaned her head against her hand. Her complexion turned pale and she looked as if she were about to throw up.

I gazed out before us. Thousands upon thousands of tribesmen stood in a large sports stadium chanting in unison about how they would sacrifice their blood and soul for Ali. Others packed into the bleachers that rose up from the stadium's side walls. We sat in box seats, set above the masses, surrounded by Yemeni journalists and important GPC loyalists. A podium stood unused ten feet to our right.

Ali Abdullah Saleh's suave and Westernized public relations assistant, Faris, had offered to bring foreign journalists to see the president speak to this crowd of adoring fans, to show us that not all Yemenis supported the protesters at the university. Who better than Faris, the handsome face of the Saleh regime, to try to convince us that the president wasn't so bad after all? He glanced at Haley, Portia, and me from a few seats over with a look that asked, "Do you see how everyone loves him? What did I tell you!"

I saw. They were the same sort of tribesmen who occupied Tahrir Square in downtown Sanaa. Some were balateja. I saw them being paid in bags full of qat after the rally was over. How was I supposed to think this was a good thing? They reminded me of the two men I saw shooting at the protesters in the Square—the first time I'd ever seen someone shoot a gun—two weeks prior. The tribesmen only stopped chanting when an imam began singing out the introductory Quran recitation over a loudspeaker, the guttural melodies of classical Arabic resonating across the stadium.

After another ten minutes of introductory pomp and speeches, a man climbed up to the podium to address the crowd. He had to stand on a box so he could reach the microphone. A short man with slick sunglasses and short black hair. It was Ali Abdullah Saleh. This was the first time I'd ever seen him in person. He leaned over and kissed the head of a little girl who had come up to greet him.

I squeezed together my nose and upper lip, my slightly disgusted face, and looked over at Haley and Portia, who were both hungover and scowling. Last night had been Haley's birthday. The young, freelance foreign correspondent crew of Yemen had celebrated at the apartment where Haley lived with Portia, Oliver, and Josh, two other journalists. Jeb, an American from Augusta, Georgia, brought moonshine that his Russian roommate made in a large cooking pot. There was dancing, and shots, and joking about tear gas. Only Haley, Portia, and I managed to scrape ourselves out of bed this morning to make it to the rally so that we could show Faris we didn't want to only cover the antigovernment activities. But we all were beginning to regret the decision and envied Oliver, Jeb, and the rest of the bunch, who were still asleep in their beds.

Saleh spoke about upholding the constitution, the need for democracy, and the crowd of the illiterate roared. A correspondent for the *New Yorker* who was in Sanaa for a short reporting trip leaned over my shoulder and whispered, "this reminds me of what Sadaam Hussein used to do."

I squinted some more at Saleh, the country's leader for more than thirty years, although Yemenis had assumed his assassination was inevitable, because that's what happened to their presidents. He was a man who worked his way into the presidency only after first getting rich as a whiskey-smuggling army officer. I was told he was taught how to wear the suit he had on by another whiskey smuggler whose son was wanted for murder in the United Kingdom. Saleh used al-Qaeda militants against his personal enemies when it suited him and American military aid against his enemies when that suited him more. Sometimes he used both at the same time. He assassinated and he promoted. He connived with the veneer of humility, acting like the average Mohammed's president. Saleh had about five different ages, according to the media. He probably didn't know how old he was, because few uneducated tribesman of his generation did.

It's all there in that short man with a bad lisp, I thought. Who would have guessed? He doesn't look like an evil dictator. The tone of his voice was far from stately, low, and rhythmic. Instead, he sounded like an aging high school principal in a fuss over the state of the modern adolescent. A lecherous old man who drinks too much whiskey, maybe I could see that. Was he in charge of the balateja who shot at the protesters? Was it on his direct order? Should I hate him, then?

"I'll tell you what I am going to hate," I leaned over to Haley and Portia to say. "Getting out of this stadium with all these gross *qabilis*," referring to the tribesmen.

"Oh my God," Haley and Portia said in unison.

Portia went over to talk to Faris after Saleh's speech was finished, while Haley and I headed down the back stairs, eager to leave. This all had felt like such a waste of time, listening to state propaganda and witnessing the people paid to cheer it on. Well, at least I finally was able to put a human face to a man I wrote about every day, I thought, the man whom Yemenis both vilified and glorified. I still felt far from being able to figure out the hazy truth about him.

As Haley and I approached the stadium's main lobby area, a look of dread spread simultaneously across both our faces. Tribesmen had already amassed, smelly bodies shoving and elbowing, eager to get to their qat in the parking lot. They squeezed out the main door, dozens at a time.

I looked at Haley. Haley looked at me. *Let's do this*, we both understood. Let's do this despite the high level of inappropriateness for women to be squeezing through a crowd of men. *It doesn't matter, we're hung over,* I told myself, *and they're just a bunch of paid thugs anyway.*

"Whoaaaaah," grunted a tribesman from the small, drab lobby below.

We descended the stairs and shoved through. Tribesmen did double takes, cocked their eyebrows at us, and then turned again to concentrate on getting out the door. To the qat! I tried to ignore their sweaty bodies pressing against my own and looked back at Haley just as we were finally making it through a crevice of an opening to the outside. Through the big sunglasses, she looked like this was the last place on Earth she wanted to be.

• • •

"Wait, so what is your lead going to be?" Portia asked me during a late night mafraj work session a few days later.

"Uh, um, that there's a plan. He's, like, stepping down, though he's, like, not." I fumbled for words. I was a freelance print journalist because, for one, I didn't like collaboration. And after all, she was writing for the *Washington Post.* We couldn't have identical leads.

"Guys, so he's definitely stepping down by the end of this year. If he agreed to the JMP five-point plan, then he is definitely stepping down," Oliver said from his cushion on the other side of the mafraj, confident as always.

"This is so confusing," Portia moaned.

"Guys, I don't think we should be so hasty about this," Haley piped in.

We were all sitting together this evening, trying to work out a potential story in the fifth-floor mafraj of Oliver, Haley, Portia, and Josh's apartment. The walls were an eggshell white, the cushions, red. Colorful stained glass decorated the windows that lined the two walls of the room, and an ornate, carved wooden door opened into the rest of the apartment. A photoshopped poster of Obama dressed in Yemeni garb, a turban and janbiya, hung on the wall. The apartment was one of the highest points in the old city, a tower of brown brick and white gypsum frosting. We had to trudge up six floors in a narrow stairwell of uneven ledges to reach it. From the windows, we could see the glimmering lights of all of Sanaa spread across the valley and the dark, looming mountains past them.

It was our bureau, the bureau of the journalism crew of Sanaa, all under the age of thirty (all but the older and more serious Iona, at least). It's where we wrote for the United States and United Kingdom's major newspapers: the

Wall Street Journal, *Washington Post*, the *New York Times*, and the *Guardian* among them. Occasionally, a publication snuck in a staff reporter, but he (rarely she) never stayed for long. There were too few of us to seriously be competitive with each other. We each had as much work as we could handle.

The mafraj was also where we partied. It's where we drank the beer and vodka that we crammed into our suitcases every time we flew into Yemen from abroad. After that ran out, we begged diplomats and United Nations employees to give us some of their alcohol stash. (Oliver and I had shamelessly stuffed beer bottles into my purse after one party at a UN official's house the previous fall, only to be discovered when a bottle came tumbling to the ground as I was saying goodbye to our host.) When even more desperate, we drank foul-tasting King Robert whiskey that we could always buy from an Ethiopian liquor smuggler or the red-tinted Chinese restaurant in Hadda that appeared to double as a brothel. We joked that it was made in a bathtub in Djibouti. But we drank it by the glass anyway.

This night, though, we all had our computers on our laps, cell phones to our ears, going back and forth with editors in America and London. News had spread a few hours earlier that Saleh had agreed to a plan the JMP had created that called for him to step down by the end of 2011. It was portrayed as a fair deal to steer the country out of the chaos that everyone predicted would erupt as more and more protesters were killed at Change Square. I received a news tip from a JMP source that Saleh had agreed to the plan during an hours-long meeting between the two sides. Then a Yemeni official called us to say Saleh hadn't yet agreed to the plan. Or maybe he had. He wasn't sure. Our editors caught wind of the potential news story and were pushing for reports. Another country in the Arab world ousts a leader—or at least it was supposed to oust him in about nine months. As if this was the way that Yemeni politics worked.

"Well if you report it, I'm going to have to report it," I said to Oliver, only half joking. Oliver was writing for the *Wall Street Journal* and I had recently learned through experience that this was the way major papers worked: if a competitor of the *New York Times* covered breaking news, I'd have to tackle it as well.

"He said he was stepping down," Oliver reiterated.

"I can't believe Saleh's going to leave office early," Portia said.

"Well, I wouldn't necessarily call it early, thirty years later," Haley chimed in again.

We received a phone call from a Yemeni official. Saleh had agreed to the JMP plan, the person on the other end was very happy to tell us. See, he wasn't a hard-nosed Arab ruler after all.

I looked up the JMP plan in its original Arabic version online, more detailed than the English translation. I read it over again. There was one point that kept jumping out at me.

"Guys, it says here that Saleh only has to agree on how he will step down at the end of the year. *How.* Not that he actually *will.* This is stupid. It's like the vaguest thing ever. I hate this."

"Argh!" Portia moaned, holding her head in her hands.

"The official said that Saleh was stepping down early," said Oliver.

"It's not early," said Haley.

A few minutes later, a major American news outlet one of our cohorts reported for ran, on its main webpage, that Saleh had agreed to step down at the end of 2011.

"Shit! My editors put that up without me realizing it!"

We all panicked. This was huge news for Yemen. And we were the ones delivering it. Us sitting together in a mafraj, my friends, we held the key to the English-language news consumers of the world. We could make them believe that another Arab leader was forced out by protesting young activists.

A phone rang. A Yemeni official was on the other end.

"Why did you write that Saleh was going to step down at the end of this year?" he yelled.

"Because that's what you told us."

• • •

It was a drab morning. It had rained overnight and the clouds hadn't yet cleared from the sky. Oliver and I had shared a taxi to the Square later that week after receiving phone calls that a band of CSF had approached the demonstration's southern edge, seeming like they were going to storm it.

Two shots echoed from just a few blocks south of where Oliver and I stood on Ring Road. We could see a large group of protesters gathered there, looking around a street corner at what we assumed were CSF soldiers. I wanted to press forward because I had grown used to gunfire over the past few weeks and it no longer made me flinch like that morning in the computer shop. The Yemenis around me were used to gunfire too, but that's because it's what they grew up with: guns at weddings, guns for fun, guns to solve disputes. The United States is the most armed country in the world. Yemen is the second.

Oliver and I walked toward the protesters. The gunfire was coming from around a corner, on a street perpendicular to Ring Road. Every few minutes, a protester or two would run out to face CSF squarely, taunting them, throwing stones.

Boom. Boom. Boom.

Were those shots fired into the air, or at someone? The sound is a bit different depending on the angle at which the rifle is pointed, but I hadn't become so professional at deciphering the sounds of the gun yet.

Two Yemeni tribesmen warmly embraced in front of Oliver and me as we approached the crowd, friends who found each other at the Square. As the gunfire rang from less than a block away, they kissed each other's cheeks and looked as if they could be anywhere, like two friends running into each other at a party. At parties in Yemen, there is gunfire anyway. I smiled. I loved them for it. I loved how, to Yemenis, the joy of friendship can take precedence over one's own safety. This can also cause heartbreak, but my thoughts were more optimistic at this stage.

Then a low, echoing boom—a tear gas gun. Oliver and I walked briskly back with the crowd of men getting away from the spreading white cloud of smoke. Protesters hooked their thobes over their janbiyas to run more freely, their white cotton knickers–like pants exposed. They held their turbans around their mouths to breathe more easily. Oliver and I did the same with the scarves we were wearing.

"The army is gonna come over," Oliver told me. "Let's go back to the field hospital. If we just wait there, we'll see who's been injured and with what."

I wanted to stay with the protesters, though. My cheeks were red from the chilly air and the burning of the tear gas, my eyes tinted the same color. Oliver pointed his camera at me to snap a photo when we stopped for a moment to gather our breath. I smiled broadly. We were still young people. We still would post scenes of our lives on Facebook.

And anyway, I told myself that this was all okay, as long as we stood back from the line of fire.

Oliver and I coughed louder, the stinging in our throats intensified as the gray cloud of gas moved toward us and a Yemeni handed us cut yellow onions to hold to our noses to relieve the stinging.

"*Shokran*, thank you," we said.

We quickened our pace away from the cloud of gas along with everyone else. We were a part of this, too. I was a part of this. A voice from the stage shouted directives on a megaphone, imploring protesters to take care of the injured. "*Hasbun Allah wa naim al-wakeel!*" he then yelled, God is our guardian and he is all we need.

An hour later, Oliver and I were crouched down in a circle of protesters just outside the gates of the field hospital, examining bullet shells and used canisters of tear gas all laid out on a blue-and-white striped tarp. Four were dead from gunshot wounds that morning, but we were already getting used to the army killing a few protesters here and there.

"Oliver, can I see that?"

He handed me a metal silver cylinder with blue print on it.

I held the small metal cylinder in my hand. Tear gas made from a factory in Pennsylvania, the state where I am from.

"Is that a bomb or what?" the Yemeni beside me asked in English.

"No, it's tear gas," I said. I read the print: MILITARY GRADE.

"Look, Oliver. The tear gas expired ten years ago."

"There also were unmarked black things here." He held up a rubber ball.

When we got up to leave, we could still detect the metallic taste in the air from lingering gas. But the protesters were not budging. They regrouped and then chanted against Saleh in front of the center stage.

• • •

Haley, Portia, and I sat around a table in the back room of Coffee Trader in Hadda, drinking pomegranate-flavored smoothies. It was a week later, though each day that had passed seemed to encapsulate so much emotion, so much learning, so much praise and stress, and so much experience because we felt we were on the front lines of social change in the Middle East. All of this made it difficult to keep track of time.

We were aloof to the Yemenis around us, the hip, educated crowd typing away on their laptops, or the young guy with too much cologne chatting with the girl in the brightly flowered hijab and overdone eye shadow. This was one of the few enclaves in Sanaa where such public flirting was permissible.

We had just gone on a girls' shopping trip at the Libyan Center, one of Sanaa's only malls. Two floors, an escalator, about three clothing stores that existed outside the Arabian Peninsula—we ran around it with childlike glee as if we were in one of Dubai's mammoth shopping centers, and we came away with new nail polish and lipstick, makeup that we would never use in Yemen.

"I just needed this." I leaned back and took a sip of smoothie through my straw.

"Ooh, so did I," Portia said.

Haley's eyes grew big and she nodded in agreement.

"Let's just be girls," laughed Portia.

"I know, right," Haley said. "Show me which color lipstick you bought again."

It was early March. Our lives had become the protest movement, trying to decipher statements from officials, trying to stay safe, and trying to appease editors. The late night parties were becoming more infrequent because we had no more time to party. None of us had any real conflict experience. Some of us, me included, never wanted to be a war correspondent, and now there was fatal gunfire and dead bodies.

To continue doing what we were doing, we had to suspend a piece of our humanity. We had to refrain from becoming overly upset when interviewing a volunteer doctor standing beside a man who had just died moments ago. Day in and day out, we had to encounter, ruminate on, but try to stop ourselves from getting caught up in, the hopes and fears of the protesters who seemed increasingly willing to sacrifice their lives for this cause. Otherwise it would have eaten us alive.

But, while we may have been running from the Yemeni army's tear gas during the day, at least we were running together.

And then there were these moments, a rare afternoon off from the work, when our collective need for a break could find solace in companionship.

"This Islahi I met at the Square keeps sending me text messages about wanting to marry me. But I swear, he's like some religious dude with a long beard. This is the third text message. He keeps writing about my eyes," I said to them, laughing. Then I held out my cell phone. "See, look."

"Oh my god, yes," Haley said.

"I wonder how many collective marriage proposals we've all gotten here?" Portia asked.

"There's this kid in the old city who keeps buying me presents, like cheap, disgusting chocolate. He's too shy to do anything else, but he, like, stares at me, open-mouthed." Haley demonstrated the expression on her freckled face. Portia and I giggled some more, and I couldn't have been more grateful for their companionship.

• • •

I sat up from the hard concrete that I had curled up on only three hours earlier. Fuzzy, thick blankets lay beneath and over me. *What woke me up?* I stared blankly for a second or two at the blue tarp enveloping me in this tent, my mind confused. Then I reached into the pocket of my blue hoodie and pulled out my buzzing phone.

I had come to the Square the night before after hearing rumors that protestors might come under attack again. As a consequence, I had missed drinks at Oliver's apartment to celebrate Portia's birthday, which would almost certainly have ended with me crashing with them for the night, as I frequently did.

I had been at the Square so late into the night, I just decided to sleep there, in the tent for young female activists. Except I was the only woman in it; all the other women slept inside a nearby mosque. They hung out in the tent during the day, but it would have been inappropriate for them to sleep outside, so close to all the men at night. I looked down at my phone. It was about seven.

"Hi, Oliver," I answered.

"Laura, we're on our way to the immigration authority."

"What?" I threw the blankets off my lap, leaned forward, and gripped the phone.

"Men showed up at our apartment this morning and said we had to go with them."

"What? Are you guys okay? Who's there?"

"It's all of us. Haley, Portia, Josh, and me. It seems legit. It seems like we are actually going in the direction of the immigration authority."

Good, so it's not a kidnapping.

"Okay, okay. Do you want me to call the American and British embassies?"

"Yeah, do that. Okay, I have to go now."

"Okay."

I overturned the thin mattresses that lined the floor, picked up the cheap, dirty blankets I had been sleeping under, searched the entire blue tent. My purse, a brown satchel that held my wallet, camera, and notebook, was missing. I had set it beside me when I had fallen asleep.

I walked outside into the morning to tell the male protesters about my stolen purse. They accused the cleaning lady, a poor woman from the lowest caste in Yemeni society, the *mohamisheen*, who are said to be descendants of Ethiopian slaves who came to Yemen around the sixth century AD. She denied any role in the affair. She probably did it, but I didn't really care. There were more important things going on. Like the fact my friends had probably just been arrested. A man from the lawyers' tent drove me home. He pulled up the slope into the old city from the saila and reached into his pocket to pull out two one-thousand riyal notes, about ten dollars.

"No, no. I can't accept."

"No, keep it. I am sorry for what happened to you at the Square."

"No, it's okay. Thank you."

I called Oliver again. No answer. Haley, Portia, and Josh, the same. Their phones were switched off. What was happening to my friends at this moment, I did not know. The thought was alarming, but I assumed they would not be harmed because we were in Yemen, and I trusted Yemenis still, despite what I had seen balateja do.

Thus my mind focused on what I considered to be the worst-case scenario: that my friends were going to be kicked out of the country for reporting on the protests and I would be the next to go. I gazed up the brown brick front of my building at my apartment on the third floor. I opened the front door, walked up the two flights of stairs at a slower than my usual jumpy pace. Normally I stubbed toes on at least one step on the way up, but this time I was methodical. I had to drag this out as long as possible. I prepared myself mentally for soldiers to be waiting inside, ready to cart me off too. I imagined what they would look like. They would hear me coming, so they would stand, side by side, in front of the doorway, holding their AKs across their chests in a somewhat official manner, as if they actually had real training. I wouldn't be able to run, because they would chase me. I would just have to succumb to my fate.

I approached my large, wooden door with its heavy, metal lock. I checked to see if there was any sign of forced entry. There was none. I knew that didn't mean anything. I had probably forgotten to lock my door anyway when I left, as I frequently did. I placed the key through its insert and turned the latch to the left. I swallowed and held my body like a board as I pushed the door open. I was alone.

I searched the house to see if there was any sign that a stranger had been inside, perhaps looking through my belongings. There was nothing. I went over to sit at my desk for a moment and closed my eyes. I tried to calm myself but felt like I had nothing to grasp on to. So I called Erik, who at least would listen to me, which was better than obsessively cycling through the thoughts in my head.

"Have you heard the news?" I asked him.

"Yeah," Erik told me. "You think they're getting chucked out?"

"I guess so. What else would this be?"

"What are you going to do right now?" he asked.

"I know this sounds crazy, but I'm going to up to my roof and lie out."

I hung up and ascended another flight of stairs to the top floor.

The high walls provided a refuge, for however brief a moment. I knew I was going to have to leave this apartment. I couldn't just wait here for the soldiers. I pressed the back of my head into the hard concrete and looked at the sun. The shouting, car horns, and motorcycle engines of the old city told me that Yemen was around me. Yemen my home. Yemen that wasn't so fun anymore. Part of the reason this was all possible was because of our community of friends, and now that was going to disappear. Hours upon hours spent in their apartment, telling jokes with Oliver, gossiping with Haley, getting advice from them all, and then there was the socializing via work gatherings that took place at the foursome's apartment almost every night. Sure Erik was still here, and I was becoming closer with Tom, Jeb, and Iona, but the two women with whom I shared most were no longer going to be here for support.

And I might get kicked out of the country, too. I might have to leave my home without a chance to say goodbye. I tried to fully understand that reality, but it was impossible to imagine that life as I knew it could be radically changed against my will. I am an American—I've been told I can command my own destiny. I was afraid that I was going to have to face that lie.

I went downstairs and scrambled to think of what I would want to take with me, stuffing essential belongings into a suitcase: notebooks, one pair of jeans, one pair of loose linen pants, two long tunic t-shirts, my long beige trenchcoat-like jacket that came down to my knees, and the green scarf I wrapped around my neck every day. *What if I can't come back here? Think, Laura, think.* I grabbed my recorder and a handful of pencils, the mechanical pencils that I bring from the States. *What else do I have to have?*

I carried my bag over to Erik's house across the old city. On the way, I waved hello to the boys who run the corner shop below my home, but it wasn't the same as before. The cacophony of the old city suddenly felt foreign, like this world I loved had turned against me. I walked hurriedly, though nothing should be hurried in Yemen aside from the post-lunch qat market rush.

Erik greeted me outside his house and we trudged up the narrow stairwell in silence. I paced the apartment's sparse kitchen, biting each nail off one by one. He sat slouched on a stone step on the floor in front of me, smoking a cigarette.

"This is really bad," I said.

"Yeah, it's really bad that they're doing this now."

"What do we do?"

"Just lay low. If they are going to kick us out, then they are going to kick us out. There isn't a whole lot that we can do about it."

I gave Erik an unsatisfied look. I needed action. I needed to fight this unjust system. I just felt so helpless.

"Can I borrow some money?" I asked. "My wallet's been stolen. I woke up this morning at the Square and it was gone."

"Dude, that sucks," Erik said. "Yeah, here. Take what you need." He reached into the back pocket of his blue jeans and pulled out his wallet. I grabbed it and then just collapsed on the gray floor, pulling at my hair. I looked out a large window at the gingerbread homes of old Sanaa and shook my head at them.

About half an hour later, we got a phone call from a friend at the American embassy who had heard that the journalists were on their way to the airport to be deported. Just like that. Bye Yemen, maybe forever. The walls were closing in. Our little club had come to an end. I sat with Erik for an hour or so and we got calls from our Yemeni friends asking us if we were all right, as local websites were carrying news of foreign journalists' deportation.

"No, no. It's not me. I'm fine." I was spared, I told them.

But did that mean I was lucky? I didn't have to leave the country that I loved, a reporting opportunity like none other, but the pressure that we had all been sharing, it was more concentrated now. I could feel it in my chest.

"*Alhamdullah*, thank God," the Yemeni friends replied. "Well, be careful. Don't say where you are going on the phone."

We never know who's listening to our phones.

An editor called. The *Times* wanted a story about today, a story about my friends. It felt like I was on the outside looking in at the movie version of my life, or like I was trapped in a car driving toward absolute chaos. I couldn't veer from this path, and, in some strange way, I had chosen it. It was now into the third week of March, and each day since Mubarak's resignation on February 11 had grown increasingly more turbulent.

After a few hours, Haley and Oliver answered their phones while they sat at the airport, guarded, waiting for the flights that would take them away.

"Are you okay? Good. Listen, what do you want to say about this to the *New York Times*?" I spoke with them professionally. The only way to write about them was to treat this like work. The suspension of humanity we adopted so we didn't fall apart during the violence against the protesters—now I had to do it with regard to our friendship.

Four days later, fifty-three protesters were killed at the Square, shot by snipers firing from nearby rooftops. Over one hundred others suffered gunshot wounds. It happened in a space of a few street blocks over about an hour. Someone was trying to send a message: Go home. We are in control here. And we think you are worth nothing, which is why we won't think twice when we shoot, even if it's at the head of a teenager.

It was hard to believe the deportations and the massacre weren't connected. There were even fewer of us left to report on it for the world. And so the young freelancers that were left grew even more determined. But at least for me, it was partially because I grew angrier. That people were capable of committing such a massacre on innocents made me feel humanity had betrayed me. Of course, I heard about atrocities on the news. Of course, I theoretically knew that they happened to other people in other places. But seeing what it looks like when so many are killed in such a short period of time in one small area, I wondered where the happy ending to all of it was.

The feeling of fear was no longer so acute. There was a dull weight in my gut that reminded me to be alert to the possibility of danger. It kept me on an edge more than I realized. But I had now learned from experience that being near violence and being shot were two entirely different things. In one you may be dead, and in the other you get to truly experience life. Not just the adrenaline. There is that, of course, but I got a chance to experience that frame-by-frame wonder that plays out in a time of emergency. Everyone was living for a purpose—protesting their brutal dictator, saving lives, reporting on atrocities so the world can see, trying not to die—and each person was putting every bit of themselves into that purpose. It felt like I was seeing a whole multitude of people truly come alive, in one moment, together. There was something inside of me that longed to see it again.

CHAPTER 11

I trudged out into our living room where cigarette smoke hovered like a cloud of tear gas. Jeb was awake, making coffee in the kitchen. Empty vodka bottles were on the floor. Another day, another crisis. Let's wait for more people to be killed. That's what dictated our lives now, anyway.

After our fellow freelance journalists were deported, Jeb, Iona, and I, no longer feeling safe in our own homes, had moved into the house in Hadda of a UN worker who was out of the country—and who was told to stay on vacation after the March 18 massacre. There was a concrete wall around the house and a guard who manned the door. He was small and didn't appear to have a gun, but his existence made me feel better. If soldiers forced their way inside the house to deport us, at least someone's yelling would warn us.

Jeb, large, bearded, and a proud Southerner, and Iona, a tiny Irish woman with brown hair cut short like a boy's, endlessly bantered about reporting obligations and how they had managed to narrowly escape gunfire. "Honestly I'm only staying in this house because there's a nice bathtub," I wrote to a friend. But it was also because I was too scared to live alone in my apartment. Iona and Jeb's presence was a mixed bag; the endless talk of work and violence was anxiety provoking, but their companionship was comforting, so for now this was home.

"Morning, Jeb," I called to him in the kitchen.

"Morning. How'd you sleep?"

"Eh, you know."

"At least I can understand you now," he remarked.

"Yeah, it's getting better."

The day after the massacre at the Square, I had tried to answer a phone call and discovered I couldn't speak. Just because I didn't fully acknowledge the extent of the trauma caused by what I'd been witness to, it didn't mean my physical body wasn't reacting to the violence, and so my vocal chords cut out for the ensuing twenty-four hours. My editors weren't deterred from trying to get information from my scratchy whisper of a voice, so I forced myself to talk, straining with the pain. I found that focusing all my energy on work was the easiest path forward. It gave both me and the trauma purpose.

Since the massacre, Saleh had been losing allies by the day, creating lots of breaking news to stay on top of, which was a welcome distraction. There was a tidal wave of defections and resignations: ambassadors, ministerial leaders, members of parliament. "The president has committed an act of suicide that reminds me of the final trip that salmon make upstream before they reach their dying location," a Yemeni official told me.

I had hardly slept since March 18, either. I closed my eyes, but my mind never thought it was time to rest. There was so much I tried to but couldn't remember, like the scene from the field hospital from just three days before. I tried to force myself to recall it, but instead I only remembered bumping into my friend Hassan outside the hospital, and his tears. I wondered for a moment how he had fared since the massacre and if he was feeling slightly unhinged as well. Nevertheless, I was sure that he was still filming every day at the Square, because that was what Hassan always did.

Iona walked out of her bedroom and we all sat down in front of our laptops, drinking coffee and eating toast. Iona had bought the bread and butter. This house had a toaster! None of us had had a toaster before in Yemen.

We, three of the ten or so foreign journalists left, were also coming under more scrutiny from the government. Yasser, my fixer, had received a text message the day before that the secret police were going to round us up for deportation. Later, I received a text message from an unknown number reading: "Hi Lora. This is Zaid. Call me." Tom, the youngest of the remaining freelancers, who had moved to Yemen only four months ago at age twenty-one, was receiving mystery calls from a middle-aged man who told him in formal Arabic that he knew Tom was working in the country illegally, reporting from Change Square, and that he had better stop.

It wasn't only the death that we had witnessed stepping across bodies at the Square's field hospital that pierced the thick skin we all pretended to wear—that we all had to wear. At every moment we also worried that the life we had come to know would be taken from us by deportation.

What we didn't know was that we would soon become low on the list of the government's worries.

"Holy shit. Guys, we gotta turn on Al Jazeera," Jeb said. He walked over to the living room and found the TV remote, switched on the screen, and flipped through channels.

"Why, what's going on?" Iona asked, coming over to watch as well.

"People are tweeting something about Ali Mohsin . . ." Jeb replied.

"No, I don't want anything else to happen," I moaned.

Al Jazeera was reporting that Yemeni Major General Ali Mohsin al-Ahmar had announced his support for the protest movement and vowed that his soldiers would protect the protesters.

"What? This is a big deal, right?"

"I think so."

"Who the hell is Ali Mohsin anyway?"

"I have no clue. I need to call Yasser," I said. "Where's my phone? Has anyone seen my phone?" I frantically searched the crevices of the big leather sofa. It was the sort that none of us would ever dream of having in our former apartments, but it adorned the living room of this expensive UN house.

Five minutes later, I had Yasser on the line. "Good morning, Yasser. Ali Mohsin says he supports the protesters. Who *is* Ali Mohsin?"

"He is the leader of the First Armored Division, the *ferqa*. He was an ally of Saleh, a friend of Saleh, you know. He is from Sanhan, Saleh's village."

"Is this important? Is it something big?"

"Yes, it's very big. He's considered the second most powerful man in Yemen."

"Why do people say his last name is al-Ahmar? Is he related to the Ahmars? Like Hamid?"

"No, no. But some say Ali Mohsin is Saleh's half-brother. It's not exactly true."

"What? So they're related? How?"

"You know. Everyone from the village is related. Marriage and cousins and stuff."

"Do you think there will be a military coup?"

"Maybe."

I put down my phone and laid my forehead on the large wooden dining room table.

"Argghhh," I moaned. "I just want a day off."

Jeb chuckled. "Well you ain't gonna get that, now are you."

I looked up at him with a half-joking scowl.

Then I got a call from a Western diplomat who used to party with us freelancers.

"Have you guys heard the news?" the diplomat asked.

"Yes, of course. This is a big deal, we think," I said.

"Yeah, you should get out of the country. See if there's a plane ticket out tonight. But all you guys should get out."

After Ali Mohsin publicly broke allegiance with the president, long-range weaponry from his base on a hill beside Change Square was aimed across Sanaa at the Republican Guard, the division of the military commanded by Saleh's son, Ahmed. The Republican Guard bases, on hilltops on the southern rim of Sanaa, in turn aimed their artillery at Ali Mohsin's First Armored Division. The capital sat in between. Non-essential embassy personnel and foreign aid workers fled the country.

"What if Saleh fights back against Ali Mohsin? There will be war," I wrote online to a Yemeni diplomat who was following the situation from his post in Europe.

"Saleh won't fight," he responded. "He won't fight because he can't win."

• • •

"Did you hear the news?" I asked my taxi driver. We were on the way to the Square an hour later.

"Yes. It's big news."

"Do you think there will be a coup?"

"Yes, maybe a coup." He was either too scared to talk politics with a foreigner or not interested in contemplating the situation further.

Sanaa was already bracing for the worst because everyone feared the tribesmen who had been killed on March 18 would retaliate. Such was their custom of *ithaar*, revenge killing. Few understood or believed in the protesters' commitment to peace.

Now with Ali Mohsin's defection adding to the uncertainty, the hustle and bustle of the city was temporarily muted. Women stayed indoors and shops remained closed. When men dug their hands into plates of rice for lunch, there was less laughter and fewer smiles, replaced by talk of politics in hushed voices.

Ali Mohsin had been Saleh's right-hand man. He had known the president for decades, had risen up through the ranks of the military with him. He and Saleh were partners in their oppressive power consolidation endeavors: stealing land, exploiting southerners, fighting the Houthis in the North. But then the men started to get competitive for power, and Ali Mohsin particularly resented Saleh's maneuvering to put his son, Ahmed, in line for the presidency.

Still, Ali Mohsin's reputation was tarnished because of his exploits. He had many more enemies than friends. Supporting the protest movement, the youth, those fighting for democracy, was a chance to repair his image and put him on what he appeared to believe was the winning side of this political battle.

On the way to the protest, Yasser called me with news that Sadeq al-Ahmar, Hamid's eldest brother, had gone to the Square this morning to announce his support for the protesters. Sadeq was the head of the Hashid tribal confederation, which meant that the most powerful sheikh in the country, along with arguably the most powerful military commander in the country, had just announced they wanted Saleh to step down. Men who fought wars and killed now said they believed in peaceful revolution. It was a bizarre turn of events, and all I could think about was the diplomat's warning to get out of the country, and whether I had time to do my reporting for today.

I paid my driver and walked down the street that ran perpendicular to Ring Road. First Armored Division soldiers were already standing in clusters on the outer rim of the Square by the last line of tents. They were armed with assault rifles and dressed in sandy-colored camouflage uniforms. One of them looked like he was about thirteen. Ali Mohsin was known for employing child soldiers.

"Who are you with?" I asked three soldiers, sitting side by side on the curb.

"With the people," two of them responded in unison. They didn't want to say anything more to me than that, though.

The protesters were slow to move this morning. Men sat on the ground in their tents, with only a thin, dark carpet beneath them, opening their eyes to the new day, digesting the news. They had been slowly regaining their energy over the past few days. The massacre had sucked the joie de vivre out of them and made them angrier. The news of Ali Mohsin changing sides might tip the scales in their favor. Yet it also meant they were partnered with one of the most corrupt, evil men in Yemen.

I walked down the space that ran between the two rows of tents toward the stage, and as I did, the sense of celebration grew. I spotted an old man pushing along an ice cream freezer between the lines of tents. He yelled in a voice of a merchant at a fair hawking his goods, "Change comes from ice cream! Ali Saleh is going to leave and it's because of ice cream!" No one apart from me appeared to pay him much heed.

When I reached the central area where the stage had been set up in front of the main gate to Sanaa University, I found men singing and dancing as sheikh after sheikh stepped up to the microphone on the stage to announce his support for the protesters at the Square, which meant they were officially calling for Saleh to step down. They dressed traditionally, of course, in thobes, suit jackets, and janbiyas at the belt. Yemeni journalists crammed together on the stage's edge, snapping photos. I wondered why the protesters weren't more unhappy to be partnered with Ali Mohsin, but I couldn't help feeling excited with them. Everything had been going so badly, and now finally a glimmer of hope—hope that this would be what finally forced Saleh to step down, that those killed would be vindicated.

But does partnering with the devil offer vindication? This wasn't what the protesters had been on the streets calling for over the past months, what they were shot and killed for. People now had to decide if the goal was only removing Saleh from power—in which case Ali Mohsin was a good ally—or if maintaining the purity of their peaceful protest movement was more important.

I paused to interview a few men. It was always a challenge to figure out which ones looked like they had something relevant to say. I found a man with an intelligent-looking face standing back from the dancing, watching the festivities with arms folded across his chest.

"What do you think of Ali Mohsin's announcement?"

"The army knows that its correct place is to protect the people," the man, Fawzi, told me. He was from Taiz originally and had been living at the sit-in for weeks.

"So you think this is a good thing."

"Yes, it's a good thing."

Nothing more insightful than that.

I walked to the tent where youth activists, mostly university students, ran one of the Square's social media campaigns. I ducked through the tent's front flap and found everyone sitting on low cushions typing away at laptops, a small satellite-powered TV switched on in the corner. A young woman dressed in full niqab, Nadia, sat on a chair across from the bunch, flipping through photos on her camera screen. I was learning to identify her by her eyes alone.

Adel, a bespectacled, scrawny university student with a mustache had just gotten off the phone with a TV station. He spoke English well, and I had given his contact to the BBC and CNN as a good activist to interview.

"Adel, what do you think of all of this?" I asked him.

"Now we just have to wait to see what Saleh will do," he said.

Everyone's apprehension to speak freely made me more nervous. I figured that I should at least go to the EgyptAir office and see if they had any seats left on tonight's flight to Cairo.

• • •

"Zubairy Street," I told the driver. I leaned back in the seat and called everyone who I thought could provide any insight, but no one knew quite how to read the situation. A standoff had begun in Yemen. And it could last for months. But I thought the artillery shells would start at any moment.

Then I received a call from a Washington, DC, area code just as I was stepping out of the taxi.

"Hi Laura. It's Chris. Are you okay?" The familiar voice on the other line was Chris Boucek, a political analyst at the Carnegie Endowment for International Peace who worked on Yemen policy. My family lived close to DC so I met with Chris anytime I was back in the States. Chris was always supportive of me, despite my young age. I didn't find the same from other analysts in Washington, who were protective of their careers. But Chris just wanted to gossip about Yemen and learn from what insights I could offer.

"Yeah, I'm okay," I told him, trying to control the shakiness in my voice. "I don't know if I should stay or go, though. I'm headed to the EgyptAir office right now just to see if there's a flight to Cairo tonight."

"You aren't a war correspondent, Laura. You can leave if you want to. It's not your job to cover this."

Chris's words played on repeat in my mind as I stepped into the ticket office. *I'm not a war correspondent, I'm not a war correspondent. Chris is someone who knows me, understands why I am living in this country. I should take his advice seriously. War isn't my job.* I thought about my family, my parents, and how I owed it to them to leave. I thought about how leaving was the smart move. *It's what any rational person would do in this situation.*

There were still a few seats available on a flight to Cairo that left around midnight. I bought the ticket and went back to the house I was sharing with Jeb and Iona. They weren't home. I called them to say I was packing up, heading to my apartment to grab some things, and then flying out.

They told me they had decided to stay. They were at the grocery store with Erik stocking up on canned goods. Erik was going to crash with them for a few days. At that moment, I couldn't afford to think about how much I would miss them all. I had to stay focused on filing the day's story and getting packed, like I was wearing blinders, purposefully ignoring the ramifications of my choice to flee. I didn't call other friends to tell them I was leaving. I couldn't bear it. I'd deal with that once I got to Cairo.

Then, for the first time since I started writing for the *Times*, the foreign editor, the chief of all international reporting, called me.

"If you feel like you should leave, then leave," she said. "Your safety is the most important thing." As I hung up, the lights in my apartment and outside on the street flickered off. Then on for a second. Then off again.

It was like a bad omen. There had been plenty of power cuts in Yemen in 2009, but electricity hadn't gone off in a while. The government really was breaking down.

After another taxi ride to my apartment, I packed up my belongings as the sky outside was getting dark. I used the light of my cell phone to go through my drawers.

Where did I put that flashlight? Why couldn't I be prepared for stuff like this? It's because I wasn't a real war correspondent, that's why.

I did a phone interview with a syndicated radio show standing in the middle of my darkened mafraj right before I locked the door for what I thought might be the final time. I tried to talk slowly and not sound panicked. I didn't tell the producer I was leaving. I didn't want the stranger on the other end of the line to think I wasn't cut out to do this work.

I walked up the stairs to look at the roof, where I used to lie trying to get a suntan, concealed by high walls. The peace of an afternoon in Sanaa. Not a thing to do in the world. That all felt so long ago, like a more innocent version of myself. In Taiz, Fahd had revived that old Laura for a brief moment, but she was long gone now.

I took my two bags outside, looked for a taxi to take me to the airport, and didn't look back to wave to the two young men who ran the corner shop beneath my building.

• • •

Am I actually going to go through with this? Leave Yemen, my home, and all the people I care about? Maybe this is the only way I can actually leave, in a huff, a harsh sever of ties. Maybe if I don't leave now I will be way in over my head in the coming weeks. I woke up so exasperated this morning by life and now here I am at the airport, prepared to check in. This is the universe providing a path out for me. But what if I'll regret this decision forever?

I stood at the first security check at Sanaa airport, where officers examined passports and a dingy, corroded metal detector assured them no one was carrying a bomb or a gun. I looked down at the ticket to Cairo I gripped in my hand. A group of German aid workers scurried in a neat line past me, evacuating the country. *I hope I don't see anyone I know here*, I thought.

I recalled the advice of my friends in more official positions: aid workers and diplomats. "If I were you, I'd get out of here," they had said.

But what do you know that I don't?

Impending war. That's what they knew. But what did that mean? An army commander had sworn allegiance to the opposition days after the massacre of March 18. Well, Saleh wasn't going to go down without a fight. That's what I figured, despite the words of a Yemeni official who told me Saleh wouldn't pick a fight that he couldn't win. I only knew of war from movies, so I had an image in my head of what was going to happen in Sanaa, and that image was the reason I had bought the ticket to Cairo. My plane left in two hours, but I just couldn't bring myself to check in.

I was afraid of disappointing everyone. I was afraid of not appearing tough. That was part of why I had moved here after all, because I thought I was tough. I was afraid of what people would think of me when I fled. I was afraid of letting the Yemeni protesters down. And I was afraid that this was all a big bluff. I listened to others' advice, but what if they were wrong?

I gripped the plane ticket tighter in my right hand, creasing the thin card-stock down the middle. I looked at it again, just to confirm the time of departure. I had two hours to make this decision. Well, actually less. An hour and a half because it took no time to go through what was meant to be security (ha! what security?) at Sanaa airport.

I hauled my suitcase over to a row of gray chairs and sat down. I hung my head low and cried. It was the second time I cried since the protests began, and the second time I cried that week.

If war doesn't start by the time night falls, then it won't start.

The words of one Yemeni friend ran in a loop in my mind. I looked out through the front doors of the airport and saw that the sky had already grown dark.

Yes, there is potential for real danger, he had said, *but . . . but . . .*

But *what?*

But no one can predict what's going to happen in Yemen. I should have known that already. That was one of the first lessons I learned about life in Sanaa, and certainly one of my favorites. Yet here we all were, waiting for war. And war meant I should leave. That was the only logic my brain could produce. But my emotions were strong, too. They implored me, tugging and weighing me down, preventing me from walking through that security check. What was happening here had become my life: the story of the uprising in Yemen. Fifty-three people were killed at Change Square a few days ago. Didn't I owe it to them to stay?

On the day after the March 18 massacre, I had entered a green tent with two new bullet holes through its roof from the previous day, the punctured fabric fraying. Tribesmen from Hamdan, a poor, dry region of rocky villages, sat cross-legged on the hard concrete floor around me. Rays of sun shining in through the bullet holes left two circles of light on the face of the man who spoke. He swatted at the light when it shone in his eyes the way one would shoo a fly. Despite one of their relatives having been killed by sniper fire, he told me they would not fight back. They would remain peaceful, "because the world will see us, and then the world will be on our side."

Didn't I owe it to them to stay?

The sundown call to prayer rang through the nearby neighborhood of Hasaba, as well as over the intercom in the airport. *Allahu akbaru. Allahu akbaru.* God is great.

I continued to cry. I willed the tears to stop, but the weight of this moment was squeezing them out of me like they were a noxious substance that needed to be released to keep out infection.

Oh, please let there not be anyone I know here, no one to see me slumped on a chair red-eyed with tear-soaked cheeks.

I needed an intervention. I needed friends. And I needed someone who understood the sort of predicament I was in. So I called my friend Liam in Cairo, who was a fellow young *New York Times* stringer.

"If I were you, I wouldn't leave," Liam told me. "The American government has ways of getting its people out of bad situations. There's little chance you would be absolutely stranded during a war, you know."

I imagined heading down an empty Sanaa street in an American humvee while gunfire rang out and bombs exploded around us. We would get to the airport right in time for the last flight out. It would be a heroic escape, my imagination told me. Much more heroic than sitting at the airport sobbing.

"Thanks, Liam," I told him. "You're probably right," I said and hung up, though neither of us had any experience in the sort of war fought between two armies. I sat up straighter in my chair and wiped my eyes. I stared across at the metal detector again. One of the security guards gave me a puzzled look and I quickly turned my head the other way, toward the airport exit. It was fully dark outside now. I didn't hear anything outside that sounded like war. Then, I looked down to my phone again. Jeb had texted me.

"Are you REALLY going? We got a house full of food and booze here!"

He made me smile. The more dangerous life became, the more fun there was to be had as well, especially if Jeb was along.

I tucked my wrinkled ticket into the pocket of my purse, just in case I decided to change my mind in the next hour, stood up, and walked out of the airport.

CHAPTER 12

In the days after Ali Mohsin's announcement, the crowds in the Square only grew while the rest of Sanaa remained temporarily calm. Yemenis proved that even war happened on their own schedule, not the West's.

I was ashamed about my instinct to bolt, but didn't have time to waste on my embarrassment. Work was the only thing that mattered, so I tried to be good at it. I tried to pitch interesting story ideas to New York.

I had just finished an article about tribesmen who, though their tribes were at war, sat together peacefully inside tents at the Square. They created a contract amongst them that revenge killing would be eliminated after the revolution succeeded. I saw people who, having little in which to put their hope, put it in each other, and I wanted to show that to America.

One evening, I was on my way to the Square to do some interviews for a new story I was working on about how the demonstration had yielded business opportunities for entrepreneurial merchants. The Square was a mini society within Sanaa where thousands lived and slept—of course they would have to buy things.

Like always, upon arrival at the expansive demonstration, I first made my way to the media tent to say hello. I lifted the blue canvas flap and walked in.

"*Salaam aleikum,*" I said enthusiastically to the group of five or so young men. Three lounged in front of laptops on a row of cheap cushions with a dark blue rug laid on top. Most picked at qat leaves with one cheek stuffed full of the drug.

"*Waleikum salaam*, Laura! *Kayf enti*, how are you?" Salah replied, the most gregarious of the bunch. He was dressed in a blue button-up shirt and slacks. A beige blazer hung over his shoulders, as if he was a preppy kid in California instead of a poor Yemeni college student who couldn't afford a laptop like his other friends.

"Guys, you expanded your tent," I said in English. "The tent is bigger!" I then proclaimed in Arabic. About half didn't understand the former.

"The rain," one of the men muttered looking up from his computer. "We need protection."

Their tent was newly reinforced with wood beams, khaki-colored cardboard walls, and gray concrete blocks around the edges. Photos of martyrs—protesters who had been killed over the past month—hung on the walls and the door of a filing cabinet in one corner. The small TV still sat in another, near the young men.

"We built this tent because we will stay here until everything changes in Yemen!" Salah proclaimed.

"Everything? Even qat?" I joked.

Salah chuckled demurely and I managed to get others to break into grins as well. I had spent so many hours in this tent with the young activists. I can't even remember the first time I showed up here, nor really why I knew to come to this tent versus the hundreds of others. So many of the hours I had spent here were just me witnessing their lives, learning their stories, and thus becoming part of them. There were so many people coming and going, there was always someone new to grab a quote from. I do remember when wise and skinny Mohammed told me the story of the balateja beating him up with the sort of amusement that only a Yemeni could conjure when talking about a misfortune. We had sat cross-legged on the ground across from one another. The day was bright and the sun's warmth could be felt through the tarp. Mohammed acted out the incident as he recounted it to me. He circled his hands in the air to gesture his tumble to the pavement as the balateja started their pounding.

"What did you do?" I asked.

"Oh, I ran out of there fast." He said. "Those *balateja*, *whew-wee*, they are bad."

We both laughed and then I told him a story of when balateja that I ran into near the old city threatened me verbally. "They said to me, 'We know you are the girl with Tawakkol Karman.'"

"Next time they say anything to you, you come to us. I'll take care of them," Mohammed said, seemingly forgetting the tale he had just told me. I still trusted him, though. While he may have been in over his head as a young university student standing up to the paid thugs of a dictator, it was a situation we were all in together.

"Did you hear what the president said about mixing?" asked one of the activists, Bassem. He was sitting on a floor cushion in front of his laptop that was propped up by a small particleboard table.

"I did. What do you all think about that?" I asked the group. Saleh had recently said in a public speech that Change Square was a place of loose and corrupting morals because young men and women mixed inside the tents.

"He's stupid. He isn't one to talk!" the young activists yelled back.

"Let's take a photo with mixing," one of them suggested. "Yeah!" the others yelled. So we all gathered together—of course, there was still a good six inches between me and the closest male—and snapped a photo of me surrounded by the group of boys making peace signs.

"There's your mixing, Saleh," Mohammed said under his breath.

I stood up after the photo and brushed the dust off my jeans, realizing that I needed to get to work.

"Salah, will you help me?" I asked. "I need to go find people to interview for this story about businessmen who make money from the protesters at the Square."

"Of course, your wish is our command."

"Salah, don't say that," I said.

"No, but really," he replied.

We exited together and passed the row of tents that lead from the side street where the social media tent was placed to the main drag on Ring Road. I saw a man selling cotton candy to a father who held his young daughter in his arms. She was dressed in a black-and-white dress with white tap shoes. When the father handed her a fistful of pink fluff, she grasped the wispy treat in delight.

Around the corner, tribesmen were performing a dance from their village while others watched and learned. They waved their janbiyas with one arm, the blades outlining small ovals in the air above their heads. They picked one knee up at a time and moved in a circle. Onlookers clapped while others sang a hauntingly melodic tune in low, nasal syllables that provided rhythm to the dancing. After Ali Mohsin's soldiers began protecting the Square—they always stood guard at all the main entry points—the atmosphere had turned into a carnival in the evenings, a place where Yemenis could gather to relax, celebrate, and have fun. Sometimes I felt the political agenda of this space disappeared with such festivities, but then I would look up and see a printed poster of Saleh dressed in the attire of an American professional wrestler and remember exactly why Change Square existed after all.

As we made our way south down Ring Road, Salah made sure to point out signs that protesters had posted on the outsides of their tents.

"Look, the Yemeni unity coalition and peace organization!"

"Salah, they spelled *coalition* wrong," I laughed. The sign read COLLATION.

"Oh," he said and moved on.

After we walked about twenty more feet, we noticed that a younger, attractive-faced boy with bowl cut hair and large brown eyes was following us. He was dressed like an older tribesman with a suit jacket over his short white thobe. I wanted to pinch his cheeks.

"Why are you here? You live here?" I asked him in sweetly-toned Arabic.

"I am with the people. I am with democracy," he said, looking up at me. "Are you a journalist?"

"Yes, I am."

Salah ran behind the boy to point out a sign that had been posted on a gray brick wall built to keep rainwater out of a nearby tent. The sign read, ONE OF OUR GOALS IS TO FIGHT TERRORISM AND ELIMINATE ITS ROOT CAUSES, in large black font on computer paper. Salah tried to scrape off some of the mud that smudged the sign's bottom corner. Another protester who stopped to see what the fuss was about handed him a tissue to rub at it.

"Salah, don't worry about it. It's fine."

"This is the demand of all Yemenis," he said proudly, rubbing some more with the tissue. "And I am one of the Yemenis. We will protect Yemen as our mother, our mother. Yes, our mother," he fumbled with the English knowing that the metaphor worked better in Arabic. "Our mothers and our families!" he proclaimed.

"This is what Ali Saleh is marketing for. That there is a fight with terrorism. That there is a fight between terrorism and peace. Well we will see who is the victor." Salah smiled broadly, content with his declaration.

"*Tamam*," I told him with a fully warmed heart. "Okay, great. Now let's go find some people to interview."

• • •

A few days later, on an early April morning, I returned to the Square to interview Tawakkol. Her tent had a thin wooden door built into the side of it. At its center, it stood about ten feet high and consisted of several rooms: sleeping quarters, a TV room, and a reception room for guests. It had become her home at Change Square. Many of the other prominent, older female activists didn't live at the Square day in and day out like Tawakkol.

I slowly pulled back the door by its edge, trying not to get a splinter in the process, and poked my head inside.

"*Salaam aleikum.* Tawakkol?"

"*Ya Laura, ahlan, ahlan,* welcome. Come in," came a voice from inside. It was smooth and welcoming.

"Hi, Tawakkol. How are you?" I said in English.

"*Alhamdullah,* praise God. We are doing well."

"You were safe on March 18?" I asked her.

"Yes, yes. *Alhamdullah.* Were you at the Square?"

"Yes, I was. It was horrible," I said.

"A crime. This is Ali Abdullah Saleh. Here, sit," Tawakkol pointed to a small wooden chair in the tent's reception room. She pulled up an identical chair from the other side of the room and sat in front of me. I pulled out my laptop and set it on the tops of my thighs. The intensity of the dry sun shown through the tarp and I had to squint through its brightness.

Tawakkol stood a little over five feet. She had a friendly face with a large, welcoming smile and soft brown eyes. Her colorful hijab wrapped around her head, concealing all of her hair. I wondered what it looked like underneath.

"So I wanted to interview you about American policy in Yemen, with regard to the protesters," I said to her.

Tawakkol's smile disappeared. She sat up straighter and looked for a moment to the roof of her tent, collecting her thoughts.

"Despite that the United States stresses freedom, we are very mad at them because they haven't stood with the revolution in Yemen," she said in English. "They are not working with the Yemeni revolution like they worked with the Egyptian and the Tunisian revolutions."

"Why do you think that is?"

"They are afraid of instability in Yemen. They are afraid of al-Qaeda. And yes, there are those things, but who wants to develop them? Ali Abdullah Saleh. The first step for killing al-Qaeda is this peaceful demonstration, this sit-in. I want you to say that to the *New York Times*." She had switched into Arabic for this part. She wanted to speak faster, clearer, break into one of the impassioned diatribes for which she was known.

Tawakkol leaned forward and grabbed my arm just like Boshra did in Taiz. One of the things about being so young in this job was that people didn't take me seriously, or rather, they treated me like a friend. I'm sure my relaxed, happy-go-lucky demeanor contributed to this. I wasn't one to shove a recorder in someone's face and ask questions with a show of officialism. Sometimes my amicable relationship with Yemenis was unproductive. But other times, it meant that interviewees would open up and say things they would only say to a friend.

"You see, *habibty* Laura," Tawakkol said, using a term of endearment, and then she delved into a story about how she and the protesters wanted to march to the presidential palace after Ali Mohsin's declaration that he was supporting the protest. They had thought that this was finally their chance to truly pressure Saleh because one of his most important allies had just deserted him. But Tawakkol told me that someone from the US embassy called her to tell her she should call off the march, because Saleh was close to stepping down and the march to the palace would have hurt those delicate negotiations.

"But Saleh didn't agree to leave," I said after the story.

"That's right! He is a liar."

In the days after Ali Mohsin had first announced his support for the protest, my understanding was that he and Saleh met at the house of the vice president, Abdu Rabbu Mansour Hadi. The men sat around a mafraj and tried to sort out a deal for Saleh to leave office. The idea was that Saleh and Ali Mohsin would retire from their positions simultaneously, and then presidential powers would be transferred to Hadi, who was deemed a more neutral party because he largely stayed in the background during his career as Saleh's deputy. The only other person who had been Saleh's vice president, Ali Salim al-Beidh, ended up fomenting the 1994 civil war against the Saleh regime, and now was exiled.

The US ambassador, Gerald Feierstein, was in the room at Hadi's house too because Saleh trusted him. Feierstein was the international community's representative to the transition agreement. That's why a US embassy official had called Tawakkol to urge her to call off the march.

Only it didn't. The United States had misjudged. The politicians ended up hitting a brick wall over what would happen to Saleh's son and his nephews who also held important military positions. Negotiations came to a standstill.

It felt to me like Tawakkol still resented the US ambassador for such a blunder. It was like she held it against him that a wily dictator acted dishonestly, or at least erratically. Yemenis knew they could never take Saleh at his word, but the international community was still struggling to learn that lesson.

Tawakkol told me of new plans for a march. "We will move to his palace, soon," she said. "America was very clear with Egypt. We will force it."

Force what?

Force America to also stand by the Yemeni protesters. To make a public announcement that now is the time for Saleh to step down. While the US ambassador was surely working to this end behind the scenes, Saleh officially was still an ally of the United States. How would that have to happen? Lots of protesters would have to die. That's what I believed would happen on such a march across the city. The army would surely attack with ferocity.

I stared at Tawakkol, wide-eyed. I wondered where she planned to stand in that march. She normally had a getaway car at such events. I wondered whether she was willing to die and leave her three young children behind.

I thanked Tawakkol for her time and we said our goodbyes. She was so uncompromising in her approach. It's what made her such a tough activist, but I also wondered why her hatred of Saleh was so strong. It seemed as though any sacrifice was worth it as long as Saleh suffered. And while Tawakkol insisted on and spread the idea of peaceful resistance in Yemen, I wondered if this plan was truly peaceful.

CHAPTER 13

I was eating fava beans for dinner with Tom at a small restaurant in the old city. We sat across from each other on long metal benches. Two Yemeni men sat at the far end of our table, leaning over their shared plate of ground meat. Three other tables sat unused around us. The dirt on the floor or occasional cockroach on the wall were of no concern to either of us. Rather, we relished how the restaurant's stone walls contained the warmth from the kitchen, where cauldrons of beans, meat, and spices stewed. Large copper kettles sat against the back wall on a portable stove, boiling water for tea.

One side of the restaurant opened into a square public space called, rather uninspiringly, *soq al-baqr,* or Cow Market. During the day, goats herded through the square and merchants sold egg, cheese, and boiled potato sandwiches from food carts. In the evening, young men loitered beside their motorcycles, hoping that someone would ask for a ride. Lining the square were small food shops, a pharmacy, two stands where men sold freshly squeezed mango juice, a small, dirty-looking hospital that I hoped I would never need to visit, and this restaurant.

I reached into our cast-iron bowl with a piece of white bread, trying to scoop up a green hot pepper slice along with the brown mush of beans. Tom asked the waiter for two more cups of milk tea. He served them to us in small clear cups. I watched the bits of cardamom in my tea float to its creamy surface.

I used to eat at this restaurant every day, roast chicken for lunch or beans and eggs for dinner. I didn't eat dinner much anymore, and anyway I hadn't been back to this place since I jokingly and loudly chanted an anti-Saleh protest slogan to Erik while eating lunch one afternoon. We received angry looks from both staff and clientele in return. Erik rolled his eyes at me. "Smooth move, LBK." The old city was almost strictly pro-Saleh. I knew that. I didn't know why I never used my brain before opening my mouth.

"Do you remember what it was like last fall, when we were just searching for stories all the time, trying to get editors interested?" asked Tom, with a hand full of bread and beans. He was tall and thin, with a long face and spiky brown hair that came out of his head in poofs. Tom, more than all of us, was growing up in Yemen. It was his first post-college experience. He came to Sanaa from London to work for the *Yemen Times*, a local English-language newspaper, and found himself writing front page stories for the *Guardian* in a conflict zone a few months later. While working, he tried to give off an air of composure and seriousness—I figured it was to act older than he really was—but Tom's vibrant youthful energy always seeped through, as well.

"In some ways, I wish it were like that again," I said. "I don't remember what it is like to feel bored. I kind of want to feel bored again, just chilling around the mafraj with Oliver."

"Jeez, I know. I miss those chaps. I just keep needing to remind myself that this isn't our revolution, you know? Like to not feel so disappointed when everything seems impossible."

"I know, yeah. You're right, but it's hard."

Tom looked up and signaled for a waiter to bring us more bread by raising his hand in the air and pointing to our pot. "*Ya Huboob. Khoobz*!"

"At least you're gonna get to have a break soon," he said to me.

"I know, it's nuts. I can't really wrap my head around it. In a few days, I'll be in my hometown."

I had recently received news that my mother, who already suffered from an array of health problems, was going to have surgery to repair two herniated discs in her neck. Her rheumatoid arthritis might be causing the cartilage in her neck to wear away, doctors told her. She apparently was feeling very poorly and in a great deal of pain. I was flying back to the States in a week to be there for the operation. I was always there for my mom's operations, and for some reason this one seemed more serious than any of her previous surgeries: hip replacements, foot surgery, and more.

Tom's phone buzzed on the table. As he read the text message, his eyebrows furrowed.

"It's Adel," he told me. "He says that the protesters are marching down to Kentucky Square and there are CSF down there."

"Oh crap, really? Call him."

Kentucky Square was about half a mile down from the last row of tents on the southern edge of Change Square. It was a large intersection where Ring Road hit Zubairy Street. A Chinese-built bridge arced over the intersection. There used to be a knockoff Kentucky Fried Chicken on one of its street corners, which is how the area got its name.

Tom called Adel, who repeated the story. He asked if Adel thought there would be violence. It sounded like it.

"Do you want to go?" Tom asked. "We probably should go. Right? We, like, need to be there. Right?"

"Yeah, but I don't have my purse or anything on me." I had come to eat beans with only my keys, phone, and a 1000 riyal bill tucked into the front pocket of my blue hoodie. I still had never replaced my stolen wallet and never carried ID on me since I lost my driver's license and didn't want to carry around my passport.

"Well, do you need anything?" Tom swung his leg over the bench and started pulling riyal bills out of his wallet.

"Eh, I guess not. Right? Let's just go," I said with a shrug.

"Do you want to take a motorcycle? That'll be the fastest."

I grinned at the idea. Sanaa was full of motorcycle taxis, but it wasn't appropriate for women to ride one. If I took one with Tom, though, he could sit in the middle behind the driver and I could be in the back. It would still be inappropriate, but I had been less concerned with abiding by society's rules ever since the first protesters had been killed.

We paid the three dollars or so it cost for both of us to eat dinner and approached one of the motorcycle taxis in the *soq*.

"Salaam. Will you take both of us?" Tom asked the driver, a scrawny teenager, pointing first to himself and then to me to emphasize just who "both" was.

"Yes, of course," the driver shrugged.

"Me? You'll take me?" I asked.

"No problem," he said.

"*Tamam, yalla*! Alright, let's go!" yelled Tom, swinging his leg over the center of the bike's seat. He was ready for some action. I got on behind Tom and grabbed hold of his tall shoulders.

"To Kentucky Square," Tom told the driver in a serious tone and we set off through the night. I put my hood over my head, hoping not to be identified as a woman.

"This is kind of shameful, right?" I asked the driver just as we were descending into the saila from the old city's small, winding streets.

"No, it's not shameful. I take my girlfriend with me on the bike all the time."

"Your girlfriend?" Tom yelled above the roar of the engine.

I couldn't stop laughing at the idea.

• • •

As the motorcycle pulled to the edge of Kentucky Square, a large intersection, Tom and I spotted balateja already pacing the area, assault rifles held at their sides. They were flocking in from side streets. They had nastiness in their eyes and gripped their guns tightly. Many had bandanas tied over their faces. CSF were standing in a line directly under the Chinese bridge in the center of the intersection, lit by the bright light emanating from the top of a water cannon truck, a green box-shaped vehicle stationed behind them. We could hear the protesters nearby chanting anti-Saleh slogans. We walked to them on a dark side street. When we had to pass a few balateja, we didn't make eye contact and quickened our steps.

"It's really tense. I definitely think something is going to happen," Tom said.

"I know. I'm going to go try to find something I can write on. Can I borrow an extra pen?"

I went into a small food shop. The man in charge was just locking his front door.

"*Salaam.* Hello, excuse me. Do you have any paper?"

"What?"

"I'm a journalist, but I don't have any paper."

The shopkeeper gave me a puzzled look and walked over to the cash register. He ducked down under the front counter and pulled out a small white envelope. He handed it to me.

"*Shokran.* Thanks. You're a big help!" I told him and the shopkeeper brushed me off.

I stepped out onto the street and looked for my friends. Tom was standing in the middle of the street interviewing protesters. Jeb and Iona were by the curb, talking. I saw Erik near them. Ali Mohsin's soldiers were nowhere in sight among the clusters of protesters, mostly college-aged youth dressed in Western clothing.

The shooting started faster than I had expected. It was directed into the crowd of protesters who began shouting angrily, some fleeing, some standing their ground. I didn't take the sound of gunfire seriously enough, or give it the respect it deserved, because I had heard the sound so often already. I had followed the same routine so many times: the moment when the first shot rang out, then the next, either I got out or I found a hiding place until things settled down. My body knew what to do.

I could hear that bullets were being fired from above street level. There were snipers, perhaps shooting down into the street from atop the bridge. Tom, Erik, Iona, and Jeb all scattered in different directions. They made it out safe, but my first instinct was that I shouldn't flee down a side street because that's where I had seen the balateja. Balateja concerned me. Despite knowing the vast majority of Yemenis would never attack a Western female, I didn't trust that balateja abided by any traditional moral code.

I scanned my surroundings for a shop to run into, but didn't see anything open. I had always found something open before. My confidence in my ability to always escape waned and fear started to creep in, but I forced it from clouding my thoughts, I clung to the belief in my ability to stay out of harm's way.

I saw a shack next to a mechanic's cluttered work yard about twenty feet ahead of me. It was haphazardly made of corrugated metal and an old rusted car with its wheels removed sat outside. The shack seemed my only option so I ran to it and ducked through an open door to find three other men sitting on the ground, also hiding. They didn't appear to be protesters, but rather men working in the mechanic's yard who were waiting out the night's violence—annoyed, certainly, but not too frightened.

The shed was probably where the mechanics chewed qat during the day. I walked to the back corner and had to crouch down because the roof was so low. There was a small wooden table placed in the middle and a tattered rug covered part of the dirt floor. A calendar from a local bank hung on one wall and Islamic calligraphy declaring in gold Arabic letters that there was no God but Allah hung near the door. I sat down on the ground, sinking into the dirt, and tucked my head between my knees for a moment. The banging was so close. I wondered whether the walls could withstand gunfire from an AK-47, and, realizing they might not, I wanted to lie on the ground and cover my head with my hands. But I knew the men hiding with me would think I was ridiculous if I did, so I stayed sitting upright. They sat stoically, speaking very little. It was the close sound of gunfire that unnerved me more than anything else, and the helplessness I felt stuck here in the shack.

I closed my eyes. *Why would I put myself in danger like this? This was so dumb.* This is not what a smart reporter would have done—there was no real need for me to be here. Just Tom and me being careless—wanting to be where the action was. Stuck inside the thin walls of the shack, the sound of gunfire was no longer innocuous. Each boom had become a beacon of potential death. Images of shot protesters, the limp, bloody bodies of March 18, crowded my mind.

Would this be the mistake that would cost me everything? I had nothing with me, no identification. I could still hear the yells from protesters outside, not running from the gunfire, but holding their ground. They blew whistles and taunted their attackers.

The sound of a tear gas gun boomed and soon gas was leaking into the shack, making us all cough. One of the men started closing the thin wooden door at the front end of the shack just as a young protester, probably a teenager, ran in, hacking and holding his eyes closed tightly. He collapsed to the ground. The men held him, tore off his backpack, and poured water over his eyes, spilling it across his white T-shirt. I had learned that this only exacerbated the stinging.

"No, no. Do this," I said, and fanned the teenager's eyes with a piece of cardboard I found lying on the ground. "This is what helps. The water makes things worse."

"Like this?" one of the other men asked.

"Yes."

The protester continued to squint and cough.

"Are you a journalist?" the man fanning asked.

"Yes, I am."

He nodded and looked back toward the door.

"Who did you see shooting the guns?" I asked the young activist, his eyes red and bleary.

"*Balateja, balateja*," he replied. "And also, the security."

I took his name and scribbled his words on the back of the envelope before tucking it into my hoodie pocket.

Then more gunfire outside. It wasn't stopping. The distraction the teenage protester provided dissipated. More yelling. It sounded like someone had been shot. The yelling was full of both shock and anger. My fear escalated. I wanted to cry, but couldn't. I thought I might die in that mechanic's shack. For the first time since I'd been in Yemen, I considered this a real possibility. Yet all I could do was be angry with myself. I was frozen in space, waiting for my environment to dictate my next move. *I am supposed to be smarter than this*, I thought. This wasn't supposed to happen.

Minutes later, two CSF soldiers stuck their heads into our hiding place. The gas masks they wore made them look like aliens. They pointed toward me.

"We want the foreigner," one of them said.

I threw both hands high above my head. "With peace, with peace. Just take me peacefully," I cried with the desperation of someone pleading for her life.

I stood to walk out of the shack, and one of the soldiers grabbed me by the arm. He yanked me away and I didn't have time to look back to see the reactions of the other men. Were they scared for me? Were they happy to be rid of me? It didn't matter. Now I had to concentrate on what these soldiers were going to do to me. In the heat of the moment, I had been afraid of their bullets. But because they didn't shoot me on the spot, I sincerely doubted it would happen later. A soldier would never intentionally, with premeditation, kill a Western foreigner. The repercussions would be too great.

The soldier pulled me down the street. It was empty at this point, aside from the cloud of tear gas hanging in the air, its stinging smoke working its way into my nostrils, down my throat. I hacked as we walked through the gas for half a block until we were under the bridge, the water cannon truck still lighting up the area. Balateja were loitering in the middle of the street, chatting, as if deciding if today's punishment was sufficient. I was in their territory now.

A group of ten CSF soldiers surrounded me like a pack of dogs. They were charged up from the shooting. They were all dressed in their green camouflage uniform. I felt one grab my ass and worried that maybe I wasn't as safe in their custody as I had assumed. "I'm an American," I told them all in Arabic, normally a golden ticket for decent treatment, but it didn't stop them.

Then a large, fat man, spotting me surrounded by soldiers, came over to us. He was dressed in civilian clothes, a long white thobe, and had a walkie-talkie in his hand, bossing around other balateja with an air of authority. The sweat droplets on his bald head reflected the glaring light from the water cannon truck. He reeked of strong alcohol.

"Where are you from?" he asked me in English with a strong accusatory tone. His gold-framed glasses were practically falling off his face as he talked.

"*Ana Amrikeya,*" I said.

"Speak to me in English, you fucking bitch. Where are you from?"

Caught off guard, I yelled back in English that I was American.

"Come with me." He grabbed me by the arm and pulled me across the intersection, away from the soldiers.

"Why are you here?" he hissed.

"I was just around this area and the protesters came. Then they started shooting so I hid."

"You're lying. Why are you here?"

"I'm a journalist! I write for the *New York Times.*"

"I knew it!"

We were headed down a dark side street and leaving the pack of CSF soldiers far behind now. I had no idea where he could be taking me. Still, the intense fear I felt in the shack had receded, and that fear had far outweighed my current concern over my unknown fate.

"You're an Islahi bitch. How much does Hamid pay you?" He was beginning to noticeably slur his English and I noticed that our path was more meandering than a straight line.

"I don't work for Hamid."

"Tell me how much do you get paid?"

"Well, actually, not very much."

"You're a liar! You work for Hamid. You're an Islahi bitch."

The ridiculousness of his accusation annoyed me more than it scared me. He couldn't believe that this was actually true. He was just regurgitating ruling party rhetoric to me about the opposition being supported by foreign elements, as if I was part of a large network of American spies aiding the Change Square protesters. I wanted to ask him how I, a woman dressed in western clothes, could possibly be an Islahi, an Islamist, but I figured that provoking him probably wouldn't serve my interests.

The man stopped in front of the metal gate of a small, walled residential compound. He reached into this thobe's pocket, pulled out a ring of keys, and spent the next ten seconds trying to match one of the keys with the lock below the door handle. I almost wanted to help him. Finally the lock clicked, and he lifted his leg to enter only for it to slide back down the front step to the street, and had to start again. To make up for himself, he looked back at me and said, "You're a very bad girl. What you do is very bad." He grabbed my arm again and gave it a yank, a signal that I should follow him without question and without putting up too much of a fight.

From what I understood at this moment, the nervous energy I felt upon entering this balateja leader's home was left over from the time in the shack, though fear is hard to sort out. What I knew for certain was that once the sound of gunfire stopped, I could think more clearly. I wasn't out of trouble completely, but at least I could negotiate this problem as long as I remained clearheaded—as long as I didn't freak out and compromise myself. I hadn't been able to negotiate with the gunfire—with being stuck in a dangerous position unable to flee. I had been helpless, and that's what frightened me the most.

The man took me inside the large yard and we walked up his driveway to stand next to a black SUV. He started making phone calls while I just stood there, waiting for what would happen next and reviewing my options for how to get out of what I was imagining as a string of events that would lead to my deportation. The Yemeni government didn't have time to hunt down foreign journalists anymore, but if one was delivered to the political security apparatus, caught in the act of hiding out with the protesters, she could be removed without much effort.

It was time to utilize the unorthodox problem-solving skills that Yemen had taught me—how to get from point A to point B in a line that curved and zagged, but got me there nonetheless. I wracked my brain for an idea while avoiding the man's gaze and focusing instead on the large house, with its well manicured bushes growing beside its walls and its colorful Sanaani stained-glass windows. Sanaa was so terribly dry; those bushes would have to be well watered. This man was clearly wealthy and well educated, definitely not the sort of person normally associated with kidnapping foreigners.

"What are you doing in Yemen?" the man asked me after putting his cell phone back in his front pocket, though we had already discussed this on the walk to his house. I figured he didn't believe me when I said I wrote for the *New York Times.* I was suddenly self-conscious of my age and inexperience.

"I, umm . . ."

"Shut up!" he yelled. His sweaty, whiskey-saturated breath traveled the small distance between us like a cloud of tear gas. I pressed my back to the front door of the SUV in a futile attempt to escape from it.

And that's when I realized that this man's drunken mistakes could work to my advantage. I still had my phone, my most obvious ticket to salvation. Remove phone from victim: that's kidnapping 101. That's political arrest 101. That's why I was supposed to always carry a back up phone on me while in Yemen. But what if it wasn't a mistake? After all, the drunk man did take me away from the marauding CSF pack and hadn't done anything overwhelmingly lecherous yet.

"Excuse me. But I really need to use the bathroom. Please can I?" I said in the most pitiful voice I could muster.

"Alright," he grabbed my arm again and pulled me up the house's front steps. "But you are very . . ." he looked as if he were holding back a burp. His eyes glazed over. "Very . . ." He swallowed deeply as we stood on the porch just in front of door. "Very bad."

When we entered the living room, which was Western in style with couches and a coffee table, I saw framed photographs hanging in a line on the wall of this man standing with Saleh, or some other leader from the ruling party, the GPC. He was clearly an important figure in Yemeni politics.

"Here's the bathroom." The man indicated a door just off the living room. "Go."

I stepped inside and pulled the door closed behind me, not daring to look back at him in case my plan had been written on my face. The bathroom had blue tile and a real toilet. Not a Turkish-style squat toilet that many Yemenis had in their homes.

I pulled out my phone and quickly typed out a text that read: "I am being held in a balateja leader's house next to Kentucky Square. He is important in GPC. He is very drunk and I am very scared."

I sent it to Erik and Mohammed Abulahoum, a sheikh I knew who lived in Sanaa. Sheikhs had sway, and I had just spoken with Abulahoum on the phone, so his name jumped out at me as a person I should contact.

I leaned over to press the silver button on top of the toilet. It flushed. I ran the tap in the sink. I looked squarely into my eyes in the mirror and took a deep breath, then turned off the faucet and stepped out of the bathroom. The man was waiting for me directly outside, his arms folded over his big belly.

"Sit here," he said to me, pointing to his couch in the middle of the living room. As I walked over to it, I heard a scuffle on the stairs and saw two girls appear on the second floor, leaning over the banister and looking down at us. I was grateful they knew I was here because they confirmed my feelings that no physical harm would befall me in the house. That would just be such an affront to Yemeni culture. Even now, I still trusted Yemenis more than that.

"You know who I was on the phone with?" the man asked, standing in front of me. "Abdu Borgi. He wants me to send you to political security." I knew that Abdu Borgi had some high-ranking role in Yemen's security apparatus. I had never met him, which I knew would not work to my advantage in this situation because it made me a faceless foreigner meddling in Yemeni affairs, not a smiley young woman whose love for the Yemeni spirit oozes out of her and helps win over the most cold-hearted of men.

My right knee trembled involuntarily as I sat on the couch. I didn't know if it was leftover energy from the time in the mechanic's shack or if my body was experiencing fear that my mind hadn't recognized yet.

"Stop shaking!" the man yelled in a tone of voice that was more worried than tyrannical. As if by trembling I confirmed that he was the bad guy doing bad things, and I was the innocent victim. In his mind, that wasn't the way this was supposed to play out.

My cell phone buzzed.

"Give me your phone," the man demanded. I held it out to him. He answered. It was Erik. I recognized Erik's voice yelling through the speaker, telling the man that he needed to let me go right away. I didn't think it served my interests so much for Erik to yell at him, but felt quite powerless to do anything about it.

"What this girl is doing is very, very bad," the man told Erik over the phone. He hung up and hit the button that lists whom I called last. I was lucky that none of the most recent names were leaders from the JMP. That would have only confirmed his suspicion that I was a foreigner working on behalf of the opposition, which could have made this situation take a drastic turn toward the political security police.

"Is this Mohammed Ali Abulahoum?" the man asked, staring at my phone.

"It's Mohammed Abulahoum, I don't know what his middle name is. He's a sheikh."

The man looked at me like I was an idiot. I looked at him as if to say, *well, what do you expect?* He called the number and spoke on the phone with Abulahoum, who fortunately had seen my text so knew about my predicament. Abulahoum told the man that I worked for the *New York Times* and that I was very important and valuable to the embassy, and that he had better not let anything bad happen to me.

"Okay, if you come pick her up, then I'll give her to you," the man told Abulahoum.

After he hung up, my phone rang again and the man answered.

"Hi, this is Kevin from the US embassy. We've heard you've kidnapped Laura Kasinof."

"No, this is not a kidnapping!" the man yelled. "What she was doing is very bad."

I held my head in my hands in exasperation.

Erik told me later that he had called the number for American citizen services at the embassy and got hold of the young diplomat, Kevin, who was manning the phones that evening and who in turn called my phone. Kevin told the drunk man he would come pick me up, but that he didn't know where Kentucky Square was.

"Just ask someone!" the man yelled into the phone.

I sat on the couch at attention like a pupil waiting to be admonished while the man continued to curse at me and tell me all the reasons why what I did with my life was very bad. A flat screen TV sat in the far corner of the living room facing another couch, a wooden coffee table in front of it with two television remotes placed neatly on its surface beside what looked like an expensive glass vase. More framed family photos, along with a painting of the old city of Sanaa, hung on the walls. It really felt like an American living room, as though the two of us were connected in this small world of elites in Sanaa who spoke English and preferred couches to mafraj cushions.

Ten minutes later, the man's guard knocked on the door to inform us that two pickup trucks full of armed tribesmen from Abulahoum's house had pulled up outside the front gate. They were asking for *Looora Kasinova.*

Still, the man refused to let me leave.

"I will only give you to Mohammed Ali himself!" he told me. He called Abulahoum back to tell him that he would be the one responsible for me from now on, that Abulahoum no longer had to worry. My momentary relief that I would be leaving soon was replaced with renewed worry, not that any physical harm would come to me, but that I would be delivered to the political security apparatus, ripe for deportation. I started to see it clearly: events had been put in motion that would lead to my life in Yemen ending. If only I hadn't gotten on that motorcycle with Tom.

And then the proverbial light bulb came on; you could have drawn it above my head. Thankfully, my kidnapper and host was too intoxicated to notice.

"I mean," I said, "if you did that, you know . . . I don't have any identification on me. If you give me to security they won't know I'm an American. Bad things could happen to me."

His alcohol-greased wheels started spinning: Abulahoum knew I was with him. Kevin knew I was with him. Yemeni culture dictated he was responsible for my care.

"I do write for the *New York Times,* you know. Just like Sheikh Mohammed Ali told you . . . If anything bad happens to me, other people know I'm with you . . ."

My phone rang again. Kevin was calling back to say that he still couldn't find Kentucky Square.

That's when the drunk man declared he would take me to the embassy himself. He had had enough of this bullshit, he told me. He was sick of having me on his hands. He was so frustrated that he seemed to be having a fight with himself, muttering and making sharp, jerky movements. I tried not to show the excitement at my imminent release. I was still in his custody after all, but I saw that a positive ending was in my grasp. I imagined this was going to turn into one of those entertaining stories I would recount at qat chews in the months to come.

The man called to his son to come downstairs to drive us. A twenty-something emerged from the steps. He had large brown eyes, thick black hair, and a nice profile. He gave me a look over, put on his jacket, and we all walked outside together.

"Call the embassy and tell them we're coming," the man said to me.

"I can't. I don't have any credit left on my phone."

"I can help," the son volunteered. He called a friend who worked at the cell phone company who put credit on my phone number. I thanked the son for his generous help. I told him I didn't know what I would have done without him.

Then we all climbed into the SUV in the driveway, the man with markedly less agility than his son and me. The son drove and the man sat in the front passenger's seat. I later learned that he was one of Yemen's most prominent wheat importers and a member of the Yemeni version of the House of Representatives. That's why he was leading the balateja from his neighborhood that night. Only important Saleh allies were given that role.

I sat in the middle of the back, leaning forward between the two front seats as if we were all old friends.

The man bent over his big belly to reach under his seat and grab something. He pulled out a Kalashnikov and swiveled at the waist to hand it back to me.

"Here, just hold this," he said to me as if he were giving his incompetent child the lowliest task possible. "And for the love of God, don't talk."

The son cracked a smile at his drunk father. I gripped the rifle awkwardly in both hands and focused my attention on trying not to touch any levers.

The son drove manically through Sanaa in the dark. It had been about three hours since Tom and I had gone to the protest together and was approaching midnight. The city was quiet. We zoomed and weaved through the streets. The dull street lights shone on the fronts of buildings of brown and white brick. Soldiers had just used live gunfire at unarmed youth, killing a handful of them, but you would never know it from the peace of Sanaa at night.

"You know I saved you from the *balateja*," the man leaned back to say to me as we drove. "Do you know what the soldiers were going to do to you?"

"I know you did. Thank you so much," I responded. I just had to keep him appeased until I got out of his car.

We arrived at the front gates of the embassy in the far northeast part of the city. I was relieved I hadn't been shot. I was relieved I wasn't being handed over to political security. I was relieved I was out of the house. But complete, true relief wouldn't come until I was handed over to someone I could trust. In fact, it wouldn't come for a very long time; not until after I had moved back to the States and learned to drive at night without looking in my rear view mirror on every empty street.

One of the embassy guards standing watch sauntered over to the SUV to speak with us. The man rolled down his window. The outside was still and quiet.

"*Salaam aleikum*," the man greeted the guard.

"*Aleikum salaam*," the guard replied, bending his neck to take a look at me, the young foreign woman in the backseat. I gently dropped the gun to the floor.

"Listen, I saved this girl from the *balateja*," the man told the guard. "She is a very important person. I want a certificate. Who do I talk to about that?"

CHAPTER 14

When I traveled back to the US for my mom's surgery, I decided to keep everything that happened over the last few months stowed away in a little locked box. That seemed simple enough to do when the worlds I was traveling between were so outwardly different. It was like there was a me who existed in Yemen and a me who existed with family, and I could swap them during a transcontinental flight. The chaos, sadness, and at times absolute absurdity that Yemen had pulled me into were not to be unveiled in America. Why live through that again anyway? It would just be easier to forget about it. It's not like I had ever intended for it to happen.

When I first moved to Yemen I had been afraid of what America had told me to be afraid of. Then I began to see that those fears were inconsequential and I only had fun in Yemen. This was often heightened by the riskiness of the place, like drinking beers in the middle of Hadda Street at three in the morning and then hitchhiking back to the old city in the back of a qabili's pickup truck. It was especially fun because it was taboo in both of the worlds where I existed. Then the risk increased once the protests began, but I was still having fun. Then everything became horrible. But even in that there was the fun of surviving amongst the chaos, because although it was difficult, the mind can shut the bad out for a while, and instead I concentrated on the good, the fun, the friendship, and the praise

I was receiving for my work as a journalist. It was easy to convince myself that it was worth it. Yemenis had a lighthearted touch in dealing with heartache, and it helped keep my heart light as well, for as long as it could.

Yemen was relatively calm when I left, with Saleh still in power, Ali Mohsin's soldiers guarding the Square, and protesters not staging any more marches outside their protected areas like Kentucky Square. There was talk of Saleh signing an internationally brokered agreement that would eventually hand over the presidency to his deputy, but I doubted that would happen. So I felt some peace with leaving for a few weeks. I was calm just like Yemen was calm: artificially.

• • •

"Ladies and gentlemen, welcome to Washington, DC," the flight attendant announced over the intercom. She repeated the same message in French.

I turned my phone on as soon as the plane touched down. I had been in the air for around eight hours.

"Please remain in your seats until the plane has come to a complete stop."

My phone slowly captured the signal. I waited impatiently.

"It is now safe to use all approved electronic devices."

If I were in Yemen, I would have taken out my phone while we were still descending.

Three bars appeared in my phone's top right corner. My email loaded. I scanned through the messages. There were two from the *Times*:

"Laura, can you call us ASAP when you land?"

"Laura, possible agreement to hand over power reached. I know this has happened before, but this time seems serious. Please call. Thanks."

I glanced over to the polite looking man sitting beside me. He sat with his hands folded in his lap, patiently waiting for the plane to reach the gate, totally unconcerned that the president of Yemen might be stepping down. I resented him for it.

There was an Associated Press story pasted at the bottom of the second editor's email. Saleh had finally agreed that he would sign a transfer of power deal. The plan stipulated that he would step down in a month's time. It was called the GCC Initiative, short for Gulf Cooperation Council, the league of oil-rich Gulf States that excluded their poor neighbor Yemen.

I knew that what wasn't reported openly was that the plan hadn't really been concocted by GCC leaders. As if they cared that much about Yemen to begin with. Instead, the deal was drawn up by a Yemeni official who was an advisor to Saleh, with input from the American and European Union ambassadors. The men had decided it'd be better to put an Arab face on the whole thing and brought the GCC on board. If it were called the American Plan or the European Deal, it wouldn't have been so catchy.

So, the article claimed, Saleh had agreed to sign this plan. That's what my editors were in a hullabaloo about. It happened while their beloved Yemen freelancer, the young woman who knew everything about the country about which they knew little, was crossing the Atlantic on an airplane.

All our hopes and dreams and headlines were based on Saleh's signature alone.

The plane came to a stop at the gate. A text came through from my mom.

"At baggage claim. Can't wait to see you!"

I sighed. I had arrived a few days before my mom's surgery because tomorrow was Easter. Easter was a big deal in my mom's family. I'd get together with my large group of aunts, uncles, cousins, and cousins' spouses. I'd be looking for Easter eggs with cousins who'd never left America, who'd never read the *New York Times*, and who didn't really get what I was doing with my life, all while I was trying to figure out if Saleh was sincere in this latest promise to leave office.

I slowly disembarked. As soon as I stepped onto the solid ground of the airport, I called the foreign desk.

"Listen, do you think you can get us something on this," an editor asked.

"Yes, sure. I'll do what I can."

I walked to immigration and waited in line to get my passport stamped while looking up news in the Yemeni press on my phone.

I hoped security couldn't see that I was looking at websites written in Arabic. Or maybe the National Security Agency could tell I was logging onto Yemeni sites while waiting in an airport. Everything about Yemen was suspicious to the American government.

I stepped up to get my passport stamped. The TSA officer looked me over after going through page after page of my Yemeni visas.

"Why were you in Yemen?"

"I'm a journalist."

"Who do you write for?"

"The *New York Times*."

Does he believe me? I can't look old enough.

"What's the purpose of this trip back to the US?"

"My mom is having surgery in a week."

He scanned my passport and stared at his screen. This was the point when many of my American friends who lived in Yemen were told to step aside—marked suspect for having set foot in the country of al-Qaeda. Potential security threats. Extra screening necessary.

The officer stared at the screen some more, appearing to be reading. Then he grabbed his stamp and pressed it onto my passport page.

"Welcome home," he said.

I retrieved my suitcase and pulled it out of baggage claim. I walked through the big swinging doors with NO RETURN printed in giant letters and saw my mother standing among the crowds of greeters, her face contorted with emotion. My eyes started to well with tears once I saw her. I wanted them to stop. I was never one to get homesick. I'd lived abroad for years; homecomings were normal. But this time I couldn't stop the tears. We hugged tightly and she felt frail in my arms.

"I'm so, so glad you're home. How was your flight? Are you doing okay?" she asked. Her short, wispy, auburn-dyed hair stuck to her cheeks. Her arthritis-crippled hand grabbed my suitcase. I could tell it was more shaky than normal. It trembled, even.

"I can pull it, Mom. Thanks," I said. "I'm good. I'm good. Saleh may be stepping down."

"I know, I just heard the news on the radio."

"I'm gonna have to work on the way home. Can you drive? I'm so sorry. I would normally drive. But I'll have to do some reporting from the car."

"Oh, that's okay, honey. I'm so, so glad to see you. Do you have to use the restroom?"

"No, I'm okay, Mom. Let's just get going. I need to work."

• • •

I sat in one of the spare chairs in my mother's hospital room. It was the kind sold in bulk: blue patterned fabric and beige wooden armrests that curved down to the floor. The kind that countless family members have spent countless hours in, waiting at their beloved's bedside. I propped my feet up on an identical chair in front of me. My mom, connected to too many wires to count, watched CNN from her hospital bed. A screen beside the IV drip read out her vitals. I stared up at it as if I could decipher the numbers and lines. I never remembered what a healthy blood pressure was.

I looked back at my laptop, the browser open to a Yemeni news site. I had told my editors I wouldn't work for a few days while my mom was in the hospital—my big vacation—but I couldn't stop following the news from Yemen. Logging on to Twitter had become one of life's necessities.

The surgeon knocked on the room's door and pulled back the long plastic curtain that shielded my mother from the hospital hallway outside. It was one day after her surgery. She seemed to be faring well, except that, to our surprise, the shakiness in her hands hadn't dissipated. We both had blamed the trembling on her herniated discs, her impinged spinal cord.

"Hi, Amelia, how are you doing?" the doctor asked kindly, leaning over the bed. His gray hair was combed back neatly.

"I'm doing well. The nerve pain and tingling down my arms has completely gone away."

"That's wonderful to hear, Amelia."

"But I have a question for you. Look at my right hand. Do you see how it still shakes? Why is it still shaking?"

"Amelia, the surgery isn't going to correct that. I greatly suspect that you have Parkinson's."

The doctor stayed with my mom a while. He said that the way they would know for certain of her new diagnosis was to give her medicine that acted as a replacement dopamine. If it corrected the Parkinson's-like symptoms, that meant she had, indeed, developed the chronic condition. I listened, but the words felt impossible. I could not contain the tragic story of the past few months to Yemen alone.

I wanted to deal with this news the way I had learned to cope with events during Yemen's upheaval: by seeing it, registering it, and trying not to be too affected by it. I'd rather deal with people dying in Yemen. That I could treat like work.

After the doctor left, my mom looked over at me and started to cry. Her eyes couldn't produce tears, though, a symptom of her rheumatoid arthritis. She was so sick, all the time. I didn't know what to do. I couldn't write about it for the world and thus feel like I had accomplished something. I couldn't do anything but sit here and cry with her.

I told myself that I couldn't cry too much. If I cried too much, she'd know that I was in a bad place. She'd know that my chest was heavy with the trials of the past few months. I didn't want her to know. It would break her heart.

My dad came into the room an hour later. We told him the news. My father and I moved to the unused room next to my mom's. We sat and cried together. Salty tears. Tears that had been so rare these past months. A war correspondent should not cry. It was one of the few things I knew about reporting on conflict. I mean, it had to be true. My instincts told me that. If a war correspondent cried, then she couldn't report. The shell that protected me from the realities of the outside would have to grow thicker. I had to avoid a meltdown. But that shell couldn't protect me forever; it was fragile at its core.

The white barren walls surrounded my father and me. Next to us was an empty hospital bed where people got better or died. The sterile needles. The heart monitor. The pain pump hanging to its side. Everything was organized. Where was the blood? Where were the bullet wounds? I would have preferred them to this.

"You know, when I first met your mother, she told me that when she got old, she would be really sick," my father said to me.

I started sobbing at this remark.

After a moment, I caught my breath. "She'll be okay. The surgery was successful. So that's good."

"Does she say her neck hurts her as bad?"

"She says she can already feel an improvement."

"That's good. Well, we'll do the best we can," he said and then paused. I could hear him swallow. "I'm going to go get a coffee. Are you okay for now?"

"Yeah, Dad. I'm fine."

I walked back into my mother's room. She told me she was going to try to fall asleep. I told her that sounded like a good idea and returned to my chair. I opened my laptop and checked my email. A message from a Yemeni official source told me that there was more political finagling before Saleh would sign the GCC Initiative. This time it was about whether the JMP would take part in the government in the thirty-day interim prior to the president stepping down. Saleh responded with the demand that he wanted all protesters off the streets before signing. I wondered if the two sides would ever reach a deal. It was easier to wonder about that.

Next, I read an email from a friend from high school with news she had just gotten engaged. I couldn't care less. I felt that celebration was something merited only by matters of life or death; revolution or illness; the end of great sorrow or the defeat of a dictator. I deleted the email.

Then, Erik chatted with me online from Yemen. He was about to leave the country for good and was staying in my apartment during the few weeks after his lease ended and before his departure. We had said goodbye in Sanaa the way two people who have experienced the best and worst of life together often do: anticlimactically and in few words. When I told Erik I'd see him later, I knew that it was true. We were both Americans, but when we moved out of Yemen and said goodbye to our Yemeni friends, "see you later" rarely applied.

"Someone was in your apartment," he wrote.

"Really? How do you know?" I asked.

"I came home and there were paper towels in the toilet."

"Weird."

"Does the landlord normally come in uninvited?"

"No, has never happened."

I imagined soldiers breaking in, looking for me. Or maybe my landlord opened the door for them, not wanting any trouble.

"Email me tomorrow, okay? So I know you're okay," I wrote.

"Sure, will do."

"BTW, my mom has Parkinson's."

"What?! I'm so sorry. How do you know? Are you okay?"

"Not really."

• • •

Ali Abdullah Saleh finally agreed to sign the GCC Initiative in a big ceremony full of pomp and praises and attended by many foreign diplomats on May 22, 2011. It was to take place inside the richly decorated walls of the embassy of the United Arab Emirates, a more benign Gulf power than Saudi Arabia (which supported dictators like Saleh) or Qatar (which supported the Islamists).

An Arab leader was going to hand over power peacefully, or so it was declared. Never mind that dozens of protesters had been killed in the process. Everyone had to pretend that Saleh was a good man for agreeing to step down. Yet the immunity for the president that this deal provided, that it essentially kept his government intact and only handed over power to Saleh's ally, Vice President Hadi, was far from what the protesters had sacrificed their lives for. There was little guarantee much would change in Yemen after Saleh signed this plan. He could still rule from behind the scenes. A civil society instead of a military dictatorship was a long way off. It certainly seemed like the only reason Saleh was signing the transfer of power agreement was that he felt cornered by Ali Mohsin after the army divided. This was the best the president could ask for.

Saleh and his GPC leader cronies planned to meet at the presidential palace prior to the signing ceremony. Then they would drive to the Emirati embassy together. But once the officials started gathering, they realized that one man was missing: the president.

In the meantime, thousands of pro-Saleh tribesmen, the balateja type, protested in the streets of central Sanaa. They yelled that they did not want Saleh to hand over power. They loved Saleh. He was the savior of Yemen. Yes to stability! No to terrorism! They waved their Kalashnikovs in the air.

Finally, late, while the foreign ambassadors were already gathering at the embassy awaiting Saleh's arrival, the president showed up at his palace. He said that he was just about to head out the door for the signing ceremony, in a little bit, soon, when news spread that the protesting armed tribesmen had encircled the embassy, yelling threats. Many foreign ambassadors were inside, including the American ambassador, Gerald Feierstein. The tribesmen moved closer. They weren't letting the ambassadors leave. The day was turning into a diplomatic fiasco.

The ambassadors had to be airlifted out of the Emirati embassy in a helicopter a few hours later. And Saleh never signed the GCC Initiative. Whether he had ever intended to in the first place was certainly left to question.

• • •

After Saleh proved that his promise to hand over his presidential powers to Hadi had all been a charade, war broke out in Sanaa.

At least, I guessed it was a war. I wasn't quite sure what made a war. Had protestors being killed by the dozens not counted? I was watching it all from my parent's home in rural Pennsylvania, and it looked like a war when I saw five-second clips of artillery fire in Sanaa on the evening news.

The Saleh family lobbed artillery fire and mortars at the heart of their enemies, Ali Mohsin's army base and a compound close to it owned by the al-Ahmar family. Sometimes there were firefights in the streets. The crux of the battle was in the neighborhood of Hasaba in northern Sanaa that was controlled by the al-Ahmars and Ali Mohsin's troops. Civilians died in the crossfire, of course. Artillery fire was extraordinarily inaccurate and would sometimes cut through a family's living room.

My plans to return to Yemen had been postponed, and I didn't like it. I wanted to jump on a plane immediately. I wanted to go back to do the noble work of reporting, because I felt like I owed it to Yemenis, and because reporting for the *New York Times* was glorious work. It was an opportunity like none other. I had received praise nearly every day when I had been in the field, accolades for my bravery and insight. I had been subsisting on the high of one sustained adrenaline rush.

Yet here I sat in Pennsylvania, afraid.

My friends in Sanaa told me they still went out to eat in Hadda at night with only the faint boom of artillery fire across the city to remind them there was a war going on. They told me it wasn't so bad, that the men stopped firing at each other in the afternoon during qat chewing hours. They told me war looked scarier from afar than it actually was. But I remained confused. If I went back, then I'd truly be a war correspondent. But did I want to be a war correspondent? I worried for my family. My mother had just found out she had Parkinson's, and I wanted to return to a city at war. It seemed cruel for me to be so callous toward her feelings, but Yemen was pulling me toward her, too. The tug of war was chipping away at my sanity.

• • •

I was sleeping in my childhood bedroom one morning in early June when I was awoken by the beep of a text message. I grabbed my phone from the nightstand. It was sent from a Yemeni journalist:

"Palace attacked in Sanaa. Saleh is killed."

In what felt like a second I was downstairs, sinking into the soft leather cushions of my parents couch, in front of my laptop. I begged, implored the universe for this news not to be true. I couldn't comprehend a world in which Saleh was assassinated without me in Yemen to report on it, as if my presence were necessary for the passing of events there. It's so easy to fall into that mind-set as a reporter, which is why the text message was a punch in the gut. I had already missed the faux signing ceremony—wasn't that enough penance? I emailed Jeb, Iona, and Tom: "I heard Saleh's been killed. What's happening?!" I desperately wanted to know the details, like I was the one reporting it.

Moments later, I found out there had been some sort of explosion inside the mosque at the presidential palace during Friday morning prayers. Saleh might or might not be dead. Probably some people were.

Later, I would find out the explosion was caused by a series of bombs smuggled inside the palace. And even later, I would learn they were hidden inside the *minbar*, the wooden lattice structure at the front of the mosque from which the imam orates. The explosion burst through the minbar, sending shards of wood through the air, while the men were standing side by side, neatly in rows, praying.

I called a Yemeni official, a spokesperson for the government.

"Is Saleh dead?" I asked.

"No. He's not dead."

"What's going on?"

"He is injured, but he is okay."

"Some news reports are saying that he will go abroad for medical treatment."

"No, he's staying in Yemen."

"Tell me for real."

"I am."

"You sound tired."

"I am. How's Momma?"

"Better. I know you're busy."

"*Tamam, yalla.* Bye."

My mom appeared in the kitchen. She went over to the counter to make coffee.

"Morning. How are you doing?"

"Would you like some coffee, sweetie?" my mom asked.

"Yes, sure. Thank you. Saleh may have been killed."

"Oh wow, really?"

"Well, we don't know if he's dead yet."

I noticed my mother's movements, still slow and shaky, but better than before. I wondered how she was doing. I wondered how my friends in Yemen were doing. It was all too much to be happening at the same time.

Jeb chatted with me online to tell me he had nearly died, too. He had been out in a big square adjacent to the palace compound that Friday morning to attend the weekly pro-Saleh rally when he heard the first boom. As he tried to leave what had become a chaotic crowd of Saleh supporters, an RPG whizzed past the front of his taxi's window.

"My driver was like 'holy shit!' It's the most scared I've ever seen a Yemeni."

The RPG had been targeting Hamid's house from the presidential palace, but was way off target. Minutes after the bomb had exploded in the palace, the Republican Guard pummeled Hamid's mansion in Hadda with artillery fire from a nearby hill. The sheikh probably wasn't even home. It was a symbolic shelling since Hamid was the most obvious person who would be behind the assassination attempt.

The names of the confirmed dead from the mosque bombing came in later that morning. I learned that an official I had once interviewed had been killed. Many leaders of the GPC were severely maimed or dead. The political leadership surrounding Saleh had been removed from existence that Friday morning. Yemen's power structure had at first fractured with Ali Mohsin's dissension. Now it was crumbling to pieces.

Later that afternoon, I learned Saleh had shipped off to Saudi Arabia for emergency medical treatment. I departed for Sanaa a few days later. I could only take part in family life tangentially when I was so invested in the day-by-day, hour-by-hour events in a country on the other side of the world. It was no use to be home anymore.

CHAPTER 15

When I went back to Sanaa, the war had stopped. It stopped the day of the explosion at the mosque, after Saleh went to Saudi Arabia for medical treatment and his army pummeled Hamid's house in Hadda with rockets.

But this didn't feel like the recipe for a lasting peace. It was now that I truly understood that I was living in a military dictatorship because it felt that the only part of the government that survived the collapse was the armed forces. The capital was divided. The lines of who controlled what were delineated by checkpoints where soldiers monitored each passing car. I knew whose territory I was in by what color uniform soldiers were wearing at the checkpoints: dark green camouflage meant I was in a Saleh family–controlled neighborhood, while sandy tan camouflage, the sort American soldiers wore during Desert Storm, meant Ali Mohsin and his partner, Hamid, were in charge. Neither side showed any indication that they were about to pack their bags and return their armored personnel carriers and long-range weaponry to their bases anytime soon. I had to always be alert to my surroundings to understand the political ramifications of my current location. If I was in Ali Mohsin and Hamid's part of the city then I could openly tell the soldiers I was coming or going from Change Square. If I was in Saleh family–controlled territory then I never said that I was a journalist and just smiled like a demure, confused foreign woman.

The social fabric of Sanaa was tearing as well. Some started to resent the protest movement that had only brought trouble to their lives. Others wished the Saleh family would just concede power already, since it was clear that they couldn't win against Ali Mohsin and the al-Ahmars. These two dissenting opinions split friendships, even families. The remarkable unity that I had once witnessed at Change Square even started to unwind as problems began to rise between al-Islah activists and the others.

This is why, in mid-June, when I landed an interview with Ali Mohsin, I didn't just go out to the street and grab any taxi to take me to his base. The driver could have been vehemently pro-Saleh and refused, caused a fuss, or even driven me to the police. No, I had to search through my contacts to find a driver whose number I had saved who once spurted pro-protester rhetoric to me, hoping that he wouldn't mind driving a foreigner to the headquarters of the man whose army now controlled half of Sanaa, and who seemed positioned to expand his territory even further.

I had covered myself up more than normal for the interview. Yemeni friends had cautioned me to do so. Ali Mohsin was a very conservative fellow, they said. He had been, after all, one of Saleh's main liaisons with the Arab mujahideen, who moved to Yemen from Afghanistan to fight against the godless communists of South Yemen. Though the general still belonged to the ruling party—at least technically—his heart was with al-Islah, the party to which Hamid al-Ahmar, Ali Mohsin's partner in bringing down the Saleh regime, also belonged.

I brought a translator, Abdulsallam, along for the interview. I only did this during the most important of occasions, and I could tell he had dressed in one of his finest suits this morning. He tried to hide his excitement about meeting arguably the most powerful man in Yemen at the moment.

"Have you ever been inside *al-ferqa*?" I asked Abdulsallam on our way to the base.

"No, I haven't." He sat up straighter. His oversized suit fell off his tiny frame.

Abdulsallam and I reached the bottom of the hill in northern Sanaa on which the al-ferqa base sat. A small dirt road wound its way up a steep rocky outcrop in front of us. Soldiers stood around an armored personnel carrier. Abdulsallam leaned his head out the taxi window and in a professional voice explained that I had an appointment with his Excellency, Major General Ali Mohsin al-Ahmar. A soldier made a call on his cell phone, after which we were told to get out of our taxi. I told our driver to come back in an hour. Another soldier pulled up in a jeep and we were told to get in. We drove up the hill and, as we reached its top, a small expanse of barren, flat, and dusty land came into view. Ramshackle buildings and ominous tanks spotted the area. A broken down basic training course sat unused.

This, apparently, was what a military division ready for war at any time looked like. The soldiers—and there seemed to be a lot of them—were sitting around as if they had nothing to do. After lunch, they'd all chew qat and sit around some more. Some were newly recruited protesters who were tired of the peaceful resistance of Change Square and wanted to fight.

We reached one of the largest buildings on the base, a square edifice made of dark gray brick, still adorned with the colorful, angular stained-glass windows that decorated nearly every building in the capital. When we got out of the jeep, I felt the gazes of the nearby soldiers. I was the only woman around.

Once inside, Abdulsallam and I were passed off to another soldier who led us up to the second floor. At the top of the stairwell still hung a large picture of Ali Abdullah Saleh. I pondered its existence for a moment, wondering what kind of fight this was when Saleh's enemy still paid homage to his presidency in such an official way. Then we were ushered into a small side room where a group of older men in uniforms adorned with military regalia sat around a rectangular table, drinking red-tinted tea. A shelf full of books with small golden Arabic letters inscribed on their bindings sat behind them.

Abdulsallam, who was exactly my height, looked back at me.

"I guess we'll wait here," he said.

Two of the men around the table said hello to me in English.

"What's your name?" one asked.

"Laura."

"Laura, what?"

"Laura Kasinof."

"Kasinof! You're Russian!" he declared.

"Yes, but . . ."

Before I had time to answer, the officer launched into some speech in a language with Slavic-sounding vowels.

"I'm sorry. I don't understand Russian," I interrupted him in Arabic.

He looked at me, disappointed.

"What do you think of Barack Obama?" another officer asked me in Arabic.

"He's better than Bush."

"Ah, Bush loved war. It is not a good man who loves war," piped another one from across the table.

I stared at his military badges and then out the nearby window at an armored personnel carrier.

"Do you think Obama is a Muslim?" the first general asked me, but before I had time to answer, a soldier popped his head in through the door to tell Abdulsallam and me that Ali Mohsin was ready for us. We left the generals to their tea and walked a short distance down the hallway and into a larger office where I was to meet the Yemeni leader infamous for corruption, murder, and supporting fundamentalism.

Ali Mohsin sat behind a table at one end of the room. He had dark skin with fat wrinkles and a big, toothy smile. Behind him were colorful stained-glass windows, alight with red- and blue-tinted sunshine. He looked like a jolly grandfather.

Beside the general sat a man with a more serious expression and a notebook in his hand. On the other end of the room was a stately desk with papers spread out on it. Above it hung another large framed photo of Saleh.

Ali Mohsin looked proper and prepared for his interview with the *New York Times.* The *New York Times* reporter was trying very hard to also look proper, but she was unnerved by the biggest interview she had ever done. We sat at the table across from one another. Ali Mohsin answered questions only after first consulting with the man to his left, Abdulghani al-Shumeeri, who, as his spokesperson, guided the commander in exactly what he should say to the American journalist. It was my introductory lesson to the sad truth in journalism that important figures will rarely say anything worth recording while on the record.

"As long as this regime is in power, al-Qaeda will continue to exist in Yemen," Ali Mohsin told me. "Counterterrorism cooperation is now based on material cooperation only. It is for the exchange of funds: how much will you give me if I can kill a person for you?"

And Ali Mohsin, who had a relationship with the old jihadists, would be a better ally than Saleh? To these leaders, al-Qaeda was merely a tool. To Yemenis in Sanaa, al-Qaeda was a myth. To the American government, it was the only reason to care about Yemeni politics.

"Why did you join the revolution? You know, some protesters accuse you of being associated with things like corruption . . . ummm . . . and the war in Saada . . ." I asked in English, before looking over to Abdulsallam, feeling bad I was making him translate accusations. Abdulsallam translated my question with similar hesitations.

The general held out his hand, palm up, and gave me a friendly smile, as if he were explaining something ever so basic to me.

"I joined the revolution because I felt our democracy was threatened," he answered. His niceties were convincing. I wondered if he had said this so many times he actually believed it.

"Well, what about the people who say you are doing this because you want to have a position in the government after Saleh leaves?"

"I don't have any desire to keep my position in power, and no aspirations for more power either," Ali Mohsin answered. "Our genuine aspiration is to steer the revolution into a safe harbor. And to ensure its success. And to help the revolution realize its objectives and to maintain democracy and a peaceful transfer of power."

Is that why your soldiers and their guns are spread out across the northern half of the city?

"Do you think Saleh will return from Saudi Arabia?"

"We have no information on this," he said.

Ali Mohsin leaned back slightly in his chair as if to think for a few seconds. He was no longer consulting with his PR manager.

"We hope his health is well," he said before pointing toward the stately photo of Saleh hanging above his desk. "See?"

"I know. I saw that when I came in," I said.

He chuckled a bit while staring at the portrait. It was a hearty, old-man laugh. It didn't sound sinister—but it very well may have been. Maybe the portrait was just to remind Ali Mohsin of how he was conniving against the president. How he had the upper hand in this fight against his old friend, who still lay on a hospital bed in Saudi Arabia, whose future was uncertain.

• • •

I sat cross-legged on the orange carpet of al-Masdar's office a few days later, pulling qat leaves from a bag Yasser had bought me. My laptop was open in front of me. The power was out, but Yasser was letting me use his USB connection so I could still work online while the Internet was down. I always felt like I was taking advantage of my fixer's generosity—it verged on chivalry—but I couldn't stop myself. I needed so desperately to be taken care of. And Yasser seemed to be the only person attuned to that need, though our relationship, of course, never stepped past the communal qat chew.

Yasser sat diagonally across from me on thin cushions. A young reporter who was uploading photos from his phone onto his laptop sat beside him.

I was engaged in the sort of work a reporter hates: trying to figure out what was happening hundreds of miles away when there wasn't a lot of accurate news coming out of the area. In the wake of the political breakdown of the last few weeks, gun-toting militants had taken over large swaths of land in southern Yemen. They created their mini-states in cities like Zinjibar, the capital of Abyan province, and started enacting sharia law (they let the no drug consumption rule slide for qat, of course). Every week or so there was news of militants taking over a new town and all government and security officials fleeing their posts. The exact nature of how this happened remained a mystery. So did whether the militants, who called themselves Ansar al-Sharia, were affiliated with al-Qaeda and why the Yemeni government seemed to let them have their way.

Opposition supporters believed that the Salehs intentionally abandoned these cities to the militants, or even that Saleh's nephews were funding and supplying them, because if the international community believed Yemen was seriously under threat from al-Qaeda, then they would no longer be pushing for Saleh to abdicate power. Meanwhile, Saleh loyalists believed that Ali Mohsin was funding and supplying the militants, since he was the one who was supposed to have all the jihadi connections anyway. I considered the possibility that al-Qaeda could actually be taking advantage of the lack of government control in the South, partially because Ali Mohsin and the Saleh family seemed fairly distracted with their standoff here in Sanaa.

"Yasser, do you know how I can reach anyone in Hawta?" I asked before sticking my index finger in my mouth to pack the qat leaves back into my right cheek.

Yasser called a friend for contacts in Hawta, the most recent city taken over by Ansar al-Sharia.

"*Tayyeb*, Laura, here is the number for the head of security."

"Excellent. Do you think he's still in town? I thought I heard that all government officials fled."

"Maybe. What do you want me to ask him?"

"Oh, I don't know. How many people in Hawta have been killed and if the militants are actually al-Qaeda."

Yasser called. The official said that he was sitting in the security building in Hawta, which of course contradicted local news reports that all government employees had fled town once the militants stormed in. I imagined a bunch of bearded guys on trucks howling into the sky as they waved their AK-47s in the air.

"Are the militants al-Qaeda?" Yasser asked the official on the phone.

"What?" the head of security replied.

"Are they al-Qaeda?" Yasser was emphasizing the first letter of Qaeda, which northern Yemenis pronounce with a G.

"What?"

"*Al-Gayda.*" Pause. "*Al-Gayda!*"

"I don't know, but if you want I can go out and ask them," the head of security told Yasser.

Yasser cackled.

"That's okay. You don't have to do that for us. *Shokran.*"

• • •

In less than a week's time, I was inside another one of Sanaa's military bases. Only this one was filled with more women. Way more women. The person accompanying me to this interview was not Abdulsallam, but rather a Yemeni woman. The rest of them scurried around carrying oversized binders. They donned a feminized military uniform—a long green camouflage cloak and a black hijab.

My friend and I were guided through the central building that housed the office of Yahya Saleh, the president's nephew and head of this institution, the Central Security Forces. Its dark, fortress-like structure took over blocks in central Sanaa. Humvees and tanks sat outside its thick walls with heavy artillery at the ready. We had entered the base through a large gate that looked like it should be the entryway to a medieval castle, only to be reached after first crossing a dangerous moat. I felt small and impotent once inside CSF, which received millions of dollars in military aid from the United States for fighting al-Qaeda in the Arabian Peninsula. Ali Mohsin's base had made me conscious that I was living in a poor, underdeveloped country. Here, I felt like I was breaking into an empire.

I had heard that Yahya was barred from talking to the media ever since, in a televised CNN interview in 2010, he had revealed details about the US drone program that weren't supposed to be made public. But I found a friend of his to set up the interview for me. "Tell Yahya I met with Ali Mohsin last week, but now I want to meet with someone from the Saleh family," I told her, "and I think the person has to be him."

"Don't worry," my friend told me. "I think I can make it happen."

Yahya was not only Saleh's nephew. He was also married to Saleh's first daughter, Bilqis, from the president's first of four wives. They had a son who attended American University in Washington, DC, named Kanaan, after the land of Canaan, meant to be an homage to the Palestinian cause. He commanded CSF but was also co-owner of al-Maz—a multimillion-dollar enterprise that consulted with foreign energy companies working in Yemen—as well as being involved in a number of other money-making enterprises.

Upon entering his large office, Yahya greeted me with a clownish smile and extended his hand to grasp mine. He was balding and cut his remaining black hair short to his scalp. His nose was long with a slight curve that was common among north Yemenis. Under it perched a well-trimmed mustache. He was of medium build, not too fat like some rich GPC leaders, but not a skinny Yemeni villager either.

Yahya then greeted my friend, and the three of us walked over toward gold-trimmed chairs placed in one corner of the room, between which a large Yemeni flag hung limply on a pole. The general's press secretary was there, as well, to record every word that was uttered during this meeting. (*Don't screw this up, Yahya!* I imagined him thinking.) A photographer snapped photos of us from ten feet away.

Yahya proceeded to snicker throughout the interview, seemingly adept at amusing himself.

"The American imperialists . . ." He let out a short, high-pitched giggle. "They are the ones behind the GCC Initiative," the transition agreement for Saleh to step down. This was actually kind of true, and Yahya was clearly annoyed about it.

"But, as well, Saleh agreed to sign the Gulf Initiative," I retorted.

"After the assassination attempt, things changed. When he comes back, there will be another discussion. He will come back, God willing."

"When will the president come back?"

"We don't really know. It depends on his health situation and what the doctors say. When he is ready, he will. I mean, you see, he will not come back to a normal situation. He has to be ready to deal with all the problems. The assassination attempt was intended to kill him and the leaders of the state. Thank God it didn't succeed, which means God loves him."

Yahya paused for a moment and leaned over toward me. He asked my friend in quick Arabic, "How old is she?"

"I understand you," I said in Arabic before my friend had a chance to answer. "And I'm twenty-five."

"Ah, you speak Arabic?" Yahya asked in English.

"I live in Yemen. Of course I speak Arabic."

The general considered this for a second. I thought to go on.

"Why don't you just take the immunity offered to you in the GCC Initiative and step down?"

"Immunity?!" Yahya became indignant. "What did I do wrong? They are liars. We did not go to the protest with arms. We don't have orders to shoot. Our conscience is at ease. We call it a revolution of liars. How many are there? Are they the majority? In a democracy, does the minority rule the majority? They should respect themselves and go home. It's been five months. It's boring."

Yahya cracked himself up at this and his mood lightened. He didn't seem like the sort to be too troubled by any one thing in particular.

"The problem is that the rest of the world believes that this is a youth revolution," he continued. "When Ali Mohsin enters the picture, it is no youth revolution."

I considered for a moment the truth behind this sentiment, but then I remembered the youth from the media tent at Change Square. Just because Ali Mohsin used them to challenge Saleh's power, just because he doesn't represent their values, it doesn't mean the original protesters suddenly no longer existed.

"Have you received money from the US this year?" I asked him.

"I don't remember these things," he said. Then he paused and looked to the ceiling as if struggling to recollect. "Eh, we only received equipment . . . like airplanes."

After I said that was all the questions I had for him, Yahya reached into his back pocket to pull out his cell phone. He leaned over toward me once again and showed me the device. There were stickers of Che Guevara plastered over it, and the iconic rebel leader's face was set as the screen's background.

"So you're a revolutionary too," I said to him in Arabic with a half-smile.

He looked at me confused and furrowed his brows. "Of course," he said.

I couldn't believe he didn't get my subtle attempt at humor. But clearly the activists at Change Square were no more revolutionaries to Yahya than he was an average citizen of his country.

"You know, I friended you on Facebook," he said to me. But your picture is not so nice. You look better in person.

"Here, take my number," Yahya said, motioning for me to pull out my cell phone. "It's seven-seven-three-six-nine-six-nine-six-nine."

I gave Yahya a cold, I'm-not-amused stare and he giggled some more. I reminded myself that behind this goofy, fun-loving smile was one of the men responsible for killing protesters since he was the head of CSF. The way he made light of Change Square seemed fitting for a person capable of evil. Did he not know that men at the Square, who once were engaged in tribal war, were now signing accords of peace? Did he not know that youth from the North and South met at the Square for the first time and debated their differences? Did he not see that young people who never had hope came together to give their lives new meaning? To Yahya, the protesters were rats—these were his words once in a social media status. To Ali Mohsin, they were a tool.

CHAPTER 16

It's one thing to watch the city that you call home, the city that you love, survive under nightly barrages of artillery fire and mortars and bullets. It's full of commotion, adrenaline, and overwhelming emotion. You can't concentrate, and you're worried for your safety and the safety of your friends, but you know that things can, and probably will, get better. War doesn't last forever. In most cases, anyway. In war there is hope for peace.

But to watch life in that city fall down a dark hole of despair, with its people left wondering not just if the sun will ever rise again, but how it will rise, and to watch that population try their hardest to keep their heads held high and persevere, understanding that life will only become more difficult, that's another thing entirely—that feels worse than war. Because in that, there is no hope.

That's what life was like in Sanaa late into the summer of 2011. Politics, be it reconciliation or conflict, were on pause. Saleh appeared on television from the Saudi capital Riyadh to show that, indeed, he was not dead. But he was badly burnt, his skin charred black, his hands wrapped in gloves. He looked far from ready to resume his duties as the country's president.

Change Square was also on pause. Protesters still lived there, but did little in the way of protest. The joy of the Square was seeping away. The economy had completely collapsed and prices for basics like food and water had in some cases quadrupled. The state no longer provided services.

Electricity flickered on for a few hours a day and offices were closed so it was no longer possible to process a birth certificate for a newborn child. Soldiers took over public school buildings, using them as barracks. Men who had been fired from their jobs by companies making cutbacks tried to drive taxis to eke out a living in the meantime, but fuel was impossible to find. The gasoline shortage meant that lines at gas stations stretched for a mile down the street, and it took over a day before a car could finally make it to the pump. Yemenis left their cars in line along the side of the road to sleep for a few hours overnight.

Black market merchants would mix water with gasoline to sell. They stood along the side of the road with dark yellow plastic containers full of it, hoping to attract a desperate cab driver. Once I was in a taxi fueled by the watered-down gas. It sputtered and stalled every minute or so. When that happened, the driver would turn around to reach into the backseat and bang the back of his car with a wrench. This worked, for another three minutes. "Excuse me," he'd say as he reached around to the back and then proceed to curse the merchants of the black market under his breath.

Tom recently had bought a motorcycle to drive around Sanaa. When he went to get gas for it, Yemenis insisted he move up to the front of the mile-long line. He was a foreigner, and after all, this was Yemen.

People started carrying weapons more openly on the streets. One day, I sat eating pizza alone at a restaurant in Hadda and saw a man walk into the shop with an AK-47 slung over his shoulder like a lady's purse. He was picking up two large pizzas to go, probably for whichever sheikh he worked for. Another day, I walked down the aisles of the grocery store, looking to see if that one type of British-made muesli I loved was in stock, and saw a man with his gun on open display, grocery shopping. At first this trend was alarming, but then I remembered that the omnipresence of weapons used to be the norm in Sanaa not so long ago. In 2007 the government began to enforce the law prohibiting the open display of weapons in the capital. After the government broke down in 2011, this ban was completely ignored, with no consequences. What government would enforce the law now?

Policemen stopped working, too. Busy intersections routinely descended into mayhem because no cop was there to guide traffic in the absence of a light or stop sign. Cars just sat there in a mismatched puzzle, creeping along a foot a minute. One afternoon I saw an old, jolly man with a whistle hung around his neck climb onto the cylindrical traffic police box in the center of a large intersection in Hadda. He blew his whistle to direct traffic and waved his arms around as if he were a drunk orchestra conductor, laughing and smiling the whole time.

• • •

A stream was burbling as it rushed down the hillside. My ears picked up its sound, such a rarity in dry Yemen. Sanaa was set to become the first world capital to run out of water ("God willing, it won't!" Yemenis always said) as underground resources were depleted by illegal wells and qat farmers used copious amounts to feed their thirsty trees.

I worked my way up a gravel path through the center of this village just outside the capital and looked down at the stream. It was tiny, but provided enough water to sustain the tall, leafy foliage growing beside me, shrubby trees and black vines sprouting tiny red flowers along the village's ancient brick houses set side by side on a rocky incline. These traditional homes resembled those of Sanaa's old city, but were falling more into disrepair because the international community wasn't invested in their upkeep. Chipped stones lay on the path at my feet. The white of the alabaster was wearing away. The village was home to around five hundred inhabitants. They could be broken down into ten families that had lived here for nearly one thousand years.

I had come to the village this morning in late August to do some reporting for a story about how Yemenis were making do despite the lack of government services and the economy falling apart. It broke my heart when my taxi driver told me the long story about how he lost his job and afterward wouldn't let me pay for my ride. I insisted he take the money, and he insisted that would be shameful since I was a foreign journalist writing about his country for the world. It wasn't fair that these hardships were happening to the people with whom I was living. It wasn't fair they were made to suffer because of politicians who cared only about self-preservation.

I wanted to find that part of the enduring Yemeni spirit that had made me so happy when I had first arrived in Yemen. And even now, in spite of scant electricity, no government assistance, no police or justice system to enforce the law, somehow society wasn't completely falling apart. I wanted to find out why.

I knew about this village with the stream because I used to take weekly rock climbing trips here with Josh, one of my four friends who had been deported in March. He had shared an apartment with Oliver, Haley, and Portia and had lived in Yemen for more than four years. Josh bought rock climbing equipment in Dubai, brought it to Sanaa and created routes on the side of a mountain outside this village. Every Friday afternoon a group of foreigners and wealthy Yemeni adolescents climbed with some of the villagers. Sometimes the villagers would climb thirty feet up the side of the mountain without ropes when Josh wasn't looking.

The villager who climbed the most was Ali, a kind-hearted thirty-something who was perpetually looking for work. And he was the one I had come to talk to this morning.

• • •

I followed Ali away from the cluster of homes that made up the center of the village and onto a rocky mound that overlooked the capital.

"You can see all of Sanaa from here," he told me, pointing out toward the city of brown, white, and dust below. I could make out the faint beep of a traffic horn. "And all of the war in Sanaa, too. When they fired at Hamid's house, it was very bad."

Hamid al-Ahmar's mansion, where I had gone for the interview months before, had been pummeled by artillery fire from a hill very close to this village the day of the attempted assassination of President Saleh.

"We were afraid that the al-Ahmars would fire from Hamid's house at the Republican Guard and hit our village," Ali now explained to me.

"What did you do that day?"

"We all lay on the floor of our house like this." Ali put both arms around his face and over his head. "One shell from the al-Ahmars hit our village," he continued.

"How do you know it was from al-Ahmars and not the Republican Guard?"

"We know."

Gunfire rang from the city below. Ali didn't flinch, nor did I.

"What do you think that was? War?" I asked, half-jokingly.

"No, it's a wedding. I am sure," Ali said.

"But you don't think that was fighting? Tribesmen shooting at each other?"

"No, I know. It was a wedding."

How did he know? How did all Yemenis shrug off danger until tragedy occurred and a son, father, or daughter were killed by a stray bullet? And even then, it was only the will of Allah. God's will rules all and there is no questioning it. Fatalism helped to survive in the worst of times. I considered that it was easier to persevere that way; to just concentrate each day on living life, on getting through that day, on surviving. In some ways, it's easier to live like that. Desirable, even.

Ali and I walked back through the shrubs and rocks to the center of the village. I stumbled over the loose ground, thinking that it would have been smart to wear tennis shoes. Ali walked sure-footedly even though he was wearing sandals much more cheaply made than mine.

We ran into a herd of bleating goats in a grove of small, leafy qat plants. Following behind them, a tiny elderly man with a staff was emitting monosyllabic yells. I wasn't sure if they were directed at us or the goats.

"That's my father," Ali said, nodding toward the man.

They greeted each other with a handshake and cheek kisses. Ali explained to his father who I was. He told him that I was not only a journalist, but also part of the rock climbing crew who used to come up to the village every Friday.

His father, who held the curved end of his staff with one hand and waved his other around wildly to emphasize whatever he was saying, welcomed me warmly. He had gray stubble and wrinkly dark skin, and the suit jacket he wore over his thobe was smudged with dirt. It was his daily uniform. His head was as high as my shoulder. I asked Ali's father what he thought of the current situation in his country.

"It is the biggest crisis ever! It made prices go up so much," he shouted back, as if eager to complain to a foreign reporter.

"What do you think will solve this crisis?"

"It is not going to go away by a political solution," he said, focusing his gaze on the ground and shaking his head. Goats bleated in the background and all at once he looked up as if he had had an epiphany. "Injuries! Injuries!" he shouted, waving his staff in the air, meaning that war would be the only solution.

"How do you survive during this time of crisis, during war?"

"Ah, we sit here. We just go with it." The father shrugged. He made me feel it was a ridiculous question. Like the whole reason I came to the village didn't even need to be discussed.

"I think Yemenis are used to living in any kind of situation," Ali said.

This rang true. Sure, I heard plenty of complaints around Sanaa about the gas lines, the lack of electricity, and the prices of basic goods, but no one did anything about it. Then again, what could they do? They could join the protesters at Change Square, but many civilians were starting to blame those protesters for causing this whole mess in the first place. The notion I grew up with, that we are the masters of our life and circumstances, seemed distinctly privileged when I looked at these villagers.

As Ali and I continued on, we ran into another elderly man who was walking by the stream in the center of town. He held a cigarette in his one hand and a qat bag in the other, and was wearing a green suit jacket over his thobe. A beige-colored scarf patterned with small rectangles draped over the back of his shoulders. I stopped to speak with him as well about the current difficulties.

"I've gone seven months without qat!" he yelled. "Qat takes a lot of money and there is no money!"

"But that's qat," I said, pointing at the clear plastic baggie in his hand full of green leaves.

He waved me off. "I got this from a local farmer," he said.

"So how are Yemenis surviving with no money, no electricity, no cooking gas, no hope for a political solution?"

"Belief in God," the old man told me.

"*Ya Laura*," Ali interrupted. "We use candles."

Ali and I walked on, following the narrow path of rubble and gravel that had been built through the village hundreds of years earlier. Ali told me he didn't think there would be school this year. He told me prices of the minibuses that cart most Yemenis around the city had gone up, so it had become more expensive to get into Sanaa from the village.

On the way to Ali's family house, we stopped at a small white building to talk to the local shopkeeper, who told me he had made about 50 percent less money this year. "I sell credit to a lot of people so they can buy things, but a lot of people, they aren't paying the credit," he told me. "I am married. I have two children. It is difficult."

"But how do you survive? How will you survive with less money?" I asked him.

It seemed a basic principle to me: things cost a certain amount. If you didn't have the money to buy those things, and there was no institutionalized plan to provide for those in need, then you went hungry.

The shopkeeper pointed toward the sky. "Allah. I don't have anyone except Allah."

After this, Ali led me to his house. In the yard sat piles of wood—another rare sight elsewhere in Yemen, but available in this water-blessed village—and an outdoor oven that seemed to work as a contained campfire, encircled by a thin aluminum wall. We entered the house through the unlocked front door and climbed its narrow stairway. Ali yelled to announce our presence to everyone in the house.

On the second floor, I was greeted by Ali's mother and one of his sisters, one of ten siblings. It was always a pleasure to meet Yemeni women in the privacy of their homes, and they were usually eager to speak with the strange foreign girl. Ali's mother wore a floor-length, black, long-sleeved dress, a sort of indoor robe. The sister dressed similarly, but with a thin black scarf draped over her hair. It didn't seem like an act of modesty, but was just part of her wardrobe. We walked into the house's mafraj together and sat down on the low cushions lining the room. They were thin and covered with a baby-blue sheet. There were no rugs or tapestries or kitchen tables, just rough white walls and a window adorned with red, yellow, and blue stained glass at its top. All was kept immaculate though, the mother and daughter sweeping up the dust every day with a homemade broom of roped together whicker. Photos of male family members, never smiling, adorned the walls or were placed on the narrow windowsill.

The mother, a tiny woman whose face showed the deep lines of decades of hardscrabble village life, sat across from me. She went by the name Umm Ali, meaning mother of Ali, a tradition many Yemeni wives still follow, adopting the name of their eldest sons. Tiny flowers were etched in dark red henna dye on the tops of her hands. Miriam, the sister, sat directly beside me, seemingly wanting to get as close as she could. Her excitement was palpable, but the necessary demureness of being an unmarried Yemeni village woman kept her from talking too much in the presence of her mother.

The mother asked who I was and how long I had lived in Yemen and if I was married and why was I not married and *inshallah*, God would find a good husband for me, maybe I could even marry somebody from the village. Yes, yes, the wrinkled old mother was insistent, that's what I would do. I tried to shift the conversation.

"I just see that it's so hard for Yemenis to live nowadays . . ."

"A canister of cooking gas is two thousand riyal! Two thousand riyal!" the mother yelled, making the gesture for number ten with her hands. "And that's when there even is gas!"

A state-run company was in charge of doling out long silver cylinders of cooking gas to Yemenis, sold at a subsidized price. But it was in short supply these days. I couldn't understand why exactly, other than that's what happens when a government breaks down.

"So how do you cook?" I asked, happy to move the conversation away from my personal life for a bit.

Miriam pointed out the colorful stained-glass window to the oven in the yard. "We use ancient methods to cook," she said.

"Do you think the government is going to find a solution to solve this crisis?" I asked them.

Miriam, growing bolder, answered the question from her heart. It's why I enjoyed interviewing ordinary people more than government officials whose responses usually had a self-serving agenda.

"What government?" she said. "Everyone makes his own law in his mind." She tilted her head to the side, pointed her finger at her brain, and gave me a look like she expected me to know better.

That's when it hit me more than ever before. I felt like an idiot for not understanding until this sheltered village girl drove the point home: Yemenis expected so little from their government. Public services were new and minimal, so life without them was much less foreign to Yemenis than it was to me. The idea of state-enforced rule of law had hardly ever existed. Yemenis were held accountable by their family, by their tribe, by their neighbors. Social cohesiveness is what kept chaos from breaking out when there was no government to enforce the laws. Tribal law had always superseded state-enforced law anyway. I remembered reading a local news article about a tribe that had been in conflict with the government leaving a slaughtered cow on the front gates of the Ministry of the Interior, the traditional way to declare that hostilities were over.

And in a way it was the same for me, albeit on a much smaller scale. Not the dead cow part, of course. But I had been learning how to negotiate this society where laws were based on custom and problems were solved via personal connections. I got access to high government officials by first befriending their close acquaintances. I convinced the drunk balateja leader that he had more to gain from taking me to the US embassy rather than political security.

Sure, I could afford the high prices, the villagers' main grievance about the current crisis, but I had to deal with the same inconveniences: electricity only existing for a few hours in the middle of each night, often flooding my bedroom with light and waking me up because I had forgotten to turn the switches to off before going to bed. I too traveled from place to place in Sanaa before or after the noon qat market rush, when the streets were completely jammed with traffic because of the lack of police. I too had gotten used to the guns in the grocery store, the military checkpoints demarking Saleh and Ali Mohsin territory, a divided city, my home.

We humans are adaptive creatures. But Yemenis' ability to adapt so seamlessly amazed me.

"Were you here in the house when the Republican Guard hit Hamid's house in month six?" I asked Miriam, using the traditional Arabic term for June.

She told me she had been. She told me it had been "terrifying." She said it in a tone that conveyed that, looking back, it had been exciting, too.

"Are you afraid the war will start again?"

"Stop it," she said teasingly. "We are used to it. It's now something normal."

CHAPTER 17

Tom had a bottle of vodka, and we had to ourselves the ground floor of a hostel that was no longer occupied by foreign tourists. Sometimes a strange, grumpy, and bearded Eastern European man, who seemed to be drunk twenty-four hours a day—and who I believed to be some sort of spy—hung around, but when he was gone, the hostel was empty.

Jeb was leaving Yemen in the next few days and we had come together on this September evening for a farewell gathering. He had decided that he had to get out. One couldn't be a freelancer in Yemen forever. It often felt like our old lives were waiting for us in our old homes. In Jeb's case, that was Atlanta.

Tom and I sat on low cushions on one side of the mafraj with Jeb across from us, legs spread out, not caring if we pointed the soles of our feet at each other, nor paying attention to other Yemenis social norms, drinking vodka mixed with Sprite or Coke or that carrot orange juice from Saudi Arabia that they sold at the local shops. Mustapha, the hostel's owner, was with us, sitting behind his large desk in the corner, disorderly stacks of papers surrounding him. He was drinking Tom's vodka at double our pace. Mustapha was big bellied and jolly, with a thick mustache over thick lips. His eyes were soft and kind and his hair was a black mop. His community had voted him the *agl al-hara*, or the head of his little neighborhood of houses in the old city. Mustapha often sat around all day on his hostel's doorstep in his oversized thobe, waving to passersby. He was missing two front teeth after a violent trip over this doorstep when coming home from Tom's recent birthday bash.

On the walls of this small mafraj were taped dozens of postcards sent to Mustapha from outside Yemen, on which foreigners declared their love for his humble hostel tucked into a narrow alleyway in the old city of Sanaa. Some were written in Chinese, Japanese, Italian, or French. The electricity had gone out, but Mustapha had turned on a mini generator, its dull humming underlining our conversation. It was difficult to obtain diesel to run the generators, but for some reason Mustapha always maintained a mysterious steady supply.

"You know why I want democracy?" Mustapha asked us all, slouched wide-legged in his desk chair, his white thobe hanging down between his thighs like a draped curtain.

"Oh boy, here it comes," said Jeb, a veteran of Mustapha's grand schemes.

"The saila will flow with whiskey," Mustapha pointed the finger of his one hand into the air and held his vodka glass in the other, "and girls in bikinis will dance beside it. This is true democracy."

"Yeah, Mustapha. That's true democracy. Right," Jeb responded. I just laughed loudly as I always did and Tom took a sip of his drink, rolling his eyes.

"Ah yes, that is true democracy," Mustapha repeated, with a tone of admonishment and pride that he had finally figured out the ways of this world. He stood up and shuffled over to his 1980s TV on the far side of the mafraj near where we were sitting, turned it on, and started flipping through channels until he reached an Egyptian music video station. A woman, scantily clad with gold tassels, belly-danced across the screen.

"Is this democracy, *ya Mustapha*?" Jeb asked between large, hearty chuckles.

"Eh, close," Mustapha said.

A knock rattled the outside door. Mustapha's buddy and handyman, Ziad, opened it slightly from the outside and poked his head in.

When he saw Jeb, Tom, and me lounging on the mafraj's pillows, a mischievous smile spread across his face.

"Ah, welcome. How are you all?" he said and opened the door wider to enter. Mustapha poured Ziad a glass of vodka with a few splashes of sprite.

"Man, I'm gonna miss this," Jeb said, leaning back against the cushions.

"Oh, come on. You're going to enjoy being in America," I said to him.

"I know. I'm gonna love me some electricity, that's for sure. And fast Internet. That's gonna be great."

Ziad stood along the wall, just staring at the TV screen, entranced. "These Egyptians can't dance," he said.

"We need to go to *nady rusy*," Jeb said, the Arabic name for the Russian Club, one of the very few bars in Sanaa. It was run by a Russian couple and located in a government-protected area on a hill near the US embassy that housed, among other people, the remaining Yemeni Jewish population.

"Ugh, the Russian Club." Mustapha made a disgusted look. "Let's just have a dance party here! Tom, do you have any Yemeni music on your computer?"

Tom turned on Yemeni *oud* music, the Middle Eastern–style lute. The singer called out to his love over the strumming. His voice reverberated with his instrument in long nasally syllables. Mustapha called out to the universe, "whoaaaaa!" and he and Ziad stood up to dance in the center of the floor between the cushions. They twirled in circles and bent at their waists. Mustapha grabbed his janbiya to wave above his head, its sharp tip making small circles in the air. Tom joined them, his blue T-shirt and khaki pants a strong contrast to their long, white thobes, trying to follow the dance steps that it seemed every Yemeni man knew by heart. He picked up one foot and then the other with the intense concentration of an intoxicated driver trying to walk a straight line. Soon I stood up to join as well, and Mustapha handed me his janbiya. I pointed its sharp tip to the sky and swung my hips to the music. "Hey! Hey! Hey!" Mustapha shouted. We were all barefoot and might as well have been at a moonlit dance on the beach. Jeb started filming the spectacle on his phone from his spot on the low cushions. It was difficult not to want this part of our Yemeni lives to go on forever, the warmth of friendship, our charades despite the ongoing crisis. I couldn't imagine how I could be having more fun than this. The good that comes out of hardship is particularly meaningful—and life was about to become drastically more difficult.

• • •

A few days later, on September 18, after Jeb had already left for the airport, Tom called me.

"The protesters are marching . . ."

"Okay, why is that . . ." I interrupted.

"No. Listen to me. They are marching down to Kentucky Square. And apparently the *ferqa* went with them."

• • •

I arrived at the field hospital and was instantly taken back to the massacre of March 18. I still couldn't fix a firm image in my mind of what the hospital had looked like that day, but my senses remembered flashes: a putrid smell, splattered blood, medics scrambling, shouts of pain and panic, not enough stretchers for the wounded. Added to that were the sounds of blasts from not so far away, though these were deep and rumbling, not as sharp as the crack of a gun. Now, the mosque had once again been transformed into a triage center where there were too many people and not enough organization. New bodies were brought in through the outside gates, protesters carried corpses and those on the verge of death by their limbs, trying to find an available stretcher or doctor to treat their friends. Shot men lay helplessly on stained, thin mattresses spread out across the dirt yard. Their blood soaked through their white bandages, but they were not the critical ones.

Change Square had been through months of inaction—boredom, really—and then all at once blood was shed again, a reminder of the days before Ali Mohsin's soldiers started protecting the sit-in. It snapped us—journalists and protesters—into action. It felt easy to find purpose in this. If Jeb had known this was going to happen, he never would have left because, despite it all, we thought we wanted to be here for these moments.

I saw the bodies of the dead were maimed not just by gunfire, but by something designed to cause more carnage. I had seen plenty of bullet wounds. If a bullet hits at just the right angle, it does a great deal of damage, but otherwise these wounds are not so gruesome, a hole, really. Yet these bodies had been torn apart. I didn't know what it was, because I didn't have experience with any weapon larger than an AK-47.

Every move that each person made in that mosque felt as though it carried the weight of life or death. And because we were walking that line, I felt that we were collectively at the pinnacle of what it means to be alive. Yet once again, it was death that brought us here. Death coming through the door, carried disjointedly in the arms of hurried men trying to save their friends, or at least trying to give them some dignity by not leaving their bodies on the field of battle.

When you are in a group of people who are fending for their lives, who have just come from an onslaught, or who are tasked with the duty of making sure as few die as possible, all the extraneous pressures of life fade away. So many people in my home country are just going through the motions, doing what's expected of them, weighed down by expectations or meaningless desires. None of us in that mosque that day suffered such iniquities. But in these times it's also more difficult to discern right from wrong because the mind clouds with adrenaline, gore, and pride in one's own bravery.

I entered into the prayer room of the mosque. In the middle were stretchers, IVs, bandages, and cases of medical supplies. Just like before, the corpses were already lined up against the wall on the cold tile floor. When I caught a glimpse of one of them, it was like a vacuum sucked all the oxygen from inside me. Half the man's head was gone. Blown away. A sliver of skull and reddish hues of sticky mush left to remind us of what was once there. This was no longer a government trying to intimidate a crowd of antigovernment protesters. This was now a war and here was the evidence. The situation had spun out of our control, and these protesters were unarmed. They had no business on the front lines, but I knew they would go anyway.

I ran around with my notebook, trying to find out how and why this new violence started, and what, oh what, could the army be shooting at the protesters. I still heard gunfire and the sound of explosions coming from the outside, a backdrop to the shouts of doctors and moans of patients. The air mixed with the smells of blood, death, and medical ointments. The smell made me feel like I had to accomplish something.

This time around, what I saw and recorded in the field hospital wasn't traumatizing in the way it would have been in the past. It didn't steal my memory away, leaving a blank space in my mind for a time that I knew existed, but couldn't recall. Dead bodies were no longer a surprise. They were just another part of life.

Anger stirred inside me like a mighty force. I wasn't upset that my choices in life had led me to this cruel reality. I was disgusted that this reality existed when compared to my comfortable upbringing in America. I wanted to be here, in this spot in this room, staring at this headless man, because of some vague notion that I was doing humanity a favor by reporting. But this task took an enormous toll on my psyche. I felt like a waif, like a half human standing here. As though part of me, the joyful part, was dying along with these men. To which heaven did this man go? This man whose head had been blown off by heavy artillery? I was taught to believe as a child that he would spend eternity in a place that was not heaven because he was a Muslim. Many Americans would turn their backs on him simply because of that. But how can anyone judge a human who has had his head blown off? I imagined his mother finding him here, his brother. They'd identify him by the shape of his torso, his arms, but not his face, because it was gone.

I left the prayer room and stepped out into the mosque's yard where I found tall, skinny Tom sitting on a gray step and scribbling away on a notepad. His brown eyes were concentrated, locked on the piece of paper he held, as if he were writing for his life. Yet I saw water welling in his eyes as well. But he was fighting it. And so was I.

"Hey."

"Hey."

"Are you okay?"

"Yeah, are you okay?"

"What are they shooting them with?"

"I think the army attacked them with big machine guns."

"What the fuck, man . . ."

"Yeah, this is really fucked up. Did you see the guy without the head in there?"

"Yeah, just blown off."

It was an uncanny experience to see a friend in such a state, when we were both are trying to keep safe, trying to do our jobs, trying to stay tough and fight, pushing the sadness away because it was like a monster that would come eat us, and we just couldn't let that happen because we had to do our jobs. *These people depend on us. The world depends on us. Who would know if not for us?* It was all there and it was just too much, but we carried the load anyway.

We both sighed deep breaths, our shoulders rose and our shoulders fell. We stared at one another for a second, but then I spun on my heels to turn away, leaving Tom to his work and me to do mine.

Through interviews with protesters, I learned that a large group of them had marched down to Kentucky Square again, outside the bounds that had for months designated where Change Square stopped and the part of the capital controlled by the Saleh family began. Soldiers from Ali Mohsin's First Armored Division followed the protesters. They marched on small side streets off Ring Road that wove around an ancient residential neighborhood.

There, the protesters and soldiers were met by scores of armed CSF, Republican Guard soldiers, and pickup trucks with large machine guns mounted on the back. Yemenis called the guns *deshkas.* In English, "technicals."

A shoot-out ensued between the al-ferqa soldiers and the Saleh forces. The protesters, unarmed men who had camped out at their sit-in for months, were the ones caught in the middle. Al-ferqa used them as human shields. They were the ones who got blown to bits.

Later, Saleh loyalists would say that it was only Islahis—who were in cahoots with Ali Mohsin and Hamid—who marched with the al-ferqa soldiers. That this was a plan by Ali Mohsin to either expand his territory or just draw CSF into a war, in either case using protesters as bait and human shields in the process. Secret negotiations were going on between JMP and GPC, and they were about to reach an agreement that would exclude Ali Mohsin from power, so he had an incentive to crash the negotiations by starting a war in the area around Kentucky Square, which is near the center of the capital. "Protesters want to be martyrs anyway!" the Saleh loyalists would say, as if this were an excuse for mowing them down on the way to Ali Mohsin's soldiers. They would say the corpses at the field hospital had been brought from a nearby morgue to be used as pro-opposition propaganda. They would deny that protesters were fired at with the heavy machine guns. "A bullet can't do to a body what I saw in that field hospital," I would tell them. And they would ignore me, because ignorance is a good way to deny the need for compromise, and I would grow angrier at them than I had ever been at anyone in my life.

Hours later, at the field hospital, I ran into two young boys, one of whom was being treated for a bullet wound in his leg. They told me CSF had nabbed them and held them hostage until they declared on the state-run news channel they had been shot by al-ferqa soldiers and not CSF, a ploy to show the Yemeni people who the real bad guys were. The boys sat in front of a television TV producer and repeated what the soldiers told them to say while armed men stood behind the camera to ensure they obeyed. Only then were they released to go to the hospital for their wounds.

I watched another man sitting on a ledge near the field hospital's makeshift surgery rooms. He leaned over slowly and slipped his shirt over his head. He grimaced slightly in the process and then craned his neck to look over his right shoulder. I saw he had been shot. A black hole encircled with red on his shoulder like a tattoo. A disgusted look appeared on the man's face while he examined the wound, merely as if this was going to ruin the rest of his day. He reached into his pocket and pulled out a cigarette, lit it, took a puff, and got up to walk around, favoring his right side. He called his wife, told her that he was safe, just shot in the shoulder and he'd be home soon.

• • •

Whenever I went to Change Square by taxi, which was really the only way I ever got there, the driver had to stop about a quarter mile away from the Square's center where the field hospital was located, as well as the activists' tent. No vehicles were allowed near the sit-in, and anyway, the tents made Ring Road almost too narrow for a car to pass through. Ambulances weaved in and out of the tents delivering the injured to the field hospital. I always believed they had to have hit some protesters in the process.

It was days like these when I wished I could be dropped off closer. I could once again hear gunfire coming from the area around Kentucky Square and the residential neighborhood to its east where the fighting had spread yesterday. I wanted to get to the field hospital so I could interview the injured about what was happening. As far as I knew, protesters had expanded the sit-in down to the intersection of Kentucky Square. They set up tents on top of Chinese Bridge, guarded by al-ferqa, but Saleh's forces were determined not to let them stay for long.

As I made my way quickly down a side street, I ran into a protester I knew from the media tent limping down the street on crutches. A smile came over both our faces when we spotted one another like two, long lost friends running into one another by complete accident.

"I was shot in my leg," Hossam told me. "A bullet. *Bzzzeroooom*!" He tried to imitate the noise of a whizzing bullet and pointed to his bandage wrapped calf.

"Yesterday?"

"Yes." Hossam looked to the street below him and shook his head.

"Down by Kentucky Square?"

"Yes."

I didn't believe these protesters were privy to some grand scheme of Ali Mohsin's to extend his territory. They were just young, independent activists taking advantage of opportunity as it came. Expanding Change Square felt like a way to put pressure on the Saleh regime after months of inertia. The action was exciting after all—even if Ali Mohsin's soldiers were around for the ride.

Even the best of intentions, though, don't stop one from being used as a pawn.

"I'll tell you what, Laura," Hossam said, "I am getting sick of the games that Ali Mohsin is trying to play with us. I think I might leave the Square."

His words broke my heart. A hopeful young activist grown cynical. In many ways, it seemed like he was one of the smart ones. Their movement was being eclipsed by the larger powers that ruled their country. Had this been Ali Mohsin's plan all along?

"Okay, I need to get to the field hospital," I told him. "But stay safe, okay?"

When I walked through the hospital's big metal gates, and through its dirt yard, past the port-a-potties lining the stone wall, I saw a few more bodies brought in on stretchers from the ambulance parked in the yard. The act was more methodical than it had been before because the protesters and medics were more prepared. I stepped up the three stone steps and through another metal gate, this one not as tall, into the mosque's open air area. It was roofed, but walls did not fully enclose it. Men kneeling on colorful prayer mats would have spilled out of the prayer room and into this area during Friday sermons if all still had been how it once was in Sanaa.

I spotted Tom interviewing Dr. Qubati, the head doctor of the field hospital, and waved to him. Dr. Qubati stood in a green smock with a stethoscope hanging from his neck. He was picking at the fingers of the thin latex gloves on his left hand.

Then, just as I was pulling my notebook out of my purse, a deep booming sound echoed from the direction of the First Armored Division base on the hill. And again, and again. I thought I felt the ground beneath me shake. The booms merited the rumble of the earth.

I looked to the closest person near me, a nurse. "That was from *al-ferqa*," I told the stranger. "Right?" Before we had time to say anything more, another deep, bellowing boom confirmed my fears. This time it came from south of Change Square, from the direction of the Republican Guard military bases that sat upon Sanaa's surrounding mountains. For the first time, the two sides of the divided army had begun exchanging artillery fire, and Change Square sat between them.

The war had started. The war for which we all had been waiting so long. The war between the divided military of a fractured country. When the fighting in Hasaba had happened when I was home in the United States, there were gunfights in the street, and the neighborhood surrounding Hamid al-Ahmar's house in northern Sanaa was shelled, but Ali Mohsin's base had not fired artillery across the city at Republican Guard bases.

I bolted toward the door without a second thought. I went without checking on Tom, without encouraging him to leave with me. I ran because I felt that was the safe thing to do. Because I knew that the field hospital was located squarely between the two army bases. I even imagined the Republican Guard firing on it directly. I imagined being stuck in the rubble. It felt so unbelievably helpless remaining there.

I ran out through the dirt yard, through the front metal gates, and into the street of tents. I was oblivious to the rest of the Yemenis, just minding their own business, looking up at each blast of artillery fire, registering it, accepting its presence, but moving on, like meditation practitioners. I saw a man sitting across his motorcycle, twisted at the waist and gazing toward the al-ferqa base as it emitted one crashing boom after another.

"Take me to Rabat Street!" I screamed to him and threw my left leg across the back of his motorcycle seat. He just nodded and revved the engine. I made sure to sit on the back edge and not get too close to the driver. I didn't want to touch my legs to his so I just let them dangle as we sped between tents. My legs occasionally felt a sharp burn from the spokes and I struggled to stay on.

About a quarter mile south, we reached the first large road that led into the Square, Rabat Street. I threw some money at the driver, not counting how much, and hurried down the street to find a taxi who could take me away from the Square as fast as possible.

"I want to go to Hadda," I said to a taxi driver sitting in his car with his left arm placed over the rolled down window ledge. He just shook his head. He told me it was impossible because there was shelling on Sixtieth Street, the main road to Hadda. The small side streets were cut off because of fighting, too, so he couldn't do it, *mostaheel*, impossible. I couldn't believe it. A Yemeni afraid of violence. This was certainly something new. What was happening here? What direction had life suddenly taken? I had been waiting for war forever, but when it finally came it took me by surprise. I made stupid moves. I stopped thinking rationally. The fighting between the soldiers yesterday, the uptick in the type of weaponry used, should have made me prepared for this, but I was not, because war is never what you imagine it to be.

Al-Masdar's office was nearby, so I followed the curb down Rabat Street in its direction while the echoing booms of artillery fire continued. It was such a threatening sound—a crash, like a firework exploding just above my head. There were other bangs, too, the steady tapping of machine-gun fire, and from who knows what else.

I called Yasser to tell him I was coming to the office. That I was outside on the street and didn't know what to do. He easily confirmed that that would be a good idea. I continued at a quickened pace over the dust-laden asphalt, focusing my gaze straight ahead, breathing heavily. I told myself that while the sounds were loud they were coming from far away. I told myself that to be near gunfire and to be shot were two different things altogether.

No one was driving, though there were men standing outside the metal gates of gray brick buildings, examining the scene, the curiosity of Yemenis never muted even in the times of danger. This is what they had been waiting for as well. This is what everyone had predicted would solve the crisis. There was no other way but war.

Two blocks ahead I saw the side street on which there would be a door that would take me inside. Inside I would be safe, and I would wait this out. I would stay safe in al-Masdar's office just like I did on March 18 after the massacre. I sped up my steps a little more, just about to break into a jog, when what was ahead of me made me stop dead in my tracks.

My eyes locked on to a flying projectile one block ahead. In the half second that it was in the air, my mind registered that it was shaped like a missile. I saw it strike the second floor of a residential building on Rabat Street. I closed my eyes for an extended blink. I questioned my vision, but I knew it was real. Its existence confirmed that the violence around me had transformed into a new type of conflict, the type that I only knew from movies—explosions all around, RPGs flying through the air, smoke-filled streets, running for cover with the cool bravery of a battle-scarred hero.

Only, I was a hysterical wreck by the time I got to the small food shop that was still open despite the surrounding artillery fire. Candy bars and potato chips sat in boxes underneath a glass counter. A carton of eggs and cheap laundry detergent were on metal racks next to the back wall. The shopkeeper and the other men whose attention I attracted urged me to relax. They shushed me gently and raised their hands in the air, palms facing to the floor, like yoga teachers bringing the energy of their class to a calming center.

"I saw an RPG!" I yelled at them.

"Don't worry, don't worry. It's nothing," the shopkeeper said.

"It's not nothing! Do you think an RPG's nothing? Let me hide . . . there!" I pointed behind his counter.

"Don't worry. Don't worry," he encouraged me. A group of men who had been loitering on the street approached the scene curiously. I called Yasser to tell him I was hiding in the shop and that I needed help and that I wanted him to come now if he could, if he didn't think it was too dangerous. It's just that I had seen an RPG and couldn't leave the shop by myself, *mostaheel*, impossible.

Yasser walked down the street, asking about the scared foreign woman, and found me still arguing with the men about whether I should be scared. "Come on, Laura. Let's go to the office. There it's nice. It's safe. Don't be scared," he said.

With Yasser as my guide, I slowly set one foot in front of the other. It was a struggle to step back out onto the street. The sound of shooting and artillery fire still punctured the air. My ears tried to trace it to its origin and calculate its distance from us—that boom came from the al-ferqa base and that one from the Republican Guard.

"Look," Yasser said while we walked past the building that the RPG had struck. His pointer finger rose above his head as if pointing out a piece of art. "It just made a small hole in the building."

"I am not going to look." I turned my head in the other direction, the ornery child.

"*Ya Laura*," Yasser drew out the last syllable of my name. "An RPG is a small thing," he said.

I still refused to look. I was so annoyed that I had to convince everyone that I had a right to be scared.

Inside al-Masdar's office, the journalists there tried to comfort me just like the shopkeeper, by telling me not to worry, that there was nothing to be scared of. I paced their office in incongruent zigzags and averted my gaze from meeting anyone else's. I struggled to be brave, but with each crack of artillery fire, I lapsed back into a state of panic as my insides did acrobatics. The men took cushions from the mafraj and piled them up in the center of the main room, farthest from the windows. They stacked them neatly and intentionally, a flat cushion for me to sit on, a hard, rectangular cushion on which I could rest my left elbow. The room was bare aside for one office desk pressed against the wall. I was just beginning to convince myself I would be safe here when the boom of an explosion resonated like a crash of thunder in my ears and the building shook as if an earthquake was rumbling beneath us and the core of my body was jarred along with it. I emitted a sound somewhere between a gasp and a scream, like I was sucking in the last molecules of oxygen in the room. I crouched down on the carpet where I was standing and my shoulders swallowed my head up to my ears as I retreated into an imaginary shell. I involuntarily muttered a prayer. That a piece of weaponry had just struck our building did not become a fully-formed thought in my mind. I didn't think it because I didn't dare to. Because that's how reporters are killed.

I was struck with the need to get down to the bottom of the stairwell. I had not wanted to burden my Yemeni friends, whose normal fatalism was upset by the needs of a frightened foreign girl, but that concern dissipated when I felt the ground beneath me shake. My fingers clenched the strap of my backpack as I pulled it off the floor and walked toward the door. I heard Samir, the publication's slightly balding, soft-spoken owner, tell Yasser in a voice that was suddenly tinged with worry that, indeed, they needed to take me downstairs, and the two men followed me.

We walked down three floors of dirty, gray stone steps with only the occasional small box-shaped window providing light for our descent, to sit in a narrow pit of a hallway that led to the outside. I crouched low to the floor, pressed the back of my head against the gritty brick wall, and attempted to slow my breath so my thoughts could come more clearly. I tried to reassure myself that this position was safe. I could wait here for hours. On the ground floor, I was safe. I willed myself to believe it.

None of us mentioned that a mortar had hit the building. No one wanted to admit the truth of what was happening around us.

Then, my phone buzzed.

"Laura, where are you?" asked a familiar voice in English, that of Abdulghani al-Iryani, an American-educated Yemeni from a prominent political family. His brother was the water minister and his uncle the former prime minister. I was supposed to be at Abdul-Ghani's for a peaceful afternoon lunch.

"I'm at al-Masdars. It's so bad. The building was hit. I saw an RPG. I don't think I'm safe." I knew the men around me couldn't understand the English.

"You're with Sameer Jubran?"

"Yes. And my fixer, Yasser."

"They'll keep you safe."

"Yes, they're being good. They're helping me."

The phone line was fuzzy and Abdulghani's words were choppy.

"Is there any way you can get out of there?" he asked me.

"I don't think so."

"Listen, I'm going to come get you. Just stay there. Where are you?"

"Rabat Street."

"Okay, I'll come from the east."

"I don't know if it's safe to come from that way. There's fighting there too."

"Oh, I'll be okay. See you soon. Stay safe."

I took a deep breath and looked up at Samir and Yasser and did what I always did when I was scared but trying to be brave. I smiled. Samir took a few steps over to the front door and leaned his body over from the waist to look out. The banging from artillery fire continued. "Oofff, today is very bad," Samir said, turning back inside. This was always the response of Yemenis. Yes, this is bad, nothing more. But this was more than bad. This was the worst it had ever been.

My phone rang again. I saw that the *New York Times* foreign desk was calling me. I tried to compose myself to not sound like I was an incompetent freelancer and a liability.

"Laura, hi, I've been trying to get through," came the voice of one of the younger assistant editors. "Where are you?"

"I'm at my fixer's office." Artillery fire blasted in the background.

"It sounds horrible. Are you safe?"

"Yeah. I mean, I think something hit our building. But I'm down in the stairwell now. Yeah, I'm safe . . . and a Yemeni friend is coming to pick me up."

"Okay, okay good. We were really worried about you," he said. "We heard that there was shelling in central Sanaa and we couldn't get through to you."

"Yeah, I'm okay."

The editor went on about when I could file today's story and how I was going to get myself to safety. I told him that I was on top of things. That was good, because there was another really important point that I needed to take care of:

"Can you start tweeting? It's really important to tweet in times like this," the voice on the line said to me. "Tom Finn is at the field hospital tweeting and he just got like two thousand new followers in ten minutes."

"Yeah, I'll try. The phones aren't really working, you know. It's hard to tweet," I replied and hung up so I wouldn't have to hear anymore.

CHAPTER 18

I never had spent much time thinking about the nuances of conflict before I came to Yemen, or that many times the simple binary of good and bad doesn't exist, and that often there's no team to cheer for. I never really thought about how two sides can wage war in a given space, while the inhabitants of that space claim neither side of the fight even though their homes now make up a battlefield. I never thought about how war can be so contained within a city to a neighborhood or section, and how, if you are lucky enough not to be living in that section, the worst part really is just the sound. I never thought about how loud artillery fire is, and how, just like using a squat toilet, it's easy to get used to.

I had this idea before that everyone who lived in a city at war was in danger. Well, that doesn't have to be true. In Sanaa, if a house wasn't within range of the al-Ahmar compound in Hasaba or Kentucky Square, life went on almost as usual, just with extra military checkpoints. And even for people who did live in the most dangerous areas, they didn't cease to exist. They still carried out their daily routines, too, just with heightened danger. The patterns of life were altered somewhat, though. Parents were hesitant to send their children to school. Families were displaced across the city. More gun fights erupted outside of the conflict zone because violence only begets more violence, and people started to become hotheaded and unnerved.

A lot of the protesters at Change Square were dying too. Snipers stationed at some of the Square's main arteries took out a few here and there. I guess Saleh's army felt that it had more license to kill freely now that they were being attacked with the force of an army. Killing protesters represented retaliation against Ali Mohsin, yet that equation was far from fair.

The war was fought mainly in the nights and in the mornings. It mostly stopped for qat each afternoon after lunch. Soldiers from Saleh's army and soldiers from the First Armored Division would sit and chew together during these times, leaning on each other in an amicable way. They also, at times, shot above one another's heads intentionally—which is why stray bullets killed civilians more often than they should have.

I had come to believe that neither army had a grand tactical plan in this war. I thought that Ali Mohsin started the fight to wreck negotiations between leading figures in the JMP and GPC. They were allegedly on the cusp of reaching a deal when al-ferqa took over Kentucky Square. Ali Mohsin wanted to make a statement that he had bigger guns and they shouldn't think for a second that they could cut him out. The reason why they were even concocting a deal to transfer power away from Saleh had to do with his defection anyway.

But aside from that, both sides of the divided armed forces were just reacting according to the situation. They knew they couldn't win over the other. And sometimes it felt they weren't even trying. I didn't understand why Saleh's army didn't just aerial bomb the First Armored Division base. They were just fighting to see who could make the most noise. Whoever that was would have the upper hand in the political negotiations and the upper hand in the new Yemen to come.

I was shaken to the core after the time inside al-Masdar's office. For nearly two days following the incident my mind raced constantly. I couldn't concentrate on others' words to me. Conversations floated past while I just sat around, detached. But then, day by day, I started to pick up the pieces and grow more curious about what was happening around me. I wanted to know who was doing what and where they were when they were doing it. The war tempted me to come closer because it was exciting to be someone who understood war and who people in Sanaa came to for answers because I was an eyewitness. That was a powerful position.

After the shell hit al-Masdar's office, I came to believe I was in control of my situation. I went to interview a sheikh who was fighting on behalf of the Saleh family at his home in northern Sanaa. In his reception room I sat in front of a gaping hole as large as my torso in the wall that artillery fire had torn two days before. I figured it wouldn't hit the same spot twice.

Tom and I had debates about how we were going to get to the field hospital as the roads to the center of Change Square had been cut off by fighting. We came up with the brilliant idea to ride his motorcycle at top speed through the Square, past the buildings where the snipers stood. We would wear flak jackets and helmets—those we still needed to procure. A security advisor for international NGOs warned Tom and me that our plan was one of the stupidest ideas he had ever heard and it was scrapped.

It was in this context that Ali Abdullah Saleh made his grand surprise return to Sanaa from his hospital bed in Saudi Arabia. We all woke up one morning and he was back, secretly arriving in the dark hours like a thief in the night. When I emailed a Yemeni official close to president to ask if he knew Saleh would return he just said, "The timing is a surprise, the idea is not."

First came nonstop celebratory gunfire for an hour across the capital after news spread that the beloved president had returned to his homeland. He still had plenty of his supporters in Sanaa, and they wanted us all to know it. I stood with a friend in her living room with our hands covering our ears, elbows pointed to the sides, gritting our teeth and mouthing expletives to one another during the worst of it. The local press reported that at least eleven people were killed by falling bullets the day that Saleh returned. And then the celebratory gunfire turned into the non-celebratory type, and then that turned into artillery fire and shelling. If Saleh had any notion that he was going to bring peace between his old buddy Ali Mohsin and his kids, it was for naught and the war only intensified. Mortars fell on Change Square too. One ripped through a tent while the protesters inside were sleeping and tore a man's body in half from the middle of his torso. Split like a piece of meat.

• • •

There is no easy way to find out a friend has died. I would become way more experienced in this as the months unfolded into years and the death of friends became less a rarity and more expected. Preferably, though, I'd rather not learn via social media. It's because then you have to start obsessively checking other sites thinking *can this be true?* And then you eventually have to succumb to the reality that it is, and that someone isn't just tweeting a mistaken identity.

The news came on Twitter in late September, the day after Saleh returned to Sanaa: a cameraman had been killed at Change Square. Shot in the head by a sniper while he was filming. I learned that the journalist killed was Hassan al-Wadhaf—the young man I had spent a week running around Sanaa with trying to figure out what footage we should capture after explosive-laden packages from Yemen were intercepted en route to the United States. The young man I had run into outside the field hospital after the March 18 massacre, tears streaming down his cheeks. It was one of the few memories that stuck in my mind from the field hospital that day.

It was not that the war became more real for me after Hassan died. The moments at the field hospital had been quite real before. It's that it no longer felt possible to separate myself from it. How can one be an impartial observer to brutality when that brutality killed a friend?

I felt too paralyzed to keep away the sadness. I had tried to teach myself not to feel. I didn't actively try, but that's what my mind did naturally when faced with all this needless death. And the way that I saw Yemeni society start to regard death as the months went on, I knew that others were doing the same. But now someone died who I knew. And I did feel. I felt so much and I didn't want to feel this anymore because I knew there was nothing I could do about the larger situation. I knew that life wasn't fair, and so I became hard. I stopped feeling even when it came to such an ultimate reality as no longer seeing a friend. More friends would die in the coming months and years, and I no longer felt anything at those moments.

Whose shoulder did I have to cry on? I would just have to get back to work. I didn't want to cry on Tom's because we couldn't do that to one another. That wouldn't be fair because it would be admitting to ourselves that we were beaten down by our jobs and the situation we found ourselves in in our twenties, and neither of us could remind the other of that. We had to keep going: for the job, for Yemenis, for ourselves, and for all the international attention we were receiving.

Hassan had died just like the others did: a bullet wound to the head. I suppose that it was one of the best ways to go. You don't even realize what has happened. I wonder if Hassan did. The finality of it all was so permanent. There was the obvious fact that I wouldn't see him at the Square anymore, but to really think that someone will stop existing in this world, that they once were alive and now they aren't, and to think about how sad his family must have been—I hated it. I thought of Hassan's gluttonous, slimy boss at the production company he worked for. How I bet he pressured Hassan to go film on the front lines when it wasn't safe to do so, and I wanted to put all the blame on him.

I would see Hassan again, though, in martyr photos plastered all over the Square. And every time I did I grew angry because it was not right for him to die. When there is a car accident, you can say, "oh, that's bad luck," or you replay in your head over and over what steps could have been taken to prevent that from happening. But when one human intentionally shoots another, then you say, "What the hell were you doing shooting that guy when you knew all he was doing was carrying a camera?" What power did you think you had to go ahead and end a life? Did you really think about what it means to end a life? If you had seen him face to face and looked into his eyes could you have done it? Maybe yes, if you believed so much in your cause. But maybe no. Maybe you are just doing this for money.

Where were the Yemenis who drew me to this place? They were still here. They were Hassan. But I no longer was naive enough to think that they were all good-hearted just because they were nice to me, the American. Could I believe that Hassan's death had a purpose? The protesters had been completely sidelined by the war. *They are no longer what are important. The war is what's important. This is the way the world works.* Meanwhile the international community and Yemeni politicians just sat around and debated "oh, should this clause in a transition agreement be called this or be called that," and they didn't care about Hassan dying. That's one of the hardest things about conflict. It's that it's inconsequential to everyone else in the world, but it was so important to me.

And then there was the undeniable truth Hassan was killed doing what we all did: reporting from Change Square. His death made the risk more tangible. Now we had an example of the worst thing that can happen; your camera can still be rolling when a sniper's bullet strikes. Sure, he was closer than he should have been, but weren't there times when we all were closer than was advisable? Sure, the sniper picked him out, but what if, for a split second, a sniper didn't realize that I was a foreigner, and shifted the rifle toward my head instead? Was it purely bad luck that had directed the gun at Hassan? Was it the will of God? I felt that Yemenis believe strongly in a combination of both those things. I was realizing more and more that you had to be unlucky to be killed in violence, as long as it wasn't some sort of onslaught, or ethnic cleansing, or the like. The chance was greater not to be in the path of an RPG, or to be the target of the bullet. But it did happen. It was happening every day in Sanaa, more and more often. And it had happened to Hassan.

I went to the field hospital to do some reporting later that day because I felt it was necessary. I got vindication through work—for choosing to live a life where friends are killed by snipers. I just walked there from the taxi, alert to my surroundings, constantly scanning my environment, but ultimately relying on the odds that danger would not strike my path being in my favor. Each time I made the walk despite the nearby gunfire, I could convince myself to do it again.

I was there for a few hours, and then left by taxi. The driver wanted to take roads through Ha'il, a neighborhood sectioned off by Kentucky Square on one end, the large Sixtieth Street on another, and then surrounded by the tents of Change Square on all its other sides. In it, First Armored Division soldiers were engaged in gun battles with Republican Guard. It was normal to hear gunfire there. I begged my driver to take the long route around Ha'il instead, but he insisted that it was safe to drive through it. "What are you scared of, the bullets?" he asked laughing. He leaned around to look at me, while still driving forward. "Don't be afraid of the bullets," he told me. "A bullet is a small thing." He took his right hand off the wheel and made a small shape with his thumb and pointer finger, indicating for me how small a bullet actually was.

CHAPTER 19

The type of Yemeni official who kept his phone number anonymous on outgoing calls rarely called me. I normally was the one begging them to get in touch. Yet here I was on a so-far-so-calm morning the last day of September and my phone was buzzing with a call from an anonymous number. I couldn't guess what this was all about. There had been no indication that a political breakthrough was imminent. The shelling continued each night in Hasaba in northern Sanaa. In fact, Saleh only seemed to be clinging tighter to power (his throne, many Yemenis called it) after he had returned. Agreeing to step down now meant he'd be letting his old rival, Ali Mohsin, win. So that was never going to happen.

Was some official calling to scold me—to tell me I was reporting events incorrectly? I figured that must be it so I reluctantly answered the call.

I was sitting on the brown wicker sofa, feet propped on a glass coffee table, at the home of an aid worker with whom I was temporarily staying because the shelling was too close to my home to feel safe. My laptop was open on my knees. A mug full of instant coffee balanced precariously on the cushions beside me. I was still in my pajamas and eager for a day off.

"Hello," I said to the anonymous caller.

"Good morning. How are you?" came a familiar friendly voice. An official who I knew fairly well was on the other end.

"I'm fine. Good morning. How are you? What's up?"

"I am fine, *alhamdullah*, praise God." He paused. "So I have some news."

"What?"

"Anwar al-Awlaki has been killed."

"What? For real?"

"What? Of course for real. Why would I be calling you if this wasn't for real?"

"Was it you guys or the Americans? Was it a drone?"

"Em, maybe it was us. Maybe it was the Americans."

"Em . . . okay. Can I use your name?"

"Of course not!"

"If I refer to you as a high-ranking security official for the story is that okay?"

"Uh, yes, okay. You are going to write in the *New York Times* that Anwar al-Awlaki is dead?"

"Yeah, if I can confirm it's true, then I will."

"It's true."

"When did it happen?"

"Just now. Just recently. Maybe fifteen minutes ago."

"Okay. Wow. Okay . . . thanks so much for calling me."

"You're welcome. Now you won't say so much that I don't help you?"

"I don't say that!"

The voice on the other line chuckled and then said goodbye. I just stared at my phone for a minute, stunned by what had just transpired. Anwar, the man pegged as the new Osama bin Laden, the only American on the CIA hit list, the man behind the failed "underbomber" attack on a US-bound airline over Christmas 2009, the infamous al-Qaeda propagandist. The United States had wanted him dead for more than a year now. And now he was? But how could I trust this information?

The United States had been imploring Saleh's government to hand over Anwar for almost two years by this point. He was believed to be hiding with his family's tribe in southeastern Yemen, but it was also believed that his location was nothing that Saleh couldn't figure out. Now that the president was back in Sanaa, now that his power was threatened more than ever before and it was obvious that the international community was actively working for his leadership to end, now was when Anwar was killed. His whereabouts had been known so precisely that a US drone could send a missile down to hit his car traversing the barren mountains. Maybe his death had nothing to do with Saleh wanting to seem like a good ally to the West, but it seemed awfully suspicious to me.

I contacted an editor at the *Times* with the news. He asked me if I could trust this source. I said I could, but that the Yemeni government had been wrong about the deaths of al-Qaeda leaders in the past. The thought of reporting in the *New York Times* that Anwar al-Awlaki was killed, probably by an American drone (we later confirmed that this was the case), an American citizen targeted by the American government without trial, made me paranoid—as it should have—about accuracy. This was front page news. The editor agreed with this idea and we worked together to write the story, waiting for the news to be verified by another source.

I hadn't written about al-Qaeda for so long. I used to only write terrorism stories because those were the only articles editors were interested in out of Yemen, yet the nebulous entity that was al-Qaeda in the Arabian Peninsula, that kept wanting to send bombs to America stuffed into printer cartridges or someone's underwear, had nothing to do with my life in Sanaa. Today though, I was happy for the break from writing about more protesters dying or never-ending conflict between Saleh and Ali Mohsin—the conflict that put me to sleep every night with its rumbles and crashes across the city. I was starting to get tired of laying that story out for American readers because it felt too much part of life to write about in a mere eight hundred words.

Anwar al-Awlaki and his death by drone had little to nothing to do with the life of the average Yemeni, especially those in the capital. He was from a wealthy family whose father had been able to move to the United States for his graduate studies. He was believed to be hiding in a far away province in southeastern Yemen that had minimal relations with Sanaa. He was guilty of encouraging young operatives to attack the United States, the most important of whom weren't even Yemeni: Nidal Malik Hasan, the first Fort Hood shooter, was American Palestinian, and underwear bomber Umar Farouk Abdulmutallab, or "Fruit of the Boom," as I heard some American embassy employees in Sanaa call him, was Nigerian.

But Awlaki was killed in Yemen. He had fled to the countryside because that's where al-Qaeda could operate most freely. That's what made this relevant. That was the only reason, really, that Yemen was relevant to the West. If there was no al-Qaeda in Yemen, surely the international community wouldn't be so vested in trying to find a peaceful solution to the current crisis. Surely, there would be less aid money. Would I have ever moved here to be a journalist if there hadn't been al-Qaeda?

An hour later, Yemeni state media reported that Anwar had been killed in the rough terrain of al-Jawf in northern Yemen—far from where he had been assumed to be, which had been Shabwa in the South. He was killed along with another American, Samir Khan, who had been running al-Qaeda's English-language propaganda together with Anwar. Reuters posted a story online about his death, and then we knew it would be safe to run the story in the *New York Times,* too.

I had been seriously considering leaving Yemen after Hassan was killed. I couldn't articulate, even to myself, the reason why I was sad or why I was angry. I was sick of the political stalemate, and all the people at the top not giving two hoots about the young men and women who had been the start of this whole thing.

But then came moments like this, when the excitement of being a reporter filled me with so much satisfaction it seemed I would never be able to tear myself away. When I was able to break news of this magnitude, news that would be the first story on the evening news, on NPR's Morning Edition, and analyzed to pieces on the twenty-four-hour cable news networks, it felt like I was part of some elite class whose work mattered more than everyone else's, like a staffer at the White House or an assistant to a Fortune 500 CEO. I was the one the Yemeni official decided to call. I got to do really important things with really important people even though I wasn't even twenty-six yet. Wasn't this what I wanted all along? Yes, it came with unbelievable stress and danger, but that could be brushed aside as part of the job, like a corporate lawyer who works one-hundred-hour weeks, neglecting his relationships and his health, but believes it's all worth it in the end.

It was so easy to think what I was doing at the time was the most important thing in the world because I lived in a bubble of politicians, activists, and aid workers whose lives were the topics about which I was writing. I was beating myself up because I couldn't say that I was the one who broke the story of al-Awlaki's death for the world, though I was probably the first journalist to learn of it. I got so caught in the race of breaking news, in retweets on Twitter, in the phrase "Laura Kasinof of the *New York Times* is reporting . . ."

The reality, of course, is that few remember the names of print reporters, and most Americans didn't even know who Anwar al-Awlaki was. His case was known because he was an American citizen, but his life would come and go. Everyone's life would continue as normal, so what was so important about me reporting it? Yes, this case would be immortalized because it was arguably unconstitutional for an American to be killed by his own government without trial, yet it was so easy to forget that behind these headlines, children just lost a father, siblings their brother, and parents their son. Hassan died last week, and no one wrote about him in the international press.

And what about the young activists I had come to know at Change Square? Wasn't trying to tell the stories of those who would not otherwise get a voice in the American press more noble? But I was getting disheartened by the protests at Change Square, and politics, and that innocents were killed and no one would ever have to pay for it. It was much easier to focus my attention on some infamous figure I'd never met and some murky issue like drones that cable news shows back home found far more important.

CHAPTER 20

"Did you hear the news?" I said to my taxi driver on the way to Change Square, leaning forward from my position in the backseat.

"No, what?"

One week after Anwar was killed by an American drone strike, another Friday surprise has gotten my editors astir about breaking news in Yemen. I was excited, too, though the story arguably had more to do with those outside the country than daily life here in Sanaa. Distractions from the war, however, were welcomed with open arms.

"You're not going to believe this," I said, "but Tawakkol Karman just won the Nobel Peace Prize."

He immediately slammed on the brakes and we came to a stop in the middle of the street. It was Friday morning anyway. The streets were empty on the holy day. And besides, there were more important things right now than traffic considerations.

The driver spun around and looked right at me.

"No," was the only word he could manage to utter.

"Yeah, I swear, *wallahy*, she won. I'm a journalist. Al Jazeera was reporting it this morning. I'm going to the Square right now to find her."

• • •

A Yemeni woman, a woman who I knew, who had once told me she supported a plan that would probably result in the death of many protesters so that Saleh could be overthrown, ends justifying the means, was awarded some lofty prize I only associated with the great political leaders of the world.

Tawakkol just won the Nobel Peace Prize. Tawakkol Karman. It was a nod to the spirit, surprise, and drama of the Arab Spring. In doing so, the committee deciding the award (I imagined them as a group of gray-haired, short, white men sitting around a table) wanted to bestow the title of laureate to an Arab woman—or so I heard—and apparently Tawakkol, the original star of the protests in Yemen, was the obvious choice. It was easy to see from the outside. She had received so much media attention over the past year. Western journalists visiting the country for a week or so at the very start of the uprising loved to interview Tawakkol because not only was she a leading female activist in arguably the most conservative nation in the Arab world, but she was an Islahi, a powerful Islamist. Such a narrative went against the way the West normally saw the Middle East. Islamists limit female mobility. But here was Tawakkol—loud, strong, and proud—in a room full of men. Her story made a great thousand-word human interest article.

Yet, here in Sanaa, Tawakkol had grown largely irrelevant to the uprising. Sure, it was her short arrest that set everything off back in January. But as the Square grew, not just in space, but as Yemenis from an array of political leanings joined the demonstration, her voice was largely drowned out. I heard nothing of Tawakkol being on the front line of the latest incursions into Saleh-controlled territory. I heard very little of her at all for the past few months except when I saw her at a Fourth of July party at the US embassy (during which she interrupted the keynote address by some benign government minister to yell from her table, "This isn't a political crisis, it's a revolution!"). Many of the independent activists rejected Tawakkol's role, ignored her in fact, because she belonged to al-Islah, part of the regime they were fighting to overthrow.

So it was quite bizarre that Tawakkol would be awarded such an honor. That's how I and many others in Sanaa felt. It was incongruous with life as we knew it. But still, I couldn't deny the excitement at the news. Just as I was one of the first to learn of al-Awlaki's death, now here I was, going to interview the Nobel Peace Prize laureate, casually, one morning. Never mind that it was a group of outsiders who gave Tawakkol this honor, or that the prize has such a blatant political agenda as to make it lose relevancy. There were numerous other Yemeni female activists who deserved this honor just as much or more than Tawakkol, but the award committee would never know about them because they were only on the outside looking in. But for me on the inside looking out, I just became caught up in the international fame to which I felt connected.

• • •

I had just arrived to the edge of the Square to see Tawakkol for the second time the day that the Nobel Prize was announced, on October 7, to shoot some video for the *Times*'s website. I needed to get in and out before the shelling started nearby in Hasaba, as it did every night, sending low booming reverberations across the night sky. Also, I just wanted to get work done because I was flying to Cairo the next day for a much needed vacation, or so I thought.

While making my way past the rows of tents, Abdul-Ghani, the political analyst and friend who came to pick me up at the Square during the afternoon of shelling, called me. He asked me if I was with Tawakkol. I told him I would be in a minute.

"Okay, great," he said. "Her phone has been ringing busy all day. Uncle Abdel-Karim wants the vice president to tell her congratulations, but he can't get through."

"I saw her constantly talking on the phone earlier today. It doesn't surprise me that it's always busy," I said, wondering where this was going.

"When you are with her, do you mind calling me? When we know you're beside her, Uncle Abdel-Karim will have Hadi call your cell phone, then you will pass your phone to Tawakkol. Okay?"

"Em, sure," I replied.

Uncle Abdel-Karim was a former prime minister, Abdul-Ghani's uncle, and an advisor to the president. He was the mastermind behind the scenes trying to fit together the puzzle pieces of Yemen that would appease the international community, appease Saleh, and still make political progress at the same time. Now this was Abdel-Karim's plan for reconciliation between Tawakkol, of Change Square, and Hadi, of the Saleh regime and potentially Yemen's new president.

And I would be the one to facilitate it. And I was eager to do so.

I walked to Tawakkol's tent, opened up the wooden door to what had been her abode for months on end, and found inside a large pack of reporters and supporters. They were all chatting, more relaxed. It seemed that most stories were already done for the day. I squeezed past a man hoisting a television on his shoulder and saw Tawakkol standing in the middle of the crowd with her orange flowered hijab wrapping her hair, bearing her large toothy smile. A few questions were still being asked of her, to which she would provide a similar answer that she had just given to the one before. She didn't ignore anyone, but her face had started to look tired. After each response to a reporter, she gave an "are we done yet?" sigh. I noticed that her smile for the cameras looked plastered on. She kept stealing glances at her husband as if to transfer a secret meaning between the two of them. Finally he shooshed most everyone else out of tent, aside from a few stragglers. Tawakkol moved to the back corner to sit down along with two friends, one of whom, Nadwa, I knew well. I followed them, believing that my special message for Tawkkol gave me license to remain.

I knelt down to sit on the ground, a blanket covering the macadam of the street below, to face the women. Tawakkol was resting her head on Nadwa's tiny shoulder. "I'm here again. I was taking some video," I said to Tawakkol, "but also, there's something else I need to ask you. Abdul-Ghani al-Iryani called me on my way here. Vice President Hadi wants to talk to you. He wants to tell you congratulations. Your phone is always busy, so they called my phone."

"*Ya Laura*," Tawakkol started, sitting up straight now, "you tell Hadi that if he wants to tell me congratulations, he needs to join the revolution." She held her finger out and pointed into the air to drive home the point.

I immediately felt deflated. Tawakkol was ruining my chance. I mean, also a chance at reconciliation with the vice president and a step toward a better Yemen, but this was my chance, too. I had hoped that Hadi would get to know who I was after setting up his phone conversation with Tawakkol. Then he would become a good source to me. I had concocted this whole unlikely plan over the past fifteen minutes.

Nadwa tried to console Tawakkol, gently telling her it would be a good idea to talk to Hadi. "He just wanted to congratulate you. What is the harm in that? It is a good thing." But Tawakkol held her ground.

This part of her personality was integral to why Tawakkol had made a name for herself as an activist. She so stubbornly stuck to her beliefs and stood up to anyone who got in her way, no matter what position of leadership he or she was in. This was the reason she was kidnapped in the early days of the protests and, ultimately, the reason she was awarded this honor of the Nobel Peace Prize. I found myself adapting to please people around me, saying what they wanted to hear. I always felt this people pleasing nature was the reason I wasn't cut out to be a journalist. I found that uncompromising women were a rare find. *Maybe,* I wondered, *we should all be more like Tawakkol and hold fast to our convictions.*

But convictions are also what start wars.

I called back Abdul-Ghani and he asked me to put him on the phone with Tawakkol. He tried to convince her to speak with Hadi, that it was good for Yemen, but she was the rock that would not be moved. And now I didn't know who to agree with: Tawakkol or Abdul-Ghani and his powerful uncle. I just wanted them all to like me, in the end.

Two women in niqabs entered the tent. They had come to tell Tawakkol congratulations. Tawakkol's husband had let them into the back room, and from their interruption I knew the matter was settled for good. There would be no compromise tonight. From the women's Arabic, short and choppy, they sounded uneducated. From their abayas, simple without adornment, they seemed poor. They walked over to us in the back corner and sat down in front of Tawakkol, their black robes billowing to the floor around them. Tawakkol held their red henna–tattooed hands and spoke with them with kindness in her large brown eyes. She inquired about their lives and if they were with the Square and said they should remain steadfast. The peaceful Yemeni revolution will succeed, she told them, because goodness always does, look at Gandhi! Look at Martin Luther King Jr.! The women may have never heard those names before, but they listened to her intently nonetheless.

CHAPTER 21

Our airplane wouldn't be landing in Sanaa as scheduled. Instead it would be landing in Aden. Sanaa Airport has been temporarily closed, came the announcement from the copilot. My flight from Cairo to Sanaa was somewhere above the Red Sea en route between the two cities.

A collective groan broke out across the cabin. This was not a plane of people who would be alarmed at this news because we already were knowingly flying to Sanaa during a war. This was a plane of people who wanted to be in Sanaa, not Aden, and understood that just because a divided army lobbed shells at one another, it didn't mean life across the city came to a standstill.

I leaned back against the seat and looked up at the roof of the plane. Then I looked out the window as if that would somehow help the situation. Nope, all I saw were clouds. That didn't help.

I had already been told by my editors last week that they did not want me going to Cairo for a short vacation. They didn't want me out of Sanaa at this time of major breaking news like Anwar al-Awlaki's extra judiciary killing by his own government and a Yemeni activist being the Arab Spring's representative for the Nobel Peace Prize. But I went anyway for a five-day trip to the Egyptian capital to see my friends there in my old home. I told my editors I could fly back quickly; there was at least one flight a day from Cairo to Sanaa.

In truth, I needed a break after Hassan was killed and I used my birthday as some lame excuse to go see friends in Cairo. In the past, I never used to think much of birthdays. I wasn't one to get excited about the changing of the seasons or to make a fuss about a holiday. But for some reason, I felt that this year my birth date merited a celebration. Perhaps it was because I needed to remind myself I was only turning twenty-six when the life I was living felt much older.

But now this had to happen. I needed to be in Sanaa to report on whatever reason the airport was closed, but here I was in the air, again, just like I was when Saleh said he would sign the GCC Initiative while I was on the way to Washington, DC, last April. Here I was, letting down the *New York Times* again.

I stood up, ignoring the illuminated FASTEN SEAT BELT sign that no one else was paying attention to anyway, to go speak with an Egypt-Air flight attendant, doubting that she would know why we weren't allowed to land in Sanaa, but desperate for information. I hoped it was just because of some misplaced shelling—the war in Hasaba was near to the airport—and not because of important news like, for example, if al-Qaeda bombed the airport, or Ali Mohsin's soldiers and al-Ahmar tribesmen took it over, or something of the sort.

I met the flight attendant while she was pouring orange juice for herself in front of the sliding doors of the bathroom. She told me the airport in Sanaa wasn't allowing planes to land because "you know, there are these . . ." she paused for emphasis, contorting her makeup-caked face into a look of disgust, "these demonstrations in Yemen."

"Yeah, I know that, but that's not why the airport is closed," I snapped back and stomped off to my seat.

My plan had been to return to Yemen refreshed and rejuvenated after a holiday spent at my favorite seedy bars in downtown Cairo and lying out by the Marriot's bougainvillea-lined pool during the daytime.

As it turned out, the pool idea was a bust because an international conference had brought dozens of Yemeni activists to Cairo while I was there. They all were housed in the Marriot for the conference and I couldn't bring myself to tan in a bikini when I knew that male Yemeni activists with whom I had spent time at Change Square, who had never seen more skin on me than my wrist, might be coming to take a dip.

And while there was no major news in Yemen during my time away, there was in Egypt. Tanks intentionally drove over protesters on Cairo's Corniche along the Nile in what would infamously become known as the massacre at Maspero, the bloodiest day since the start of the Egyptian revolution. I had been stuck in an old colonial bar in downtown Cairo while the showdown was unfolding, prohibited from leaving by waitstaff because gunshots rang down the street outside.

Sitting at a small table with two friends, trying to make light conversation to distract ourselves from the violence outside, I realized that I trusted Yemenis with their weapons to a much greater extent than I did Egyptians. Yemenis had a gun culture that stemmed from ancient tribal code. Egyptian youth were wielding handguns for the first time. I couldn't understand the violence that was happening around me, couldn't analyze or predict it, and that was so much worse than anything I had experienced yet in Yemen, except that day I was stuck in al-Masdar's office during the shelling; that had been terrifying for the same reason. Normally, violence in Yemen has an aim and a reason—and that reason was never me—so it felt much less threatening in the moment.

My two friends and I eventually were allowed out of the bar and we sprinted across a tear gas–soaked Talat Harb Street into the dark alleyways of downtown Cairo to finally seek refuge in a friend's nearby apartment. It was not how I anticipated spending my vacation, contrasting violence between Egypt and Yemen, but one can't feel too sorry for herself when people are being killed in such a violent way. People are always dying violently the world over, but when it's happening a few blocks down the street, it's more palpable.

After the Maspero massacre, I spent my remaining few days in Cairo not with the old friends who I originally had come to see, but mainly with Yemenis: youth activists and old politicians who were either visiting the Egyptian capital or in self-enforced exile until things calmed down in Sanaa. I felt drawn to hang out only with them. With Yemenis I could rest in familiarity and habit. I smoked shisha pipes with a group of parliamentarians from Taiz at a bright café on the top floor of a Nile River party boat. The black dirty river flowed upward beneath us. The smog of the city settled in our lungs between puffs on the water pipe. I told a group of them the story of my experience with the drunk balateja leader from months ago ("and then he said, 'I saved her from the *balateja* and I want a certificate!'"). They howled with laughter and so did I. The bubbling water in the shisha bowl was drowned out by the honking horns of drivers stalled in traffic on nearby Nile Street. A Yemeni businessman with whom I had chewed qat in Taiz entered the café and sat down at our table, and we greeted each other as old friends.

• • •

As soon as I felt the plane begin to descend, I started checking my phone every ten seconds for service. Others around me were doing the same. As soon as I saw the bars on the screen, I called Yasser in Sanaa to find out why the airport was closed, making a vague attempt to lower my voice when the flight attendant walked by.

Yasser told me it wasn't a big deal. He said a few shells had flown over the airport early this morning and that's why it was forced to close, that's all.

Our aircraft made a sharp right hook over the sea before it followed its downward-turned nose to the landing strip below. After it hit the runway and slowed to a humble drive, the pilot announced that the plane would return to Cairo shortly, and any passengers who wanted could get a free ride back. Otherwise we could disembark in Aden, which is what I decided to do, though I was debating what my plan should be from here.

I wondered if I should just wait in Aden until the airport in Sanaa reopened or if I should try to get to Sanaa by land. There were increasing reports of bandits on the road from Aden to Sanaa, so that was one problem. Bandits were unpredictable, and Cairo had confirmed that I didn't like unpredictability.

Also, if police at checkpoints along the road discovered I was a foreigner, it would mean definite trouble for me—potentially expulsion, but who knows. Who knew who the police were working for then?

When there are police but no government, the police are much less predictable, too.

But the last thing I wanted was to be stuck in Aden while there was news in Sanaa. My editors would be upset with me, because they hadn't even wanted me going to Cairo for the short holiday to begin with. And besides, a photographer who was working for the *Times* had just snuck into Sanaa, and I really wanted to meet him.

I walked down the aisle with my book bag in tow, weighing the options. I bent my head down to look out a side window at Aden's runway. I felt like I could see the humidity in the air. Aden's moisture was a wet sponge, worse than summers in New York. I didn't expect to be breathing in that humidity today.

As I passed by the first-class seats at the front of the plane, a tiny woman in a niqab grabbed my arm. "Laura!" she said enthusiastically through her black veil. "It's me, Sara."

"Sar . . . Yes! Hello!"

Sara was the wife of a Yemeni sheikh I knew quite well. Of course, I never would have recognized her all covered up for the outside world. She told me she was staying on the plane to go back to Cairo and then introduced me to a sharply-dressed man in Western attire and well-coifed hair sitting beside her. She said that this was her brother-in-law, Soliman.

"Where are you going?" she asked me.

"I don't know what to do. I just need to get to Sanaa as fast as possible. I need to be there for work."

"You need to get to Sanaa? Me too," Soliman said. "I'm going to go by car."

"You're leaving right now?" I asked, realizing this could really work in my favor. I knew this family well. I trusted them. I thought that this was going to be a classic example of how my vast network of personal connections in Yemen paid off, of why I was so good at navigating life in this complicated world.

"Yeah. As soon as possible. I need to be in Sanaa by tomorrow morning for business. You want a ride?" His English was clear and American accented.

"Yeah, I definitely do. That's okay?"

"Of course it's okay. I'll meet you outside the airport. We'll get some lunch, you know, some fish. We'll get you something to wear over your face, and we'll go."

I thanked Soliman. This was going to save me. I'd be totally fine to make the ten-hour ride from Sanaa to Aden with such a well-known family. I'd wear a niqab, of course, but even if at the checkpoints they discovered I was an American in hiding, I'd be protected with a sheikh.

I left the family and walked down the roll-away stairs onto the tarmac in hot, sticky Aden, where life seemed colored in a hue of gray. *I love you Aden, I do,* I told the sky. *But for now, I need to be in Sanaa.*

I entered the airport and, as I walked into the line for passport control, a short Yemeni man beside me said, with the giddiness of a schoolboy, "I am excited to get my passport stamped in Aden. Aren't you?"

I thought about it. Yes, of course I was excited, too. This was just going to be another adventure. A hiccup in plans, but I would get from point A to point B nonetheless.

• • •

Soliman had found a taxi driver—a small, wrinkled, elderly man—to take us along the northern road all the way to Taiz. From there, we would meet two of Soliman's tribesmen who would drive his car down from Sanaa. Soliman's family also owned a house in Taiz, he told me, so if we wanted to spend the night there we could, but it probably won't be necessary because we need to get to Sanaa as fast as possible.

We ate baked fish at a crowded, sweaty restaurant on the side of the road beside a rocky cliff. After lunch, I went to the bathroom and put on the niqab Soliman had just bought me. I pulled down the abaya over my head while trying not to step into the smelly squat toilet that was crusted with specks of chewed qat and material even less savory. Next, I wrapped the thin black scarf around my hair, tucked the loose end into the fabric under my chin, and draped the veil, the niqab, over the front of my face, tying its ends in a bow on the back of my head. I loosened the bow slightly against my skull, worried that it would give me a headache.

I walked out of the bathroom thinking that the only thing giving me away as a foreigner were my flip-flops, because Yemeni women would never wear such things, but Soliman looked at me disappointedly. He sighed. "Come on." He reached around and put his hand on my shoulder, pushing me along. "Just get into the car, and I'll fix it there."

"What's wrong? I thought I put it on right."

"Everything's wrong. Come on."

On the drive out of the city, past the Soviet bloc-style apartment buildings that rose out of the barren land by the sea, I learned that Soliman had spent years living in the United States. I found him less urbane than I knew his brother to be, and his words and actions were tinted with a deliberate flirtation that made me want to scoot as far away from him as possible in this small backseat.

I hated wearing the niqab over my face. It was tight and the ridges of the area that was cut out for my eyes rubbed uncomfortably on my bottom eyelid. I flipped the black flap up over my forehead, free to do as I pleased, a Western woman.

"Hey, put that down. There's a checkpoint," Soliman scolded as soon as a small band of soldiers came into view on the road in front of us. He leaned over and helped me fix the veil over my face, grabbing my upper arm as he did so. The driver slowed to a stop in front of two soldiers. A few more lounged by their weapons underneath the roof of a various-sized plywood and metal shack along the side of the road. Soliman rolled down his window to tell the soldiers who he was. They just nodded and let us go. He was a powerful person in the web of Yemeni society, especially northern society from where these soldiers would have come.

We had left Aden city limits, and small bushes and squat trees dotted the brown landscape that looked like how I imagined the plains of eastern Africa. From here, there was only one way to go, north, along this rundown two-lane road that crept up a slow incline into the central Yemeni highlands.

The driver swerved around a pot hole, jerking his clunker of a taxi back and forth.

"Watch your driving, geezer!" Soliman yelled at him, void of a respect for this southerner. In Soliman's mind, the hierarchy of Yemeni society couldn't be more clear, but he seemed to want to drive that point home to the old man by yelling at him every chance that came his way.

"You didn't tell anyone we are doing this, did you?" Soliman asked me. "You can't tell anyone. You don't know who is listening to our phones."

"No, of course not," I responded, hoping my tone of voice didn't give away my concern at his comment. Why didn't Soliman want anyone to know? Was he seriously worried? As if the government was concerned that some American was on the Sanaa–Aden highway when war was on in Sanaa.

I had ten hours in this car with this man. Ten hours. It just sank in that he was already starting to annoy me. I chastised myself for always diving headfirst into things without thinking them through. My eagerness to catch a ride to Sanaa caused me to see past the potential pitfalls of traveling overland across Yemen with a man I didn't know. Still, I pushed these thoughts aside for now because I trusted that Soliman's sister-in-law would have warned me against traveling with him had I not been able to trust him.

Soliman reached into his qat bag and pulled out a handful of small, tender leaves. He squashed them in between his fingers, then held out his arm to my face to feed them to me.

"I don't need you to do that," I told him.

"Oh come on, loosen up," he said.

• • •

Around nine in the evening, we reached the outskirts of Taiz. Over the center of the city, the night sky was set aglow by artillery fire as if we were watching a distant fireworks show. I knew there was war in Taiz, too. Soliman instructed our driver to stop over on the side of the road. A black SUV pulled up behind us.

"Get out," Soliman told me flatly, and I opened my door into the brisk, black air, around 3,200 feet above sea level. The driver argued with Soliman about how much he should be paid for the ride. Soliman cursed him and spun around to address his tribesmen in the SUV, kicking up the dust with the back of his shoes. In response, I tried to give the old driver the most sympathetic face I could offer, but I think it wasn't any use. I was Soliman's property as far as the driver was concerned. He just started his ignition and set off back to Aden.

Soliman and I climbed into the backseat of his car. The front where Soliman's tribesmen were sitting was stuffed with assault rifles of various shapes, on the tribesmen's laps, and on the floor at their feet.

"I think we need to spend the night here tonight," Soliman said to me in English. He scooted over next to me and then leaned forward between the two front seats to plug his iPhone into a car charger.

"The night isn't safe to be on the roads anyway," he said.

I knew Soliman was right. The bandits were roaming. There was no government to crack down on them, and powers within the government were potentially even encouraging their presence (the more chaotic it becomes, the more the international community will see that Saleh needs to stay in power). Perhaps more worrying, though, was that the way to Sanaa was a road of tight hairpin turns up and down mountains, hardly something I wanted to take at night with a tribesman driving who would unwaveringly obey what I assumed would be his pompous sheikh's directive to drive as fast as possible.

Still, the last thing I wanted to do was spend the night with Soliman in his family's house in Taiz, but I knew I had little choice in the matter. Soliman didn't seem like one to take suggestions well. So to calm my fears, I put my trust in Yemeni society. We would be in Taiz, and if I had to I could escape to a neighbor's house, where they would take me in with open arms. The only reason Soliman was so untrustworthy was his Westernness. He didn't behave like a Yemeni. He behaved liked a rich prick from America.

But Soliman's family house wasn't in the city of Taiz. It perched on a hilltop on the outskirts, with no other buildings, certainly no neighbors, surrounding it. The car slowed to a stop in front of the house's front gate and an elderly man met us there. He obediently swung open the metal door for his boss, his master. Then we drove into the yard and parked in front of a darkened two-story house. The tribesman in the driver's seat switched off the engine and the head lights faded to nothing. The night was nearly pitch black. The power was cut so there was no hope of illuminating the situation. The sky was clouded over. I realized that if I screamed, no one but these men would hear me. The laws of Yemeni society no longer applied to me up here. Soliman considered the two of us as Americans, and outside those laws. In the past, I always ended up okay, I always found a way to get myself out of the problems I had so unceremoniously stumbled into. I had thought of myself as invincible, but I most certainly was not.

I knew that one of the ties that bind Yemeni society was accountability. The problem was that Soliman didn't think he was being held accountable because no one knew I was with him. Did his sister-in-law know? Now I couldn't recall for certain whether she was part of our conversation about traveling to Sanaa by land. Had she stopped listening then? I couldn't tell Soliman that someone in Sanaa knew I was with him because he instructed me not to do so and I didn't want to evoke his anger. Did I have any options? Yes, I did. I had an iPad.

"Soliman, I need to work. I absolutely have to contact the *New York Times*. It's about a story I wrote from Cairo that is being published today," I lied. "I can do the work on my iPad, but it is out of battery," I lied again. "Can I use your car charger here to charge it and finish work?"

"You can connect to the Internet?" he asked.

"Yeah, for like a million bucks a minute. To satellite. It normally works everywhere in Yemen."

"Alright," he put a key into the car's ignition to start the engine. I moved into the front seat and pulled my iPad out of my backpack and plugged in the cord. I told Soliman this would take ten minutes or so. He left me and walked into the house. The tribesmen sat on the doorstep, chewing qat, guns lying at their sides, their thobes pulled up revealing their hairy, skinny calves. *What did they think of their master with his Western girl in tow?* I wondered. *What did they think of his pudgy belly and cocky attitude? Did they think anything at all?* The way they followed directions so mindlessly and talked so infrequently, sometimes it was hard to imagine they did. There were beautiful parts of ancient tribal code, but the undying allegiance to one's sheikh part was really working against me right now.

I pulled up my email on my iPad and wrote messages to a handful of friends in Sanaa, letting them know where I was, that I didn't feel safe, but that they absolutely shouldn't tell anyone right now. They should just know where I am, in case I didn't contact them tomorrow.

I slid out of the car and walked into the house past the tribesmen. I climbed a flight of stairs, touching each new step gently with my toes before rocking back to the rest of my foot. Maybe if I didn't make a sound, I could disappear.

I nudged the wooden door with hand-carved flowers indented into its frame until it was half open, and when I fully registered the scene in front of me, I found my nightmare. Soliman was splayed wide legged on a sofa, the king of his domain, drinking a glass of whiskey.

He urged me to drink, too.

"I'm really tired. I think I just need to go to sleep." I told him.

"Ah, come on. Have a drink. We are in the middle of nowhere. What else can we do?"

"No, really. I have a lot of work tomorrow in Sanaa. I'm gonna go to sleep."

"Alright, alright." Soliman reluctantly showed me where a bedroom was. He wished me a good night. I returned the sentiment. I sat on the bed and stared at the bare wall in front of me.

I went over my situation in my head: I was in a house with a man getting increasingly drunk. The only other people with us were men who would fight to the death for him. I imagined that Soliman would rape and kill me. I imagined the worst thing possible happening to me, even if the idea that he would kill me was more irrational than likely.

I closed my eyes and felt the tension rise up through my shoulders into the back of my skull. My hands trembled as I took off my abaya and lay down on the bed with my clothes still on. I stared at the ceiling. I willed myself to sleep. I had accumulated too few hours of sleep in Cairo. "Please God, protect me," I whispered, with just the aspirations of my breath audible to the outside world. My nerves were so frayed that my mind couldn't stay awake. Sleep, so graciously, was a defense mechanism to fight this exhaustion. My body dozed off to a cautious slumber.

•••

I didn't know how much time had passed when I heard the door creak. I opened one eyelid. Standing there, one hand still on the door knob behind him, was Soliman, dressed only in white boxers.

My closed eyelid swung open to meet the other and I sat up.

"Soliman . . . what," I paused a half second, "are you doing?"

"I'm just gonna sleep in here."

"What?"

"Come on, I'll stay on the one side of the bed and you'll stay on the other." He approached me and moved to the far side of the bed. I swung my legs over my edge to get away from him. I knew I couldn't run because I had nowhere to go.

"No . . . just no. I'm gonna sleep on the couch," I told him.

"That's *ayb*. You are my guest. You can't sleep on the couch."

"This is *ayb*," I retorted, repeating the Arabic word for shameful.

"Don't be ridiculous. I need to sleep in the bed . . ."

"I'm going to the couch." I stood up.

Soliman tsked, stood up too, and acted like he was going to walk out of the room. I sat back down on the edge of the bed. He made it all the way to the door when he spun around and moved back toward me.

"Oh, just come on," he said. "Loosen up."

I stood up again with the notion that I had to do everything in my power not to let us be in the same bed at the same time. I rushed to the corner of the room and felt Soliman grab my wrist but then release it. I took the abaya from the chair and pulled it on over my head.

"What are you . . ." he stuttered.

"I am going to stand here in this corner like this until morning." The ends of the dress fell to my feet. I crossed my arms in front of my chest.

"Fuck this!" he yelled. "We're going to Sanaa." Soliman stomped out of the bedroom, grabbed the knob, and slammed the door shut. I quickly gathered my belongings and peeked out of the room. I saw Soliman in the living room putting on his pants. A half empty bottle of Chivas Regal sat on the coffee table. He looked back and saw me peering at him.

"Come on!" he yelled.

We descended the staircase single file and then Soliman barked at the qat-chewing tribesmen to get in the car, we were going to Sanaa tonight. They obeyed without protest, got in the front two seats, and Soliman and I sat in the back. I had to travel the rest of journey beside the man who I just thought was going to rape me. We hardly spoke and when I did respond to his nonsensical inquiries, my words were few and soft-spoken. I didn't rehash what just happened in my head. I believed to do so was futile. I just wanted to focus on getting to Sanaa, yet I was helpless in the backseat. The only thing I could do was wish, pray, implore the universe to grant us safe travel. After two hours, Soliman faded in and out of sleep, leaning his head on the opposite door, as the car weaved back and forth up and down mountains. The car shined two beams of light ahead of us a few feet on narrow road, but that was the only thing I could see of the outside world, aside from shadows that a mountain casts. I thought I saw movements in those shadows, but I'm sure it was only my imagination. After another hour, my eyelids drooped closed as well.

• • •

The first rays from a rising sun shone across the high valley, illuminating the rocky landscape with a pale glow. I slowly opened my eyes to see the reflection off the windows of a military checkpoint just ahead, while the car gently slowed to a stop.

"This is Sanaa?" I asked the tribesman driving.

I knew his grunt in response meant yes. We had reached the capital's city limits. I straightened my back to sit up and I could just see the first signs of a city up ahead, the toasted beige expanse in the valley, my home. It never looked so welcoming.

Soliman, awake too, muttered something to the soldiers. He told them they better let us through, we had a rough night. They looked around to me in the backseat, no longer wearing a niqab over my face because I just didn't care, and signaled for us to go. I felt the sun on my face through the car window and knew that this nightmare was coming to an end. Soliman made some halfhearted comment about the previous night. "What did you think I was trying to do?" he asked. I just ignored him and stared out at the mountains. I dreamed of the cup of coffee I was going to be drinking soon, safe inside my favorite Hadda café. I would run into friends there. I wouldn't tell them what just befallen me on the road from Aden to Sanaa, though. After all, it had all worked out in the end. This would just be a good story. The gravity of the situation was from from apparent in my skewed world of shelling, balateja, and political unrest.

CHAPTER 22

Samuel and I walked toward the front gates of the al-Ahmar family compound in Hasaba neighborhood of Sanaa. Armed tribesmen, guards to the wrecked fortress, followed our movements, each with a bulging qat cheek. They wore magazines of bullets strapped into khaki vests. Their white thobes were crusted with dirt, their hair was in disheveled messes, their legs were bone-thin and dry. They were not curious about our presence. Their stares told us that we were intruders here. It was mid-October and the war in Hasaba showed no signs of ceasing. In fact it had been kicked up a notch. Such was what happened when the artillery fire flew over Sanaa airport the week prior forcing its closure. The large three-story house behind these tribesmen was that of the late father of the al-Ahmar clan, Sheikh Abdullah, and was the nucleus of government-sponsored attacks during the Hasaba war. Chunks of its walls were missing, especially on the top floors, leaving the inside of the house exposed by craters of raw, jagged concrete. Few windows remained fully intact. Bullet holes decorated the compound's outer wall that looked like an exhibit at a contemporary art gallery. I think Sadeq, the eldest al-Ahmar brother, still lived inside, like a king in ruined glory. During the war, his camels and peacocks wandered the halls of the estate in distressed confusion.

Just across the street from the al-Ahmar mansion was the headquarters of the GPC. The building had suffered the vengeance of the al-Ahmars and Ali Mohsin. It was burnt to a blackish tinge, looted to a hollow shell, and al-Ahmar tribesmen patrolled its barren grounds. A large poster of Saleh still hung from the three-story building's top floor, but it was at a crooked angle, dangling from a thread.

"I think it will be good inside there for a photo," Samuel said to me, pointing to the front gate of the GPC building's compound.

From Barcelona, Samuel spoke English with a heavy accent and had a thick unkempt black beard, tanned skin, and a long rectangular face. His dark and deep-set eyes implored others for trust. He was the photojournalist who managed to procure a visa to Yemen as an Arabic student and was working undercover for the *Times.* None of his photos that accompanied my stories carried his name.

Samuel arrived in Sanaa while I was in Cairo, and luckily for me, he lacked the cocky attitude that normally accompanied most male photojournalists who covered conflict. He didn't need to prove himself to anyone and didn't feel he deserved external praise for choosing such a dangerous profession. He was relaxed and jolly because he had let all those things go. Samuel kept reminding me that I was very "Ameriki" whenever I urged us to get somewhere faster, get work done faster, or in general move faster than his Catalan saunter. I was jealous of how much he could just sit back and chill during an afternoon cappuccino break. I would complain about editors and he would only complain about the shape of his mug: "This cup is e-stupid. Khow does anyone want to drink a cappuccino out of such a tall cup?"

Still, I enjoyed the change of pace his presence brought me. I now had a work partner to whom I could constantly explain the ins and outs of Yemen. Samuel would just listen and mutter on occasion that "This place is, like, really nuts," and I would laugh and tell him that indeed it was.

We had come to Hasaba this afternoon, when the war cooled down for lunch and qat, so that Samuel could take some photos and I could just inspect the scene and gather some color for reporting. I had come back from Cairo, tried to push what happened with Soliman far from my thoughts, and just got back to work. And work meant reporting on the ongoing war, or at least trying to find ways to report on it anew since war starts to get boring to American readers after some time.

The booms of artillery fire echoed each night, and Samuel said the sounds of fighting were worse than anything he had heard in Libya during the recent war there. He told me more people had to have died each night than the small number of a half dozen or so that local media reported each day. We even went to the local military hospital to try to figure out if the official death total was accurate. I believed it was, but Samuel kept insisting we couldn't hear that many explosions each night and there only be such a small number killed.

The main street of Hasaba had been empty aside from the occasional rebel fighter. Though I did see one small food shop that remained open, run by a man who was not eager to speak with me, the inquiring journalist. The rest of the stores were shuttered and their doors were littered with bullet holes. Most of the windows of the top floors of the buildings, small apartments, were blown out. A barrier in the middle of the four-lane road was also smashed with bullets, like the al-Ahmar tribesmen and government soldiers had a shoot-out in this exact spot, but aimed at the guard wall rather than each other. Sandbags were piled on most street corners and occasionally parked next to them was a pickup truck with a heavy machine gun propped on its bed. Most of these were unmanned.

The desolation around us, a city without its people, felt apocalyptic. The fighters, the shopkeeper, and we were the lone survivors, trying to make sense of the destruction, the might of man, what we could do to one another if we were simply left to our own devices. Not so far away from us, street markets buzzed, children skipped home from school in their green uniforms, but here we were alone with the fighters. It's shocking how war can be so contained within a city. When I heard the *rat-a-tat* of a machine gun from a few blocks away, I knew not to worry, that the sound and the destruction that came with it would stay over there, and I would be over here, and life would proceed without interruption.

A few tribesmen dressed in thobe and janbiya, carrying AKs over their shoulders, approached Samuel and me while we were inside the frontyard of the GPC building. I explained to them that we were journalists. Was it okay if we take photos here? Yes, of course, but not of the al-Ahmar house, they told us. I tried to get information about the war from the tribesmen, but their answers were limited to one word or huffs. When I asked a boy who looked to be about thirteen his age, he lied that he was twenty-five.

Samuel had walked over to the side of the building, trying to converse with one of the tribesmen in his limited Arabic. A miscommunication seemed to be brewing; I could tell because Samuel kept pointing to the man's gun, confused, and the tribesman kept looking at Samuel as if he were trying to figure out exactly what the strange foreigner's problem was. Then Samuel looked over to me and called out, "Are you sure these guys are fighting with the rebels?"

"Yeah, of course," I yelled back.

"Come here then."

I walked over to them across the dirt yard.

"Look," Samuel said and pointed to a small photo, a decal, of Saleh pasted on the stock of the tribesman's gun. "How can they be with the rebels? This is Saleh, no?"

I had to hold back a laugh. Of course Samuel would be confused. He had just come from Libya where a rebel would never dream of having Gaddafi's face posted anywhere unless it was the bottom of a toilet. But this was Yemen. This was where all the rules that govern life elsewhere have to be tossed aside.

"These men aren't fighting for politics," I told Samuel. "They are fighting for their sheikh, Hamid. Politics means nothing to them. I'm sure some man gave him that sticker like a year ago or something and he thought it looked cool. It's nothing more than that."

"Really?"

"Yeah, for sure."

"How do you know these things?"

"Because tribesmen fighting for the government would never just be hanging out in front of the al-Ahmar house."

"This place is, like, really crazy."

A machine gun sounded in the background though it was afternoon, qat time. Occasionally random violence broke out in this area. Samuel involuntarily ducked at the sound and then quickly scanned our surroundings. He had long covered war, had come in and out of conflict for a decade. Though he knew very well that we were out of range of the sound of gunfire, he had a heightened flight response, probably the result of years of an overstimulated adrenal gland. While I, who had been living in a perpetual state of high adrenaline levels for the past few months, didn't even acknowledge the sound.

• • •

I had told few about what happened with Soliman on the road from Aden to Sanaa. I had told an older American friend who had lived in Sanaa much longer than me. She confirmed that these sorts of things are not completely uncommon with Yemeni men after they have lived in the West. They understand that Western women are loose, because when compared to Yemeni women, they are, and that, paired with a sheikh's inflated ego, is a dangerous combination. It's such a shame, but it's good I was safe, she said. I agreed and pushed the event aside. I told myself it wasn't that bad after all because in the end nothing had happened to me. And how could I complain when civilians were still being killed?

So this morning, the day after Samuel and I went to Hasaba, when Soliman called me and told me to get to his house right away, and not to ask questions, but just to come because there was someone at his house that he wanted me to meet, I agreed. I agreed because he didn't sound like he was lying. I rationalized that if he didn't harm me in his house in Taiz then it didn't make sense that he would harm me in Sanaa in the middle of the day. And besides, I wanted to meet whoever was there. I wondered if it could be Hamid, who had been traveling clandestinely around the city ever since the attack on the presidential palace.

When my taxi pulled up in front of Soliman's compound in Hadda, I saw two SUVs filled with government soldiers parked outside, which meant whoever was inside was on the side of the Saleh regime, nullifying my Hamid theory and piquing my curiosity all the more.

I walked to the front gate where a guard let me in, and when I turned to the front porch, I saw Soliman relaxing in a wooden deck chair. Across from him was a man whose face looked strikingly familiar. A bottle of white wine was open on a glass-topped table between them.

"Laura, welcome," Soliman said as I climbed the front stairs. He grabbed my hand and kissed each cheek to greet me. I didn't pull back or hesitate.

"This is Ammar," he said.

I knew who this Ammar was. Like local versions of Madonna, Saleh family members didn't need last names in Yemen. And anyway, Ammar looked just like his brother Yahya. I could see it in his beady eyes, long nose, and mouth shape that seemed like it rested in a perpetual smirk. He was the deputy director of Yemen's National Security Bureau, the country's version of the FBI, and one that had a reputation for activities like torture and disappearing political dissenters. There were actually two versions of the FBI in Yemen, but the American government encouraged Saleh to create Ammar's NSB about ten years back, after it thought the other one, the Political Security Organization, was connected with Islamic fundamentalists.

"I've heard about you," Ammar told me.

"Oh, is that so?" I replied. "Good or bad?"

Ammar chuckled. This reminded me of Yahya, too.

"Good and bad," he said.

Soliman's Ethiopian maid brought me a wine glass and I sat and drank with the two men in the relaxed atmosphere of a summer afternoon at the park. I saw that Ammar was much smarter than his brother Yahya, a smooth operator really, whose words were calculated to make the exact impression he intended. I enjoyed talking to him because I felt like it was a game of how to manipulate the conversation, in which I had a formidable opponent. Ammar had information I wanted, and he knew it too. While I had the advantage of being a twenty-something female with whom Ammar couldn't hide his urge to flirt.

Early in the conversation, Soliman told Ammar about what happened between us at his house in Taiz as if it were a story to be proud of.

"It was inappropriate," I said to Soliman.

"Oh come on, please." He looked at me with a cocked eyebrow.

"This man is crazy," Ammar said smiling.

"He's just mad at me because I sold weapons to Hamid," Soliman said to me.

"Yeah, fuck you." Ammar leaned back against his chair and crossed his one leg over the other, his pressed black slacks and white button-up shirt rolled up at the sleeves made him look like a businessman at happy hour.

"You know, he really screws me a lot," Ammar continued. "Some friend."

I just laughed, unsure of what to say, slightly unsettled they were talking so lightheartedly about a conflict in which civilians were dying, that pushed their country to the verge of total collapse. Or had it already collapsed? Perhaps this was what a collapsed country looked like—the men at the top enjoying a leisurely afternoon in their oasis of life while the rest of the population had to combine resources to survive.

I was vaguely aware these men were posing. The Salehs and their friends had a reputation for inviting foreign women to their Thursday-night parties. I knew that although I had never been invited to one: I was either not cute enough or not ditzy enough—but I guessed it was slim pickings after most of Sanaa's American expats had fled. I pushed those thoughts aside, though, persuading myself that wasn't the only reason they had invited me here this afternoon. That this was mainly for work. That I was gaining a source.

"Ammar, can I ask you a question?"

"Anything. I mean, almost anything." He chuckled.

"Do you guys shell empty buildings at night? Why are there so many booms but not so many people die?"

I was still interested in Samuel's observation that the sound of shelling was worse in Sanaa than it had been in his experience of the Libyan war.

Ammar laughed so hard at my question, he had to set down his glass of wine so as not to spill it over himself.

"*Ya Looora Kasinova*," he said leaning over his thighs. Yemenis loved to call me this. "We use this thing, it's kind of, how do you say . . . sound bomb."

"So it just makes a noise?"

"Yes," he shrugged.

I was surprised that I felt a sense of betrayal with this revelation. Shouldn't I have been relieved, overjoyed, that each crack that echoed across Sanaa's night sky was not accompanied by destruction? Yet all I could think was that the fear the booms provoked—the edge that I and all of Sanaa's residents lived on because the sounds of war each night were a lie. I recalled hearing the booms when I was leaving the Square after my late evening interview with Tawakkol the day she won the Nobel Peace Prize.

How they made me walked at a quicker pace to the edge of tents to search for cab. How I begged the driver to get out of range of the war as fast as he could—artillery shells fell on the Square occasionally, it was close enough to Hasaba, yet that all could have been for naught.

People did die, and many of them were innocent civilians who lived in Hasaba, within the territory controlled by the al-Ahmars and Ali Mohsin. Some fighters and soldiers from both sides were killed, too. But much of what this war turned into was just a show. It was muscle flexing. Most important was who appeared to be the strongest in this fight, because both sides knew they were incapable of completely destroying the other. So they just destroyed one another's buildings instead. The assassination attempt against Saleh still didn't totally make sense in this narrative. It was an outlier in a fight that otherwise was just a competition of machismo.

In Ammar's cavalier attitude I saw that, to him, this was all a game. That made me feel betrayed as well. The original youth protesters at Change Square were dying for their cause, but to those who actually wielded the power, this was about a personal fight that had been boiling for a long time—a power struggle between the al-Ahmars and the Salehs that existed way before Mohammed Bouazizi ever set himself on fire in a small city in Tunisia. To Ammar, the protesters were a sidebar, an annoyance. The idea that they were a political force to be reckoned with—Ammar would find that laughable.

In the time of war, government collapse, and rising prices, many Yemenis were forgetting the original zeal of the protest movement, the way it drew out thousands to Change Square. I don't think Ammar and his family ever admitted to themselves that the energy of the protests had existed to begin with. Did they so underestimate the civilians and the youth of their country that they couldn't admit Yemenis could be organized enough to independently rise up against them? Or did the Salehs not see themselves as monarchs that needed to be deposed? If I were a better person, I would have asked Ammar these questions. I tried to remind myself to hate him, that he was a bad man involved with bad things. That he was a leader in the system that killed young men and women who I knew. The regime that shot and killed Hassan. But instead,

I just enjoyed my wine and conversation. And anyway, compared to Soliman, Ammar was a gentleman.

We went into Soliman's house for lunch and all sat at a table together. I broke bread with Ammar Saleh, potentially responsible for the massacre of protesters on March 18, as well as a man who I recently was convinced was going to rape me in rural Yemen, and who was also selling weapons to Hamid. It was so easy to be won over by the devil in sheep's clothing, especially when it entailed casual socialization with the leaders of a country. Power was attractive, and being so close to it was, too. I never could have done this in America.

And anyway, who was the devil in this case: Ammar or Hamid? They were one in the same, yet on opposing sides.

Ammar drove me home. I sat in the front passenger's seat with him at the wheel. Two SUVs drove behind him, sirens on their roofs roaring. When Ammar pulled over for me to jump out on Hadda Street, a soldier from the police car had already gotten out to open my door and lead me to the side of the road, the most well-trained Yemeni soldier I had ever seen, likely whipped into shape using American funds, if not by actual American army commanders. I turned around to wave goodbye, but Ammar and his convoy had already sped away down the street.

CHAPTER 23

Most of Sanaa's foreign residents had evacuated that fall during the war. Only the most essential aid workers, diplomats, and security personnel remained, along with the few of us freelancers, academics, and those expats who simply had made Sanaa their home. All in all, there weren't a whole lot of us, which is why we felt we had an excuse to come together every few weeks or so for a massive party—as we did this night. It was at an aid worker's house in Hadda, complete with an inground swimming pool. Outside in the house's manicured yard, armored vehicles sat guarded by the security for the highest ranking diplomats , some of them ambassadors.

Inside the front door, a stack of abayas lay on a bench, shoes were piled in a corner. Techno music blared from a small speaker attached to an iPod and the rumbles from the Hasaba war in the background provided extra bass, but none of us paid them much heed. They were now part of our day the same way the sounds of the call to prayer had been integrated into our lives. I stopped to consider that maybe the booms were Ammar's so-called sound bombs anyway.

I squeezed through the crowd of drunk diplomats in the house's large foyer. These were the men and women who sat in meetings each day trying to convince the Salehs to agree to the GCC Initiative, or trying to convince the JMP to tweak the GCC Initiative so that Saleh would agree to it, all while trying to figure out what Ali Mohsin's true motivations were. Being a Western diplomat in Yemen was like being in a popularity contest; there were so few of them and such a large political mess that it was easy to play a big role in shaping the country's future as long as the JMP and GPC people liked you. Some of these diplomats were more vested in solving the crisis than others. Some only wanted to look like the savior of Yemen to boost their career.

Then there were the humanitarians at this party, the ones trying to figure out how to get basic grain shipments to poverty-stricken governorates before eating their extravagant sushi dinners at night prepared by the Japanese ambassador's personal chef. (I wasn't above partaking in these as well.) Many of them were beautiful. Few spoke Arabic. Most of them had never been to Change Square. I missed the one who always wore a cravat and raved about his espresso machine.

Few to none American diplomats were at the party, however. They weren't allowed to go out at night. Except the one who always disobeyed security protocol to sneak out for the expat parties. I saw that one in the kitchen mixing a gin and tonic.

I found Tom standing in front of the sofa away from the dancing crowd. He held a beer bottle in his hand. I held a plastic glass filled with homemade red wine an aid worker made in her basement. Tom told me excitedly in a hushed voice about his latest romance. He was worked up about the ordeal and used lots of hand motions to convey his feelings. I told him it was great. Then I told him about a recent crush and he told me to forget that guy. He sucks, anyway. Ugh, why waste my time. Take another drink of wine and hope that this batch won't give you a painful hangover the next day when we go to the Square and see how many are dead. None of these other guys are going to the Square—obviously that makes us so much cooler than them. So much more "in touch."

One aid worker drunkenly stumbled over to us wearing a low-cut golden halter top—a ploy to grab the attention of a diplomat. That diplomat was off in a dark corner talking to one of the Yemeni women who always came to these parties dressed in sexy attire, dreaming that a Western diplomat would one day take her away from this place. Another aid worker was already passed out on the mafraj cushions because apparently the cup of homemade wine she drank was definitely not fit for consumption.

Everyone just ignored her. She does this. And here we all were, a mix of misfit Yemenis and the foreigners who make their careers from tragedy in Yemen.

Do you remember what life was like before we got to know what war was all about? I don't. This seemed like the only reality that could have ever existed. This war consumed us; it shaped everything in our lives at the moment—our jobs, where we lived, our emotional health, and our strained relationships with our families back home. We could have left, but we didn't. Why? It was a complex answer, of course, and different for each of us. But we all had to be gaining something from this war. We wouldn't have lasted otherwise. To imagine it all as altruistic would be a flimsy self-deception. One of the things we gained were these nights. They didn't exist before the fighting. Not like this, with what felt like every Western foreigner in Sanaa showing up at a party, because now there were so few of us—the remnants. Our small world was both claustrophobic and empowering.

Meanwhile, inside a small mafraj near the house's entrance sat Tarek Saleh, the third brother of Yahya and Ammar. He lounged on a low cushion in a corner wearing a gray baseball cap, its curved rim casting a shadow over the top half of his face. His arms were folded across his chest and he relaxed his legs straight outward because there was no one in front of him who he could offend by showing the soles of his feet. Tarek was the head of the presidential guard, the part of the armed forces tasked with protecting the president. Faris, the handsome and eager-to-please public relations manager of the Saleh regime, sat next to Tarek, engaging him in conversation. The two were close friends and had come here together this evening to drink and relax in a party full of the foreigners who spent their days trying to remove them from their positions of power. They ignored the blonde aid worker sleeping on the cushions beside them.

The night went on. We poured more sour red wine. A UN employee passed out brownies infused with hashish. At least this night no one got spitefully pushed into the swimming pool. Tarek moved to the dance floor. A diplomat who was trying to entice Saleh to step down was shaking her hind end somewhat seductively directly in front of him. Someone put on Katy Perry. Just dance some more. Just ignore the fact that Tarek has a pistol tucked into his belt. He always did, because that's the sort of person he was. The twenty-something child of a prominent Yemeni opposition figure was getting down in front of the speakers. Tarek eyed her curiously. While a Yemeni activist came up to me and Tom to declare she had to leave because she couldn't be in the same house as Tarek Saleh and Faris, the only voice here to remind us that the situation was politically charged. That we weren't in neutral territory. That we were living in a time when civilians were dying and these men's hands were stained with blood . . . but please for once, let's forget it. Let's forget the violence. Let's forget that I'm a journalist and all these people around me are sources and let's just let the night spin into a drunken haze and then we'll all stumble out into the reality of this conflict-stricken, impoverished, failed state. And that's what we all did.

CHAPTER 24

The divided army was at war in Sanaa. In Aden, there were suicide bombings. In the desperately impoverished region on the western coast, children were starving to death. The government didn't control parts of the north or southeast. And in Taiz—beautiful Taiz, the country's industrial heartland—the government fired artillery nightly into the center of the city in an effort to squash a violent rebellion.

After getting in touch with the governor of Taiz province, who said that he welcomed Samuel and me into his home city to write an article for the *New York Times*, we traveled there by air in early November. When our small plane touched down, the pilot had to steer clear of some goats that had wandered onto the runway. The perils of Taiz were only just beginning.

Unlike in the capital, civilians had taken up arms against the government in Taiz. Some of them were youth from Freedom Square. Others were men from surrounding villages. Even a handful of northerners who had grown tired of Change Square's peaceful resistance came down to Taiz to join the fight.

The rebellion surprised Yemenis across the country. Taizis weren't fighters. Taizis were the educated ones. Yet Taiz was the only place where part of the original protest movement fought back after brutal government attacks.

The government claimed that Ali Mohsin had sent soldiers down to Taiz to fight, and that the rebellion's leader, Hamoud al-Mikhlafi, was just a stooge of Hamid. The battle was cast as a proxy war for the ongoing political conflict in Sanaa. Saleh sent one of his most brutal officers to oversee security in Taiz and try to squash the rebellion far from the eyes of international media. Residential buildings in the center of the city were shelled at night. Female protesters were fatally shot by snipers. The fabric of the city, once known as peaceful and law-abiding, shifted towards violence. Taizis felt their government had turned against them, was punishing them even, for being the original heart of that past winter's protest movement.

Upon our arrival to the city, Samuel and I were going to lunch at the house of the governor who had invited us, Hamoud al-Sofi. Al-Sofi was on Saleh's side, and it became apparent fairly quickly that our welcome in Taiz was a ploy to try to convince us the rebels were the ones destroying the city, not the government, and that they had transformed tranquil Taiz into a city where AKs were now ubiquitous on street corners. Al-Sofi even left bottles of Chivas and expensive French red wine for us at our hotel's reception. Just a little gift for the journalists, from the friendly governor of Taiz.

Al-Sofi also sent a car to our hotel on a steep hilltop to pick up Samuel and me and take us to his house across the valley. As we drove down to the center of the city, we saw that protesters from Freedom Square were staging a march on a main commercial street. A large cluster of ragtag youth took over a few blocks, waving their banners, and chanting with a vivacity that suggested this wasn't their eleventh month of protest. Merchants stepped outside their stores to cheer them on. They raised their hands above their heads and clapped or pumped their fists with faint smiles. Taiz was still at it despite the brutal government attacks. Taiz still supported revolution. Samuel and I watched the protest march silently. We knew that protest marches begot violence, so we also scanned the scene for signs of it.

Yet I also couldn't help wondering what the point of all this was. It was the war that mattered at that point. It was whether Ali Mohsin could do enough damage to the Salehs to force political compromise that actually mattered. There were few to no journalists even broadcasting this for a the larger world to see, so why do it? I saw it over again: the need to believe one had a purpose, that he or she had a role in a greater cause. These protesters shook the core of their country less than a year ago. After being a part of that, it wasn't so easy just to pack up the tent and go home. Wasn't I addicted to it just like them? But having a purpose comes with risks. You can be shot. Is it worth it to be shot when your protests don't matter? *Have I gone hard to think that the protests don't matter?*

Sure enough, down the street, in the direction the march was headed, Samuel and I spotted half a dozen soldiers of the Republican Guard in their dark green camouflage fatigues. The soldiers cordoned off with orange cones part of the street ahead of where the protesters were marching. They were moving quickly, on a mission. We saw one raise the barrel of his assault rifle to eye level. Another soldier went to his humvee to grab his gun out of the front seat. He also pointed it directly down the street at the protesters. Then they fired one bullet after another, in the open, with no attempt to use balateja to pretend the government wasn't involved. The act had the feeling of a casual afternoon ritual, as though it was nothing to be alarmed about in the least.

We saw that the protesters didn't stop marching toward the gunfire, exactly what one would expect of Yemeni protesters.

Our driver continued to head toward the Republican Guard too, from the back side, steering us down the area of the street that was blocked off to traffic because it was the fastest way to the governor's house.

Samuel leaned forward from his spot in the backseat with me and hit the driver on the side of his arm. "What are you doing? You see those guys? Look, guns!"

"*Mafeesh moshkela,*" the driver replied, no problem. "We are in the governor's car."

Except that this wasn't the car the governor used on a daily basis, so the driver's assumption that the soldiers would recognize us and know not to be alarmed was incorrect. Al-Sofi hadn't sent for us to be picked up in his usual car just in case the rebels decided to attack it on our way to his house when we drove through their territory.

The driver continued forward, and we were about one block from the Republican Guard now. The soldiers heard the sound of our approaching vehicle, driving down the street in the area they had sectioned off for their day's protester target practice. It must have seemed quite the brazen move. Maybe we were rebels coming to attack them! The soldiers turned around, pointing their guns straight at us.

At the exact moment when my mind was able to register what was about to happen, I saw a flash of yellow emitted from one of the rifles' ends before Samuel pulled me down to the floorboard. I ducked my head as low as possible, bringing my face close to a floor dirtied with cigarette butts. My first thought was, *Wow, there's a yellow spark at the end of the gun. Just like in the movies.* But then I heard chuckles coming from another man who was sitting with us in the back seat and I knew they were because of our behavior. *Why did we have to act so scared?* I knew that we had just been shot at, but the weight of what that meant, the absolute seriousness that that bullet could have struck someone in this car—that I was far from understanding. I had seen so many bodies shot over the past year, hundreds, sometimes just in the ankle, sometimes square in the back of the head. Yet I no longer thought it was possible that the bullet would strike me.

Still, I squatted down behind the driver's seat, covered my head with my arms. There was a brief moment when I waited for impact, but when it didn't come—as I had expected—I popped my head up like a gopher to look out the car window. The driver had sped the car in reverse as soon as the shooting started, spun us around on a point, and headed down a side street, away from the Republic Guard.

No bullets hit the car, of course. If there is one thing the average Yemeni soldier didn't have, it was good aim.

Samuel and I hoisted ourselves back on the seats once we knew we were far enough from harm's way. He swore under his breath as we drove on and shook his head at such unnecessary danger. He just gazed out a side window, perhaps contemplating life: when he would finally give up covering conflict, why he was in a city at war with a reckless twenty-six-year-old. I just sat back against the seat and shrugged. I didn't feel afraid of the bullets. I really didn't feel anything at all—except embarrassment that I had reacted so swiftly to the gunfire. The chance that one of those bullets was going to hit the car in a way that would have hurt either Samuel or me—I figured it was negligible, just as the Yemenis around us did.

• • •

Hamoud al-Mikhlafi's home sat atop a steep, narrow hill just above Freedom Square in Taiz, where a few hundred protesters still lived in their tents despite the nightly shelling that periodically blasted through the surrounding buildings. A handful of armed men were standing guard outside the house among leafy Eucalyptus trees; cords of bullets hung around their necks like jewelry.

This part of Taiz was controlled by the rebels. They patrolled its streets regularly. If government troops entered, a firefight would ensue. The rebels also regularly attacked public buildings and sometimes were able to seize them entirely. The governer told Samuel and me—after apologizing for the incident with the Republic Guard—they were trying to take over all of Taiz and turn it into Benghazi, a completely rebel-held city. It had been that way more or less since early June after government soldiers set fire to tents in Freedom Square, creating a burning inferno that sent flames into the sky and killed a dozen or so protesters in the process. To retaliate against the government, a civilian rebellion was spawned in the days following "the burning of Taiz." Hamoud was the rebellion's most important leader.

All the other houses around Hamoud's were partially destroyed by artillery fire, machine guns, and mortars, peppered like Swiss cheese. Blocks of rubble had been brushed to the side of the street. Hamoud's house was barely touched, though, aside from windows punctured by shards of shrapnel. I explained to Samuel that this meant we would be safe inside during our interview with the rebel leader. And besides, it was approaching the afternoon, and everyone in Yemen knew war wasn't fought in the afternoon while everyone was busy achieving a decent qat high.

"They're not going to kill the head of the rebellion," I assured Samuel as we got out of our taxi in front of the house.

"Why not?" he asked.

"Because that's not how it works here. He's like this untouchable figure."

He just looked to the mountains, annoyed, while I reveled in the excitement of interviewing a rebel leader who didn't come with the same dirty baggage as Ali Mohsin. In Sanaa, bad guys fought bad guys. Here in Taiz, one side of the battle could be seen as noble. That is, if I accepted there was such a thing as noble violence, because even then the rebellion in Taiz had its ties to some of the ignoble in Sanaa.

One of the rebels led Samuel and me into a mafraj that was on a lower level than the rest of the house. We kicked off our shoes at the door, and Samuel made a note of the collection of assault rifles and one RPG sitting next to the shoe pile.

"Nuts. Let's just go in," I said, and we entered.

Stepping into a filled mafraj always felt like stepping into a sauna, and this experience was particularly sticky. The room was narrow, long, and crowded with men chewing. Unwanted qat leaves peppered the floor like a collage alongside the Kalashnikovs. Windows on one side looked down to the valley below and the remaining tattered tents of Freedom Square. A slight man with speckled silvery hair and a large flat nose stood up to greet Samuel and me. He was dressed in a white thobe with a pressed collar. Hamoud shook Samuel's hand, and then shook mine, which surprised me since he was an Islahi.

Then the rebel leader pointed at me and smiled. "I know you," he said. "We met before, at Doctor Abdel-Kader's house."

Hamoud's words were quiet, like a grizzly whisper.

"I drove you to the Square." He raised his eyebrows and nodded his head toward me.

"Oh, that's right," I replied, embarrassed I hadn't put two and two together before I arrived to his house. He was the quiet, mild-mannered man at that qat chew from back in February. I looked around his room full of militia men. Times had certainly changed.

"How's your mother?" he asked. "Doctor Abdel-Kader told me she had surgery."

"She's doing much better," I responded, taken aback that the leader of the rebellion would be asking about such things. A few more men entered the room and tried to find a spare spot of cushion. Some were armed, others not. Samuel eyeballed them nervously as we moved to sit down at the far end of the mafraj. I paid them no heed, but was eager to speak with Hamoud, who sat cross-legged on the floor in front of us, leaning slightly forward in eager conversation.

"I'm sorry the mafraj is such a mess," he said. "Normally this is not what it would be like for guests."

"It's okay. You're busy," I replied.

Hamoud told us the story of the rebellion—from his point of view. Three days after the burning of Freedom Square, he gathered local men at his home village about fifteen miles from the city and prepared to launch an attack against the government. The rebels, a few hundred of them at the time, stormed into the city, guns blazing, surprising the authorities. The dignity of Taiz had been squashed too much, Hamoud said. "Yes, we are more cultured and more peaceful, but bravery and manhood is in Taiz," he told us. Some of the men near us on the cushions grunted or yelled out "God willing!" in response, like an old-timey Sunday service.

"All along, Taizis were 'Yes, sir' sort of people," Hamoud said. He saluted the sky. "But all of Taiz went out on the streets. They stopped being obedient and revolted. This is the problem because Ali Abdullah was the commander of the army in Taiz just before he became president. He did not expect Taiz to say no. So he is paying us back."

When new fighters entered the crowded mafraj, they first approached Hamoud to give their greetings and he spoke back to them gently. He kissed the head of the son of one fighter like the pope. Unlike the tribesmen of the North who fought for their sheikh blindly, many of the rebels were fighting out of conviction. Some of them were from Hamoud's village, but many others were not. One man had even come from Saada in far northern Yemen to fight alongside Hamoud. Another, from Sanaa, defiantly showed me his GPC membership card to show me that not everyone in the room belonged to al-Islah.

The war in Sanaa felt purposeless, but this didn't. There was even a large segment of the civilian population that cheered it on.

The idealized image of a rebel leader had been preached to me in stories since I was young. I also heard stories about nonviolent leaders who took on the corrupt rulers of the land, but those were much fewer in number, not as full of glory. I saw within myself how easy it was to romanticize violence when it is aimed at an oppressive authority, when it is cast as the small man against an empire. But was this a just war for anyone? Who was I to judge violence that ends up in the death of another. It was a dangerous path to head down.

I realized the reality of conflict doesn't fit into a simple binary. I remembered seeing a photograph online of Hamoud wearing a vest packed with ammo, standing before a prayer rug, calling out to Allah before going into battle during the early days of fighting in Taiz. He was the image of the contemplative warrior. I knew that Hamoud probably received weapons shipments from Ali Mohsin and Hamid to continue the fight. He was a homegrown hero, but he had to also have had a close relationship with the leaders of the militarized opposition in Sanaa when he was leading such an important rebellion in Taiz. And he was an Islahi, so the political party's agenda would have had to play a role in his decisions as well. Protesters who had rejected the turn to violence were marginalized by Hamoud too. The violent always took the lead.

Hamoud insisted that Samuel and I stay for lunch. "It's a must," he said. Samuel told me we shouldn't be sticking around this area of the city too long, we shouldn't push our luck, especially in the house of the rebellion's leader, but I cared more about appeasing our host than Samuel's concerns for our safety. I assumed we were safe because Hamoud said we were safe, because he said he would protect us.

"Yeah, but the driver of al-Sofi's car told us we were safe too," Samuel said. "They always say it's safe." But he stayed with me nonetheless.

We left the mafraj full of fighters and entered the main part of the house from a side door. We walked up more stairs and entered into a small, plain room just off the kitchen that had a small section of mafraj cushions in one corner where we sat. The room and house were void of ostentation. It was certainly not the type of home a poor Yemeni would live in, but a far cry from the Persian carpets, expensive tables, and antique vases with which sheikhs decorated their homes in Sanaa.

Just then, my phone buzzed. I grabbed it out of my purse and looked at the screen.

"Oh, it's the governor," I said to Samuel in English.

He looked at me surprised when I answered.

"Where are you?" al-Sofi asked me over the phone.

"At Mikhlafi's house," I answered.

Samuel's look of surprise amplified, as if he were questioning my sanity.

"Let me talk to him," al-Sofi said to me on the phone.

I looked over to Hamoud.

"The governor is on the phone. He wants to talk to you," I said.

Hamoud gestured for me to hand him the cell phone.

"I give up," Samuel said.

Hamoud stood up and paced the small room in circles. They mainly spoke in basic pleasantries. I knew it was good the governor knew we were here. I told Samuel that it meant the Republican Guard definitely wouldn't attack this area of the city this afternoon. I don't think he believed me, though.

Two enemies in a violent war had just chatted on the phone nicely, as if it were the expected thing to do. Yemenis could shoot at one another one hour, but have common courtesy when speaking together the next. It was as if a certain amount of respect was obligatory for the enemy. There was an honor code to war.

Well, to an extent.

"That devil," Hamoud muttered after he hung up, shaking his head, though he also had a mischievous glint to his eyes when they met mine and I wondered if he said that for my benefit.

We all sat back down on the cushions and were served a large platter of lamb and rice; another meat stew with whipped fenugreek topping and a green salad were laid out on plates or cast iron bowls atop a tarp on the ground. We ate with our hands, but Hamoud made sure that Samuel and I had spoons, too, a courtesy for the foreigners.

As we were eating, Hamoud's two youngest daughters came into the living room to greet their father. They both wore matching dresses of yellow and black-and-white polka dots. Black curly hair in ribbons, they were probably around four and six.

I wonder if they understand that he is leading a rebellion? What would it be like to grow up in such an environment? I felt a tinge of jealousy for how exciting it all must be.

The girls tiptoed over to Hamoud and he gave them each an affectionate hug and kiss.

"How are you?" Hamoud said to the smaller, picked her up gently by the shoulders, and set her in his lap.

"*Alhamdullah*," she answered in a shy whisper.

"What?" her father asked.

She just smiled. He set her back to her feet and encouraged both girls to greet his guests.

They walked over to Samuel and me, extending their small hands out to shake ours just as they were taught to do.

"Why don't you sing for our Samuel and Laura?" Hamoud asked his daughters.

They held their hands and shifted their weight on their tiny black button shoes.

"*Yalla*, go," their father encouraged.

The two young girls stood before us ready to perform as if at a school concert. They sang a nursery rhyme–sounding tune about loving Mohammed and Mommy and Daddy, crossing their arms over their heart at each mention of the word *love*. First they sang in Arabic, and then repeated the song in English with an accent of rolled r's and British style "ah"s.

"Yay," the three of us said, as we clapped for them.

"My other daughter is studying to be a doctor," Hamoud told us. It seemed that he wanted us to know that he, an Islamist, believed in women's education.

Just then, a few shots of gunfire echoed not so far off.

"Bullets," the older daughter said in her little-girl voice, and then shyly curled up next to her father, not because she was scared of the sound, but because she was timid about speaking in front of foreigners.

Afterward, Hamoud went into the kitchen to bring out a large silver pan filled with flaky bread saturated with honey that Yemenis call *bint al-sahan*, daughter of the plate. We dug into the pan with our hands. I licked the remaining honey off my fingers before my ears perked to the sound of more gunfire in the background. I looked over to Samuel, who sat up stiffly.

"We really need to get out of here," he said to me.

"War," Hamoud said. "The government is striking us."

• • •

Samuel and I stood on the top deck of our hotel that evening, beside a large swimming pool that sat untouched. Its existence—for international businessmen and their families who used to come regularly through Taiz—was a reminder of another time, one in which Taizis didn't have to wake up each morning and check if any of those killed in the night's shelling were friends. It had already grown dark. We looked out at the city across the valley from our vantage high on a hilltop and could see the night's artillery fire soaring. Each flare's glowing yellow light arced across the air like a softball. It disappeared into the shadows of houses and afterward we heard the sound of an explosion echo through the city. Then we would see flashes of yellow from somewhere else and moments later hear the *rat-a-tats* of a firefight. This is what Taizis lived with night after night. There didn't seem to be any sound bombs here. The war here wasn't a symbolic fight between two leaders; it was a bloody battle between a government doing everything it could to maintain control of its territory in the face of a popular rebellion. The Republican Guard were indiscriminately shelling neighborhoods in rebel territory. Would this war just cease to exist if Saleh signed the GCC initiative tomorrow? Nearly the entire population of this city felt as victims. Could they forgive a government that did this to them even if their leaders were granted wholesale immunity? Even if Yemen did find a political solution, it felt impossible for the hatred that this year of conflict dug to just disappear. War had changed the culture of Taiz. I wondered what happened after peace—if peace ever would come.

I wanted go out and visit a family I knew in Taiz this evening. Samuel and I were returning to Sanaa tomorrow and it was my last chance to do so. Even if a dozen civilians were killed in Taiz this night, I knew that the chances random shelling would hit a moving car were slim. I called the number of Firas, a teenager who Dr. Abdel-Kader had recommended I use as a driver, and told him to come up to the hotel to meet me.

"Really, you will be fine to go out into this?" Samuel asked me.

I just shrugged and told him that I had nothing to worry about.

• • •

The soft ground was muddied from the rain and my feet sank into it so that with each step I had to pull myself away from its sticky grasp. Firas's car was up ahead and I turned to wave goodbye to the family I had come to visit. The foreboding sounds of war had continued while I had sat and drank tea with them, but I chose to ignore the booms, as if their existence hinged on my fear. Then the sounds of a thunderstorm had rumbled through, and it made the children in the house dance with excitement because these booms were fun. They didn't bring death.

Firas had dutifully waited for me in a night that, but for the glow of flying shells and lightning, would have been pitch dark in the absence of electricity. I jumped into his old station wagon and we slowly made our way down a dirt road into the center of the city. I bounced violently around in the backseat over the potholes, never considering I should find a seatbelt for safety. Otherwise, I sat quietly and reflected on how glad I was to have made the trip out to visit the family.

Now we had to drive through downtown Taiz, the rebel's territory, to make it to the hill that the hotel sat on across the city. The stores were shuttered up for the night, metal doors folded across their fronts. Few were outside at this time of night, and of those who were, it felt like they were not merely spectators to the war, but active participants in it. Some of them definitely were rebels: bandannas tied around their faces, heads constantly turning to the left and right to monitor the scene, clutching AK-47s. Firas and I heard the booms of the night that we both had come to know too well, except they were louder than in Sanaa, because they were landing much closer.

With another crash I could feel the whole car shake. We were the only ones on this road as far as I could see. I looked at Firas's reflection in the rear view mirror and saw the ends of his eyebrows creep toward one another. He leaned forward to concentrate on the task at hand, getting us both home safe.

I saw fear in his eyes, and it was only then that I realized it had been cruel to make him take me on this journey. He never would have said no. I was a foreigner and we were in Yemen, after all. I felt ashamed at myself for being so heartless. He was so frightened and I was not.

I'm not scared.

It hit me like the weight of a dying friend.

Why did I push so hard to go out to the city tonight in the first place? I didn't have to visit the family. I felt indebted to them because the father had given me much advice on the news in Taiz throughout the past year. He would have understood, though, if I had canceled because it was too dangerous to make the journey between my hotel and their house. Yet I still felt compelled to go, the visitation was just an excuse. There was something else driving me.

Another round of artillery fire exploded nearby. Its boom felt welcoming. It made me feel high. It made me feel happy. It made me feel brave. I looked in the rear view mirror again and saw that Firas, decidedly, was not any of those things.

Something's wrong with me.

Another shot of artillery fire cracked, followed by the consistent tapping of a machine gun. Firas pressed the gas pedal to the floor, willing his car to drive faster up the hill to my hotel. I stared out at the tree-lined streets and gray brick buildings and felt nothing. I willed myself to feel frightened, any bit of fear at all, but the response was hollow. It felt like what was left inside was a numbed stump. It took me until then to feel remorse for making Firas drive me across the city when it was too dangerous to do so. I didn't feel remorse for forcing Samuel to stay longer than necessary at Hamoud's. And I didn't feel afraid when the soldiers shot at Samuel and me yesterday. I was a person incapable of such emotion anymore. *Why can I no longer feel afraid?*

I knew I had been torn up by the death around me over the past year. While staring at corpses at the field hospital at Change Square, I had thought more than once that if I had to see one more dead body, I was going to go to the presidential palace and kill Saleh myself. But this response was only anger. It was only hate. I felt neither saddened by death nor fear in danger. I had already been so scared this past fall, in al-Masdar's office, with Soliman, yet I did nothing to lessen my chances of those things happening again, so the knob in my brain that switched on the flight response had been twisted in the off direction for me to go on living without bursting a valve.

In this car in Taiz, I realized for the first time that something inside of me was gravely amiss. Yet exactly what it was, I did not know at the time. I felt cracked open and exposed as a fraud. It was the fear in Firas's eyes that brought me to this point. The realization that I put another human being in needless danger. And he was Yemeni, so he wasn't complaining about it, but it was me who did wrong.

And that was the first time I realized, fully, wholly, that I needed to leave Yemen.

CHAPTER 25

I had been trying to get hold of an al-Awlaki family member for an interview over the past couple of weeks despite the family's self-imposed media blackout—encouraged by their ACLU lawyers, I assumed.

Not only had Anwar been killed extra-judicially by an American drone strike, but now his son was dead, too. A sixteen-year-old American boy, Abdulrahman al-Awlaki had set off to look for his dad in the southeastern province of Shabwa that past August. Anwar was believed to be hiding there with their family's tribe. In October, it was reported that Abdulrahman was killed in another drone strike that hit a car driving along a road in Shabwa.

Because such secrecy surrounds the US drone program, we had no insight as to why he was killed. It seemed doubtful that the United States would target a sixteen-year-old boy just because of who his father was. It was more likely that either Abdulrahman was traveling with potential targets or that it was a case of mistaken identity—the United States thought an al-Qaeda leader was in the car, but wasn't, and it was just an extraordinary coincidence that an American citizen, Anwar al-Awlaki's son, was a victim of the attack. Regardless, now three Americans had been killed by the US government and the reasons for their deaths had yet to be revealed in full.

The al-Awlakis were a wealthy and powerful family in Yemeni society. They were sheikhs from the South who moved to Sanaa after the Marxist government takeover of South Yemen in 1967 aimed to stamp out tribalism. Anwar's father had been the minister of agriculture and went to graduate school in the United States. His children were schooled in some of Sanaa's finest institutions during the time they lived in Yemen, alongside the Saleh boys. A distant cousin of the al-Awlakis told me after Anwar's death that the family was very Americanized, even in their life in Sanaa. "They ate American breakfast food," he had told me, "and ate at a table like Americans, not on the floor like Yemenis."

Yasser had just given me the email of Anwar's brother, Ammar. Al-Masdar had been in contact with him after Abdulrahman's death when the family wanted to clear up issues surrounding the boy's age (American media had initially reported that he was in his early twenties, though he was actually sixteen at the time of death, and thus a minor), so Ammar had provided a copy of his American birth certificate to al-Masdar.

I wrote Ammar a professional email this morning, shortly after I returned to Sanaa from Taiz, inquiring about an interview, praying that he would agree and I would be able to provide more detail on the family to my editors. To my great delight, the brother emailed me back. I opened the message, read the words on the screen, and had to sit back from my computer for a moment to hold my head in my hands.

Ammar would meet me, though not for an interview, just to have coffee, the email read. We had met before, actually, he continued. We hid together in the garden at Change Square during the March 18 massacre.

I read the email again and again, trying to bring to my mind the image of the Western-dressed Yemeni man who spoke English like an American who hid with me that day. The brother of the man touted as the new Osama bin Laden and the young woman who was reporting for the *New York Times* just happened to have taken refuge together when the bullets were flying during the most deadly massacre of protesters at Change Square. Ammar was the one who showed me the video on his phone of the young man sniped down right beside him. Did I ever ask him for his name? Did I ever ask him why he spoke English so well? I couldn't remember. I even thought that he was the one who told me to stand back from the garden's door. He was the one who warned me to be more careful.

• • •

I sat down in front of Ammar at a coffee shop in Hadda. His hair was jet black and slicked back with gel. He was dressed in a pressed button-up shirt and slacks. He was drinking a cappuccino in a tall white mug. I had a chamomile tea. I can't have caffeine at night.

I tried to figure out if I recognized him. He looked vaguely familiar, but faces didn't stick with me from March 18. Then I moved on to try to figure out if he looked like his brother Anwar, but Anwar was so skinny compared to Ammar's wealthy Yemeni gut that it was difficult to tell. I wondered if Ammar could tell I kept trying to analyze the shape of his nose.

We opened the conversation with mild pleasantries sitting beneath a large white canopy and surrounded by bougainvillea bushes. Pale yellow floodlights provided a warming glow. Ammar wanted to clear up the story about Abdulrahman and his family's theory on the events surrounding his nephew's death, but only off the record. He was full of platitudes for Abdulrahman and his voice softened when he explained that his nephew was just like any other kid, but one that was thrust into a very difficult situation. It was all because of the family he was born into. Ammar surely had to suffer some of that as well, but he was older and had established a life for himself outside his former home in the United States. Unlike his older brother, Ammar wasn't an American citizen.

I knew that I should be pushing for this to be an interview, that I should want so badly to land that feature exposé on the al-Awlaki family. I should have been convincing Ammar to say something, give me something on the record that I could use in a story. *That's what a real journalist would have done,* I told myself.

But I couldn't. Once I sat down across from Ammar, I no longer wanted to plead for an interview. My gut couldn't make my head make my mouth ask those questions. I knew I should have been asking when he saw his brother embrace fundamentalism, or why he did, or the last time he talked to Anwar. These were the sort of stories talking heads on TV or wonks in editorials wrote about without end, projecting opinions based on very little fact.

I just wanted to sit, chat, and shoot the breeze. After all, Ammar was quite good looking. He knew all the leading characters I knew because he had grown up with them: the Saleh boys, Hamid, many other officials and businessmen. So I sat and gossiped with the brother of the man who had been on the CIA's kill list because it made me happy to do so. I didn't want to talk about Ammar's dead family members. So many people had become dead over the past year. How many people had died over the past nine months? I was so tired of people dying. I wanted to gossip about the people we knew who were alive.

The truth was, I also just wanted to go home. I just wanted for everyone to be my friends, not sources, not people whose relationships with me were so muddled by the pressure of having a relationship with a journalist. I was so sick of negotiating that line. And Ammar was a prime example.

Every person I wrote about, quoted, or interviewed, I had some back story with. They drove me home drunk from a party; a brother put moves on me in the central mountains; I knew about their affairs, both past and current. I knew they only hated Saleh because he cheated them out of business deal in the early nineties and not because of their so-called support for democratic change. Yemen had closed in on me. It felt suffocating that everyone knew my business and I knew theirs. There were twenty-eight million people in this country, yet I always ran into someone I knew at the airport. The people with whom I interacted came from a small segment of society. They were those who weren't living in a house with fifty other members of their family barely ekeing out a living, or selling jasmine flower necklaces on Hadda street for ten cents a strand, or living in an IDP camp in the North because conflict had pushed them from their homes. And the generations of that small, elite group had known one another for hundreds of years.

I don't know if I should have done this differently—if I should have kept a larger distance between myself and the foreign society about which I was writing. Perhaps I should have stood at a distance from interviewees with a threatening recorder in hand, told them thank you, and gone my way instead of staying for lunch or a chew. My reporting would have suffered as a result. But in the end, it was also my demise.

At that moment, sitting down with Ammar al-Awlaki, I was questioning why I had accepted with open arms all the turmoil and the trauma of the past year. I was questioning why because I realized that night in Taiz—when the shells were falling and I didn't care and just wanted to be close to the violence—that I was severely, dangerously addicted to adrenaline. Yet I was only here at this moment, at this coffee shop, after all, because of killing, death, violence, and adrenaline. Because I was an American citizen, and so was Ammar's brother.

Late in the conversation, an activist friend of mine, Hamza, walked in through the doors of the café. He immediately spotted us and came over to our table in the garden. I nervously wondered if Ammar would want me to introduce him or not, but, as it turned out, Hamza and Ammar knew each other from social media.

"I'm really happy to have had this chance to meet you. I've always wanted to," Hamza told Ammar, in English.

"I don't know. It's probably not too safe to hang out with me, huh?" Ammar said.

Hamza pointed to the sky. "Oh yeah, I think I see a drone now," he said, looking up and then pretending to duck his head.

"Gentlemen," I chimed in. "We're in Hadda. At least we know we can hang out with Ammar in Hadda. There are too many embassies and officials' houses for a drone to strike. What if it accidently hit a UN car?"

We all laughed to ourselves, not so hard that it seemed affected, but honest amusement at our joke. I admired Ammar's resilient spirit, making light of his situation, even though the baggage he carried because of his brother probably will haunt him for the rest of his life and had already brought great pain. It was this pursuit of happiness that Yemenis carried, and not on their sleeves, just inherently. They were constantly making lemonade with their lemons. And in Yemen, the lemons were plentiful, yet I was hard pressed to find a genuine sulker.

I set my teacup down on the glass table, leaned back against my metal chair, and crossed one leg over the other. I remembered why I was here after all, not just in the coffee shop, but still in Yemen. Not that I had changed my mind about wanting to leave, but at least I knew why I had put up with all the pressure, the sadness, the fear that had finally had its way with me in the end. In Ammar, I saw the attitude of a nation.

CHAPTER 26

Misery, I would soon learn, was relative.

Samuel and I had traveled to Aden—by air—to do a story together on Somali refugees. It was a story totally different from the stalemate of domestic politics in which Saleh kept us all perpetually on the edge of our seats as to whether he would ever sign the GCC Initiative. And it was different from the war stories I so desperately needed to stay away from. Yemen's government had all but collapsed, the economy was wrecked, and various points of war flared up across the country. But Somalis still fled to Yemen on rickety boats across Bab-el-Mandeb, desperate to get out of the unlivable situation from which they were coming.

When I interviewed new arrivals at a Somali-inhabited slum on the outer rim of Aden, who had arrived one week prior on the shores of southeastern Yemen and who had walked ten days through a desolate landscape to reach this slum, their eyes were empty of any signs of emotional existence, hollow white shells that became neither excited nor sad. These were male teenagers. They had been conceived in the war, born in war, and raised in war. In famine, too, undernourished from the time they were in the womb. I had already heard stories from Yemeni parents who lived near Hasaba about how their newborn children refused food after the artillery fire started. Imagine years of violence. How does a society pick itself up again when it has reached such utter despair?

In my entire time in Yemen, I never saw anything more disturbing than those young Somali men's eyes. I wanted to find a sliver of hope in their existence. They were alive. That was it. Was that enough to celebrate? Where was the happy ending to their story?

In a nearby building, a woman seven months pregnant or more slept on a thin foam mattress on a concrete floor while her three other children, hair a mess, squatted next to her chewing on their thumbs. She had just arrived here from Somalia, too. Samuel took photos and I tried to ask her questions. It felt insensitive, but I did it anyway, assuring myself that giving this woman a voice in American media was a worthy cause—if an editor didn't cut her quotes, that is. She had dreams of getting to Saudi Arabia to find work. The reality is she would probably be stuck in deteriorating Yemen, with its population resenting her presence. "Yemenis don't have enough jobs as it is," they would say. The pregnant woman hadn't known there was war in Yemen, she told me. She just paid a smuggler to take her and her children across the sea.

Later we ran into a young Somali man who had been living in Taiz for the past few years. He said he was in Aden to make arrangements to return to Somalia. "There is much war in Taiz," he told us, and I told him that we knew that was true. "Why would I stay in Yemen?" he asked.

I can't believe his next best option is Somalia, I kept thinking to myself as Samuel and I returned to the official UN vehicle, leaving the Somalis behind to head to lunch. It was easier not to have to think about them or their hopelessness again. That would have been possible if it weren't for those young men's eyes.

• • •

Later, Samuel and I went to a qat chew at Bilal's house, the journalist who helped me when I was first here the past February. There I ran into Abdul-Rizaq, a journalist who once had wanted to take me to see Anwar al-Awlaki in Shabwa. Now that Anwar was dead, Abdul-Rizaq had to concoct another plan. He told us that he could take us to the house of the recent teenage suicide bomber's family. A young person killing himself in front of Yemeni police was not common in Aden at this time. In many ways, this young boy was a spark. Samuel and I agreed to go with Abdul-Rizaq after the chew. We had come to Aden to do the story on the Somalis, but were certainly open to other leads should they come our way.

With that, the conversation turned to the increase in extremist activity in the South, especially since militants had taken over cities in the southeast over the past few months. The Adeni men sitting with us on the low cushions lining the room preached about how al-Qaeda in Yemen is just a Saleh creation, how the militants are under the president's control. This piqued Samuel's interest for sure, as it was the first time he had heard such a theory. I, on the other hand, just moaned silently to myself.

"I hear that from everyone," I told the group of men. "I need proof."

No, they all retorted, it's true. And they threw their leftover qat leaves into the small trash cans in front of them.

"You think this is true, Laura?" Samuel, who was sitting beside me, asked. "It makes sense in some ways."

I sighed deeply.

"Listen," I told the men. "I need to meet someone who is in al-Qaeda, who can tell me about his relationship with Saleh. Otherwise I'll never believe this." I said it in both English and Arabic, as the room had speakers of both.

"I have a friend who was paid by the government!" shouted a short, bearded man from the corner whom I had never met before.

"How do you know him?" I asked.

"We were mujahideen in Afghanistan. He tells me all of this."

"Then I want to talk to him himself. Otherwise I don't believe any of you," I said.

• • •

She had a look of desperation, her eyes calling out for answers. Was what her son done noble? Was it a crime, a waste of life—the worst possible outcome, because by destroying himself he hurt others in the process?

Of course a mother would be clinging to the former, but would that hope push her to a more radical form of Islam, one that condones the killing of those associated with the infidels of the West, because then she can find purpose in her son's death?

She was the mother of the suicide bomber. She had answered my knock and let me in after Abdul-Rizaq took me to her apartment near the sea. The windows were shuttered with cardboard in an attempt to block the outside world after her son detonated his explosive-filled vest in front of a security checkpoint in central Aden the week before, but I was allowed to enter the house, and was given tea to drink. Probably because I was a woman. How could the mother turn away a fellow woman?

Her son rebelled and this was the form of rebellion that he knew. Where I'm from, kids moved to the city and did drugs. Here, they move to Abyan and join al-Qaeda. We are all so impressionable when we're young. I was impressionable. I still could be impressionable. I could fall for the heartbreaking tale of a mother who just lost her son, or the suaveness of a Saleh family member slowly convincing me that his family is not so bad after all. I constantly had to keep myself in check to not be won over just because I wanted people to like me. The trials of a journalist: trust no one. Sources aren't friends. But I wanted to console this mother because the look on her face begged me to.

Maybe she was lying about her son being a well-behaved child, one who cared about the needs of the poor, saw injustice in his current living situation—northerners oppressing southerners with aid from the American government—and just got caught up with the wrong crowd. But I didn't think so. Her story made sense. Should the son have had an option to rebel peacefully, a Martin Luther King Jr. figure leading the way, maybe he wouldn't have taken a violent route. But Tawakkol, with her calls for peaceful civil disobedience, was a northerner. And anyway, what had the peaceful protesters produced? It was so easy to be cynical. It was so easy to think that violence was the answer. It seemed like the only way things got done. Yet I had seen that violence only beget more violence. The war in Sanaa felt never-ending.

After their Marxist government collapsed, the population became even more disgruntled, and that's when al-Qaeda came in, with support from the Saleh government who encouraged radicals to stamp out the leftover socialism. Sure, it wasn't that simple. Or even that prolific. There were plenty of youth in the South who had nothing to do with intolerant fundamentalism, the way teenagers in America were uninterested with the outside world. And there were youth who actively rejected it. Some who would consider themselves atheist socialists, even. But it just takes one boy to blow himself up in the center of the city to wreak havoc. Then Americans would read about him during their morning perusal of news websites and think, "Those Yemenis, they sure are a bunch of terrorists."

The truth was this boy's father might have been connected to radical Islam as well. He was the imam at a local mosque that may have been preaching radicalism. I couldn't figure that out. And as for the violent fundamentalists who had welcomed this mother's son, encouraged him to run away to Abyan, and trained him there, I couldn't figure out if they were a direct offshoot of al-Qaeda central in Pakistan. The murkiness of this world made me not want to write about it because by doing so I would have to distill it down to a few hundred words for a news article. And just by looking at the eyes of this mother, I knew it was much more complicated than that, and unfair to make it seem so.

The walls of her home were sparsely decorated with religious insignia. An old PC sat in a corner with a shelf full of religious books against the wall. She had taken me for a tour around the few rooms. I thanked her over again for her hospitality. The entire time I was in her apartment, my nerves remained jumpy because I wondered if the father would come home and be upset with his wife for allowing inside an American journalist, young woman or not. But the anxiousness was not needed. It was just the mother, the daughters, and me. And thus I wished her farewell, telling the mother in Arabic, "God be with you," because I didn't know what else to say.

• • •

Later that evening, the man from the qat chew, Yassin, showed up at our hotel. We spoke with him at a picnic table far from anyone else down by the sea. He told us his friend who was in al-Qaeda agreed to speak with us and tell us about his history with the Saleh regime on the condition that we never printed his name. Samuel and I exchanged glances. The only sound was the ocean sending its waves to collapse on the sandy beach behind us.

Once Yassin got home he sent me text messages asking if we could get married, telling me that my eyes were like the moon. I read them, rolled my eyes, and switched my phone off in case he was going to send anymore. This happened to all young Western women in the Arab world, though Yassin's timing was particularly laughable since the next day, he was taking us to see his friend, who he claimed was "al-Qaeda," whatever that meant.

• • •

Samuel and I got into a car with Yassin, our new mujahid friend. We drove into a northern part of Aden filled with towering minarets and sterile concrete apartment complexes on which hung white political banners with green curvy Arabic script declaring pro-southern independence sentiment. The British colonial architecture of the port didn't make it out this far.

"This neighborhood is nicknamed Kandahar because so many mujahideen live here," our guide told us. This was ironic because the enemy who these mujahideen fought in Afghanistan, the Soviets, also inspired their living quarters back home in southern Yemen.

"Look guys," Samuel said, pointing out the window at a bunch of red-and-blue flags decorating the roof's ledge of one small store. "They are supporting Barcelona. Always the rebels are supporting Barcelona."

I rolled my eyes. He was always going on about this idea that the underdogs of the world liked Barcelona's soccer team and establishmentarians were fans of Madrid. Samuel was always wanting to find a fun story in everything. He was convinced we needed to do a story about this, though I wasn't about to pitch the idea to my editors at the *Times.*

Still, I was glad he broke the tension. I didn't know if Samuel was also having second thoughts that maybe this wasn't such a great idea. We didn't know where Yassin was taking us. I didn't want to admit that to myself. After all, he was a former mujahid who self-admittedly had some shady friends. But after our meeting with him last night, I had agreed with Samuel that we could trust Yassin. "You can see it in his eyes," Samuel had said to me. Then there were Yassin's text messages about my eyes. Evidence pointed to his sincerity.

Yassin pulled to a stop in front of one of the apartment complexes down a small alley in "Kandahar's" interior. We saw barefoot children run through puddles of water that had collected in the street's potholes. Clotheslines strung across banisters where plaid patterned mawaz, the wraparound skirt that south Yemeni men wear, hung out to dry, their bright colors contrasting with the sterile gray of the building around us. Nothing in Sanaa was built like this. There was more emphasis in the North on the aesthetics of architecture, with its gypsum-frosted archways, stained-glass windows, and brightly painted doors. Another reason the two cities feel so different is because, visually, they were worlds apart.

When we all got out of the car, I wrapped my scarf over my hair loosely, an attempt at modesty when we were going to enter the house of a very conservative man.

We followed Yassin up a set of stairs to the second floor, like a highway side hotel, all keeping an eye on our surroundings. None of us spoke. I didn't know if the tension was real or in my head. Two young Westerners were walking into the lion's den—that's how this felt. My mind started playing the name Daniel Pearl on repeat, yet I was determined not to turn back.

Yassin stopped in front of a tall brown door and knocked. An overweight man with a thick gray beard answered. He wore a thobe and a red-and-white checkered Arab kefiya draped over his head like a Saudi. He uttered a solemn "*salaam aleikum warahmat allah wabarakatu*" to Yassin, the extended greeting of the pious that wishes not just peace upon you, but also the mercy and blessings of God. He hardly acknowledged the presence of two foreigners. I didn't know if I should be overtly friendly and smiley, like I usually am upon meeting strangers, so I settled on a middle route in which I just looked at the man wide-eyed with curiosity—but he had already turned to face the other direction.

We followed the man into his home. My eyes darted around to inspect the situation, to see if there were any indicators that this was sort of trap.

Down a narrow hallway, I spotted a small boy, maybe six years old, standing straight with his hands at his hips inspecting the guests. His presence was a good omen.

We walked past a sparse reception room and into a small diwan with no adornments aside from a black banner of Quran verses.

I sat on the thin cushions, my legs crossed beneath me, slightly catty-cornered from our host. Samuel sat at the edge of the room under the only window. Yassin sat next to his friend.

The man wouldn't look at me directly when he spoke to me, avoiding eye contact. I had never met anyone so conservative in that respect aside from strictly Orthodox Jews in Jerusalem. The son brought us all tea.

We began the interview by telling the man we were journalists and that we would never publish his name. I told him I had lived in Yemen for a nearly two years. He just nodded with his chin pointed to an opposite corner of the room. I didn't know if I should avert my gaze from him as well, so when asking the man questions, I asked them to Yassin instead, who was ever so eager to keep his unwavering gaze in my direction.

The man told us he been imprisoned for involvement in the bombings at two Aden hotels in 1992 where US marines were staying. I knew those attacks were considered the first on the United States by al-Qaeda. No Americans were killed though. An Australian tourist and a Yemeni hotel employee had been the unlucky casualties. I didn't ask the man if he really did do it. I wondered if Yassin had told him that I was American.

The man went on to tell us he was released from prison a few years later to fight during the 1994 civil war alongside the very government that had imprisoned him. Saleh had used jihadis like him to fight the Godless socialists of southern Yemen who wanted their old independent state back, he said. I knew the move was pure Saleh, and mighty smart too, because the jihadis would be fighting with conviction and that was worth a whole lot when both sides were undisciplined soldiers. They also had conflict experience from Afghanistan.

The man told me that for decades the government had kept tabs on him, and even in the 1980s he lived in a house owned by the late Sheikh Abdullah al-Ahmar in Sanaa, in Hadda, alongside dozens of other men coming and going from the jihad in Afghanistan. (This was one reason why GPC supporters called the Change Square protesters terrorists—because they were associated with Hamid, and Hamid was associated with his father. And his father organized for many Yemeni mujahideen to travel to Afghanistan. History, in Yemen, was quite a burden.) Saleh, whose strength came from his ability to micromanage his population, surely had been complicit in the affair of sending the young men to Afghanistan.

"So I have heard that Saleh paid al-Qaeda. Is this true? What does this mean?" I asked the man. I now stared at the gap in the cushions between him and Yassin.

The man wavered for a second, looking out his window, which only revealed the gray concrete of the apartment complex next to his, but then decided to proceed.

The Saleh government definitely pays al-Qaeda, he told us. It started it the late '90s when militants' attacks on foreigners began in earnest. Saleh paid the jihadis on the condition that they would stop blowing up things. He also must have wanted al-Qaeda under his control. Saleh didn't like other players wielding power in his country.

Young militants were given "ghost jobs" at ministries that didn't really exist and wired money each month via al-Kuraimi, a local version of Western Union. Some of the more important leaders of the group traveled to Sanaa to receive funds and in the hopes that they would provide the government with information on who were the most active of al-Qaeda.

"Did you go to Sanaa?" I asked the man.

"Yes, twice."

"How much did you get paid?"

"Five hundred thousand riyal each time," he said, the equivalent of approximately $2,300—a large sum in Yemen.

"Who paid you?"

"Qamish."

Qamish was the head of the PSO, the rival political security organization to Ammar's NSB. It was older, more corrupt, and, just as the American government had expected, had ties with fundamentalists. The man told me he was once paid at Qamish's house and the other time at

PSO headquarters. When I asked him detailed questioned like how he traveled and who he traveled with, he answered me right away, with plain answers that, given everything, seemed to be truthful.

By this point, our conversation had turned gravely serious. It was as though, if we said the wrong thing, we would shatter this sacred space we had created in which we knew the words uttered carried the weight of an anvil. I spoke more softly than usual. I think everyone else in the room did, too.

"Some of al-Qaeda think this is an infidel government and they wouldn't take money from them. But the way I saw it, it was compensation from the government since they put me in jail for a year and a half," the man said.

"The people who don't get paid, these are the people Saleh tells America to kill," he continued, referring to the targets of US drone strikes in the country. I didn't know if that part was true, but I could see Saleh doing that fairly easily. He was a man with many grudges.

I asked the man if he knew members of al-Qaeda still today, and he told me of course he did. I asked him if the government was still paying young jihadis, he said yes.

My mind was racing, trying to contextualize all that I was hearing. I was trying to make sure I wasn't being duped. I knew there were things this man said that were conjecture, but other information appeared to confirm what I had heard all along. I recalled when members of the political opposition would rub their two pointer fingers together to infer the sameness of the two entities: the Saleh regime and al-Qaeda.

Yet now, this didn't appear to be the big story that I had expected it to be. It didn't seem so damaging. And it was because this man said that Saleh paid the militants not to attack. Not to attack. Sure, Saleh didn't subdue all of them. Sure, some would launch attacks against foreigners anyway, or even the Yemeni government. Sure this sort of temporary, Band-Aid fix to systemic problems always ends up backfiring in the long run. But Saleh paid them not to attack.

I kept trying to figure out how this could be a story. And even more so, I was left wondering if it was better to bribe al-Qaeda to try to prevent attacks or not deal with them at all. My American upbringing told me it was best to throw them all in prison. But in Yemen, they're just going to dig out anyway, with spoons, such as what happened in a famous prison escape of 2006 in Sanaa.

It definitely looked damning that the Saleh regime was so closely linked with people who self-identified as al-Qaeda. And what did he expect by encouraging the jihadis to spread their Salafi ideology to stave off the South's socialism? Saleh didn't create al-Qaeda in Yemen, as the opposition said, but he helped them proliferate. Then he tried to tame them. What could I learn from this? That Saleh is a liar. That he told the United States he was an ally in the war on terrorism when really he was going about that war his own wily way.

I asked the man if the militants who had taken over towns in southeast Yemen over the past few months had anything to do with the Salehs. He told me he had no idea. He told me he thought those militants have no morals. He fought the Godless socialists who occupied Muslim land and the Americans whose military inhabited the holy Arabian Peninsula. These were noble actions. The young men these days, "their ideas are random and disjointed. They have no goal," he said.

"During my time, no one would go blow himself up. These guys don't care that they are killing fellow Muslims," he said in a much stronger voice than before—the older generation bemoaning the ways of the new. There was something strangely familiar about it all.

What he said made sense, too. The younger lot was killing people who didn't deserve to be killed. But this man, one of the original fellows, he had morals. He fought against occupiers. His side started to look noble. *Viva the revolution!* Fight the man! But the man is me. He is fighting me. Innocent people were killed in those Aden hotel bombings. Even when looking at the world through a fundamentalist mentality that argues that the Arabian Peninsula is holy ground and that its American military occupiers deserve to be killed, the Marines staying at Aden's hotels were probably just poor guys from small town or inner-city America who enlisted, not out of a political agenda, but because it seemed like the best option for their lives at the time. And the cycle of innocents being killed just goes on when the people at the top manipulate the agenda.

"Thank you," I said to the former jihadi in front of me after we were done the interview. *Thank you for giving me this lovely cup of tea in your humble home and telling me information that could land you in serious trouble with the authorities. Thank you for being a respectful host. Now let me march out of here with my clothes and laptop and electronics that probably cost as much money as your entire apartment is worth.*

After we left through the door, Samuel leaned over to tell me. "Did you see the Barcelona flag in the kitchen? I told you. The rebels, they always are with Barcelona."

I just rolled my eyes at him and descended the staircase to Yassin's car.

CHAPTER 27

Yemenis had taught me many things. They taught me to embrace life with open arms and not to take myself too seriously. They taught me that bullets were only small things and how to differentiate between the sounds of fireworks versus artillery fire. I'm not sure if it was Yemenis who taught me how to beguile the authorities, but the skill certainly was honed while I lived there.

I had secured a visa for a *New York Times* correspondent to come to Yemen and replace me, Kareem Fahim. It was difficult and not a cheap process, but Yemen is a place where everything and nothing is possible at the same time. Technically, it should have been impossible to get a visa for Kareem. But in reality, I figured out over these last few months that by knowing the right people, one could make it happen.

On that November day that Kareem was arriving, I was a nervous wreck. Other foreign journalists had recently been prohibited from entering Yemen because the government was still active in limiting media coverage of its crises. Why they allowed the few of us foreign freelancers living in Sanaa to stay and report on the uprising remained a mystery. I think the government just didn't want to go through the effort of deportation, but turning journalists around at the airport was much easier.

Immigration officers would start rifling through passports and find past visas for other countries that had the word *journalist* on them—or if the reporters had visited a lot of suspicious places like Syrian or Libyan rebel-controlled territory, that would alert the suspicion of the airport police. Also, of course, journalists had that look—slightly worn, casually well-dressed, an air of confidence outranking their local knowledge—that would make the officers think that maybe they should run a search on this person's name before his or her passport was stamped.

I wanted Kareem to get into Yemen with all my being because I wanted to feel like I could move out of Sanaa without paralyzing guilt because I left the country uncovered in the *New York Times*. It irritated me when my friends at the American embassy bemoaned the things I did to put my life in danger because they were going to have to be the ones to pick up the pieces in the end. I felt that they should be grateful I was doing the American public a service by being here.

Friends and colleagues were curious about my plans after I left Yemen. The truth was, I had none. I just knew I had to leave and I wished that would have been enough to satiate others' prying. I just responded that I was planning on applying to PhD programs. It sounded like some sort of respectful next step that could at least stave away their inquiries for now. I felt that I had another life awaiting me in the faraway land of America, one that would welcome me back with open arms and be more gentle than Yemen was. What I didn't realize was that Yemen had become my life. I didn't switch America Laura off and turn Yemen Laura on and then vice versa. What happened in Yemen would stick with me in America, for better or for worse, but I didn't fully comprehend that upon my departure.

I went to the airport to meet Kareem, the hardcopy of his visa in my purse. He had a photographed copy that would get him through the first round of security and then I would present him and the immigration officials with the real one. I was aware this could go all wrong. They might discover that not only was Kareem a *New York Times* correspondent, but that I was abetting him in getting in the country, and we both would be forced to leave—certainly not the way I wanted to say goodbye.

I walked up to the large front door in the arrivals half of the airport. Just outside, taxi drivers stood idly smoking cigarettes and tribesmen with empty janbiya sheaths huddled in packs, waiting for their cousins to come home from surgery in Cairo. I passed by them and muttered a *salaam aleikum* to the security officer sitting in a gray folding chair by the door before passing him too. I was a Western foreigner, and such was permitted of me without question.

I was now in a bleak, white hall where airlines that flew into Sanaa maintained small, square offices that were open for three hours a day. I went to use the ATM beside a small snack bar where a skinny man sold chocolate bars and cans of soda because it was one of only three ATMs in all of Sanaa that worked with my MasterCard debit card and I needed to take advantage. My hand shook as I inserted the card into the machine and I took a deep breath, going over my script in my head. Afterward, I approached two soldiers with rifles standing in front of the door that led to the baggage claim area.

"Excuse me," I said to the guards.

"*Salaam aleikum*," they said to me, taken aback by the foreign girl. I was already looking distressed, forehead creased, lips starting to tremble.

"How are you?" I asked them feebly.

"Praise be to God," they answered.

I told the guards that I was a PhD student doing research in Sanaa and my fiancé was coming to visit me. I hadn't seen him for a year and was so missing him so much. He's my love! I began crying in earnest, desperate tears streaked down my cheeks. I was so worked up about getting Kareem in the country, and I so just needed to cry. These men were my therapists. Another one came over while I was telling the story. I could tell that he was some sort of leader because he wore a pistol, was dressed in civilian clothes, and thought he was clever. He took me by the arm and told me that I shouldn't worry. I showed him Kareem's visa. He took it and patted my hand.

"But I heard sometimes foreigners get in trouble at security," I cried.

"No, this is not true," the officer said.

We entered the baggage claim area together. It was empty aside from security officers and a few bell boys with silver push carts, trying to earn a meager living. Large windows looked out onto the runway lined the far wall. Kareem's flight had just landed. The officer and I moved up to the window, past the one conveyer belt for baggage and empty duty-free counter where stacks of European chocolate sat untouched, and watched the passengers deplane down the rollaway staircase. I had met Kareem once at the *New York Times* bureau in Cairo. I kind of remembered what he looked like.

"Is that him?" said the officer, pointing to a well-dressed, tan-skinned man with curly black hair strutting across the tarmac.

I told him it was and hoped my memory was serving me correctly this afternoon. Meanwhile, I texted Kareem that the immigration officers think we're engaged so we should act like we know each other.

CHAPTER 28

Tarek Saleh had sent a car to come pick me up on my last full day in Sanaa in 2011. He had promised to help me with research I was doing on his family. "You might as well have the facts. Why should we lie?" he told me.

I hoisted myself into the front passenger seat of a slightly beaten up jeep, its paint chipping at the sides, beside an old, skinny army officer with a bushy gray mustache—a loyal officer whose future was unraveling along with the regime he served. He wore a green camouflage uniform and appeared so tiny that I wasn't sure how his foot reached the gas pedal.

I thought the officer was taking me to Tarek's house in Hadda, but instead we made a right turn at Seventieth Square, past Fun City, with its sparkling merry-go-rounds, onto a wide, open road that had been Sanaa airport's only runway before the airport moved out to the northern edge of the city. Then this road was used for grand military parades. Now it had been closed to the public ever since the assassination attempt on Saleh's life at the presidential palace that sat just to the east of the road.

The officer I was with just flashed a driver's license–sized ID at the soldiers blocking off the road and drove through without question. We then proceeded down Seventieth Street, past a towering, white mosque that looked like it came from an Arabian Nights fantasy. Its six minarets towered one hundred meters high. Crimson lattices adorned the sandstone surfaces of its domes like veils. The project had cost the state

$60 million and was finished in 2008. Yemenis called it the president's mosque since Saleh commissioned for it to be built. I wondered if its name would change.

We then turned right, eastwards, onto Djibouti Street, completely opposite from where I had believed Tarek's house to be.

"Where are we going?" I asked the officer.

"To the presidential palace," he answered.

I had only ever been to the palace once before, for a press conference in a big hall near the palace's front entrance. The room boasted large murals of Sanaa's old city skyline outlined in gold-trimmed frames. I had to wait in a holding room with other journalists for thirty minutes to enter, as security fumbled over each recorder and phone.

On this day, once we drove past security, the driver waving to his colleagues, we hooked a right to drive down a small gravel road. We passed the conference halls, offices, and living quarters for guards. Behind them were more ornate offices and living quarters for Saleh and whichever wife was staying with him at the time. The whole complex took up about 120 acres of the city. It was strangely empty this afternoon; there were no visitors or meetings, and fewer soldiers than I had expected. The bushes were slightly overgrown, the tops of grass blades a shade of brown.

The officer stopped the car in front of a small building with two domed humps on its roof, set side by side, like a woman's bosom. I knew what this was. The officer opened his car door and stepped out into the sun. I did the same and walked to him. Side by side we stood there, staring at the tiny mosque.

"Mr. Tarek wanted you to see this first," he said to me.

• • •

Saleh had finally signed the GCC Initiative a few weeks ago, the move that would bring an end to his presidency after thirty-four years in power, numerous wars, al-Qaeda attacks, millions of dollars squandered, and now scores of dead protesters. The government made some announcement that the immunity the agreement stipulated for the president also extended to his entire government. Western analysts from the outside bemoaned the GCC Initiative, this being one of the reasons why. I knew the Yemeni government's statements were rarely to be taken seriously—and the larger worry was that there weren't functioning courts to put anyone on trial to begin with. I also knew that secretly the US government had been threatening Saleh with sanctions, and this, in the opinion of many of us on the inside, was finally what made him agree to step down, because there appeared to be little that Saleh cared about more than his money, estimated to be in the billions of dollars. He also believed that Hadi wouldn't abandon him when he became president, though on this point he would be quite wrong.

There were to be "elections" in the coming months. Hadi would be the only man on the ballot. And anyway, now the international community was in charge. The UN's special envoy to Yemen, Jamal Benomar, and the US ambassador, Feierstein, were in a competition of who would be the diplomat to take most credit for the transition agreement. German and British diplomats would begin struggling over who was to solve the crisis with the southern separatists. The Russian diplomats were allegedly put in charge of an upcoming national dialogue process meant to bring reconciliation. This would happen while Benomar would make public statements about Yemen being the only peaceful, negotiated transition of all the Arab countries that experienced protests during 2011, though I looked at the wreckage in Hasaba, in Taiz, and the war in the South with the militants and wondered what peace he was talking about.

• • •

The officer and I walked toward the mosque, which was the size of an American ranch–style home. His steps were cumbersome from age and he stared at the ground instead of straight ahead of him. In that moment, everything was silent. The palace was silent. The officer was silent. Sanaa around us was silent. I could only hear our footsteps rattle the gravel below.

The protesters weren't the only ones to die in the violence of this past year, or civilians in Taiz or the children of Hasaba who played with unexploded ordinances on their rubble-strewn streets. That's what Tarek wanted to show me. The Saleh government was struck with a deadly blow, too, and we all largely ignored it because the attack's perpetrators were never revealed to the public—it really blunted an act of violence if you couldn't pin it on someone.

The shoes of those killed were still lying in a pile by the mosque's door, black leather sandals now caked in dust. Some of them were the cheap plastic type, and some of them were expensive leather sandals once worn by wealthy, powerful men. When they slipped their shoes off that Friday morning, did it ever cross their minds that they would never put them on again? No. Because we never assume we are going to die, though we are living in turbulent times. I started to slip off my sandals as well but the guard motioned that it wouldn't be necessary.

Inside the mosque, shards of wood still lay on the floor. Some were tiny chips and others a foot long with jagged edges. The most stubborn of the blood stains still marked the carpet. I wondered if it was Saleh's blood I was looking at. Flecks of sunshine shone through a back window creating spots of light on an otherwise dark floor. The shattered minbar at the front of the mosque where the bomb had been hidden remained as well.

"Were you there that day?" I asked the officer.

"Yes," he replied somberly, obediently.

"Why didn't Saleh die? Was he praying when the bomb exploded?" I asked, bending over at my hips to show him what I meant.

"No, that's not it. Look here," he said and moved to show me where everyone had been standing that day: the leading politicians who were killed, the soldiers who were killed, and then Saleh, who was standing by the door when the explosion happened, not in the middle as everyone assumed. He wasn't struck directly by the exploding minbar, which is most likely why he survived. Was it fate or was it luck? Yemenis would claim either depending on which political truth they held on to. Would there have been war in Hasaba and Taiz had Saleh been killed? One small step to the right and history could have taken a different path.

The officer and I left the mosque in silence, once again past the piles of shoes of the dead.

• • •

I went to the media tent at Change Square to say goodbye to my friends there. I didn't really know how one says goodbye in these situations—to young people my age who I had spent hours and hours with over the past ten months, me bugging them for quotes about what "the youth believed," bugging them for their router's password because they changed it every week, demanding their attention when I was frightened by violence or had a story to tell and I wanted them to listen because it was good Arabic practice and because they always listened anyway.

Then there was that afternoon it poured rain on us, spilling water in through the tent's corner. We hid just inside the door, watching the children outside run and stomp through the puddles. Occasionally that guy who wore the tall clown wig from the tent across the way would run out into the rain as well and dance in a circle with his arms to the air, chanting "Sit-in, sit-in, until the regime falls!" which rhymes nicely in Arabic.

Then there were the times I frantically called each one of their cell phones until someone answered so I could check to see if anyone from the tent had been shot.

What did I give to them in return? I wrote about them in the *New York Times*—a band of tech-savvy young Yemenis who maintained that peaceful resistance would change their country's future. I still have much to repay them someday. And here I was, running off to America, abandoning them.

I walked through the front flap of the tent. Inside Nadia was arguing with a boy about some Facebook page. The rest sat in front of their laptops on low cushions cross-legged or leaning on their left bent knee with their right folded underneath. This was their place for social gathering. It was the first one they had ever had. They weren't rich enough to go to the Western cafés where cappuccinos cost two dollars, but were cosmopolitan, well-educated, and ambitious, so they yearned for more than everyday, traditional domestic life.

I told them I was going to America. They asked me when I was returning and I told them "soon" because I couldn't bear to say the truth. "Laura, Yemen is your home," they said. "I need to see my mother," I told them, and they couldn't argue. The photos of the martyrs still hung on the walls. There was a large poster of Hassan al-Wadhaf on the door of a cabinet, his TV camera hoisted upon his shoulder, his soft eyes gazing straight ahead.

Some of the tent's main inhabitants had abandoned the Square, either a few months back when the war started or when Saleh signed the GCC deal. I asked the ones remaining when they would pack up their tent and leave, and they told me not until Saleh's son and nephews stepped down from their positions in the security forces too. "The people want to overthrow the regime. Not just Saleh. The regime."

I wondered what they would do after this. Resume class as students? Look for jobs? What a memory 2011 was for them—this tent. Even if there hadn't been a revolution in Yemen, not in the traditional sense at least, each day of their lives over these past ten months was part of a collective peaceful resistance that surprised their countrymen and the world, those in the world who watched, anyway. Even if the Salehs never believed that independent youth who saw their regime for what it really was truly existed, they did. Right here in this tent. I just prayed that the hopes and ambitions of the *shabab*, the youth, weren't swallowed by reality.

But at least they had their memories. And I had mine too.

• • •

I stopped by a coffee shop in Hadda after I left the Square to use the Internet in case the power was cut at home, but also because I hoped to run into friends. I knew they'd be there. They always were.

Sitting outside on a patio under an umbrella were the more wealthy and more Western activist crowd—the ones who spoke English perfectly and could afford two-dollar cappuccinos. There were about five of them sitting between two tables, men and women, the latter of who didn't wear the face-covering niqab, but just colorful hijabs over their hair.

I pulled up a chair and sat down beside Ibrahim. He was slightly balding at a young age and always sweating, but I always figured it was because he was so passionate about life. Ibrahim read Nietzsche and Marx and could spout political theory as if he had a PhD.

I looked over at Ibrahim's laptop screen. He was designing a Yemeni version of a Monopoly board. The first square read FIND YOUR SHEIKH, and the Go to Jail space also told you to "dismantle your militia."

"Guys, guess where I was today?" I said to the crowd. "The presidential palace."

"How's Yahya?" Ibrahim asked me without missing a beat, without any inflection of humor in his voice. I punched the side of his arm.

"Yahya wasn't there, Ibrahim," I said with an affected anger. This was an ongoing joke. Ever since I told Ibrahim that Yahya's cell phone number ended in a stream of six-nines, he loved to joke that I was Yahya's girlfriend. It really annoyed me because I had heard there were Western girls who had been Yahya's girlfriends and I didn't want people to start spreading the rumor about me, not knowing that Ibrahim was only kidding.

"How was it inside?" Ibrahim asked.

"It actually wasn't that nice."

"*Ya Laura,* these people only will let you see what they want you to see," he said, and I knew he was right. But I didn't want to tell Ibrahim that chewing qat with a member of the Saleh clan felt easier now than visiting the activists at the Square. At the Square, I had to deal with guilt. I had to deal with uncertainty. I didn't have to feel sorry for the Salehs. I just could observe what it was like for a dynasty when it knew its days in absolute power were coming to an end.

At the Square I didn't know whether the youth should be proud of what they accomplished. I was reminded of all the death that had happened there, the immense, adrenaline-soaked death, and so much of it felt in vain. I was reminded of how their movement was pushed aside during the war, no longer considered important. Saleh was handing over his power, but he was provided with immunity, and thus the protesters would never get a sense of justice for so much needless killing. And without justice, I wondered if it was possible to truly move on. The protesters were the ones who had started this whole political fiasco to begin with, but they weren't the ones in control in the end.

In the end, everything felt like settling.

CHAPTER 29

The year 2011 turned into 2012, and I was once again in New York to celebrate.

I went to a house party with friends my age who I knew from living in Cairo. Some of them were in Egypt during the revolution there. I only wanted to be around people who had also experienced running from gunfire. Not because it was some badge of honor, but because I felt too out of place otherwise. I was afraid to talk to new people because they would inevitably ask what I did professionally.

"I'm a freelance journalist," I would say.

"Cool. Who do you write for mainly?"

"Well, I was just writing for the *New York Times* from Yemen over the past year."

"Whoa, that's so cool!"

No, it's not. It was incredibly hard, and still is incredibly hard in ways that I am just finding. And I have no idea what I'm going to do next with my life because how do you follow up a gig like that? And more than that, being there left me with a new overwhelming and almost uncontrollable anger that never was there before.

I never actually said that. But one time, after a girl in a tiny, high-waisted skirt and plastic rimmed glasses at an art show in the East Village kept insisting that I had the coolest job in the world, I told her dryly: "I've seen dead people."

How could I ever do justice to my experience over the past year in a few sentences? It felt disrespectful to Yemenis to even try. So I'd rather be around people who also lived in Arab world, who got it, who I didn't have to explain things to.

For New Years Eve, I stood on a rooftop in Brooklyn chatting with a friend. When the fireworks started over the East River, each boom made my heart race faster. My eyes looked left, then right, searching for places to take cover. I wanted to go back downstairs, inside the apartment, curl up in a ball on the sofa and just wait for this all to pass, but I kept on talking to my friend, pretending everything was fine, because that's not who I saw myself as—a person who flees.

• • •

The *New York Times* staff correspondents had difficulty getting visas to Yemen to cover the presidential transition in late February. Kareem had already left because they needed him elsewhere. I had a residency visa and could enter the country any time I wanted. When the editor called me and asked if I was willing to go cover the transition for the *Times*, he was hesitant. "You've just gotten back and had time to get your feet underneath you a bit, are you sure?"

"Yes, I'm sure," I replied. Of course I wanted to go back to Yemen. I needed to be witness to the transition from Saleh to Hadi. I had to be crazy to not want to be there. The only thing I could think to do with my life was go back to Yemen. My entire professional skill set centered around my knowledge of that country. Going back meant I could delay moving on.

"Well hopefully it will provide some closure for you," my editor said, as if I could just walk away from the country afterward.

• • •

I walked out of Sanaa airport on a February day in my new long, gray-colored jacket that came to my knees, perfect for Yemen, the brisk dry air cooling my face. There were no longer the sounds of machine gun fire coming from a few blocks away. I felt like I could conquer the world.

I walked by the tribesmen waiting outside the front door for their cousin to come home from surgery in Cairo and the skinny bell boys waiting for someone's luggage to tote, and found Abdullah, a trusted taxi driver who I had come to know over the years in Sanaa, though not the Abdullah married to Heather. He grinned at me mischievously, knowing we couldn't be too friendly between genders out here in public so we both climbed into his yellow and white taxi cab.

"Welcome home," Abdullah told me once he had put my suitcase in his trunk and settled into the driver's seat. He twisted at the waist to turn back to me and shake my hand.

"Here, you left these in my car," he handed me a packet of hair pins. The gesture took me by surprise for a second, but then warmed my heart that he saved them for me. I had belongings in Yemen. Maybe that meant I belonged in Yemen.

"Guess what?" Abdullah said next as he pulled out of the airport parking lot and paid the twenty-five-cent parking fee to the attendant in his teller box.

"What?" I asked.

"That show . . . what's it called . . . *Kinny Minny*?"

"You mean the show I'm in?"

"Yes, with Fahd al-Qarni."

"Yeah, it's called *Hammy Hammek*," I said.

"It's replaying on TV right now."

There had been a few kidnappings of Westerners over the two months I was gone, and they had seemed to be of a more sinister variety, not the usual tactic of the tribes when they wanted to bribe the government. These kidnappings were solely to procure ransom money. I assumed that the government was replaying *Hammy Hammek* as part of a renewed anti-kidnapping campaign.

"I told my wife, 'I know that girl on TV,'" Abdullah said to me proudly.

I rubbed the bridge of my nose with my thumb and pointer finger and stared out the window at small green fields of sorghum dotted with tiny stone homes in this village north near the airport. I knew what this was going to mean.

• • •

When I walked through those narrow alleyways of the old city, I saw many faces that I recognized. There was jolly Mustapha, sitting on his doorstep, legs splayed as far as his thobe would allow and little Ziad standing by his side. There were Sami and Samir, standing behind their counter of potato chips and chocolate bars that tasted like chalk, who still waved to me though they supported Saleh and saw me frequently at Change Square on Al Jazeera television clips. There was the annoying man who sold silver jewelry who always called out to me in English when I walked by.

I recalled the time when Ahmed the dry cleaner secretly told me that he was an Islahi—there weren't many in the old city—and we had red tea together in the back of his shop. I remembered wading through a foot of browning running water here during a rainstorm along with Yemeni men hiking their thobes up to their upper thighs. They had all laughed at me for my faces of disgust and I had laughed at them for baring their pale, skinny legs to the world.

If I walked straight from here, through a winding alley that felt more like a tunnel than a street, where merchants sold dates and almonds by the bagful, I would eventually reach a center square where Erik, Robert, Tom, and I used to eat kebabs for dinner at an outdoor restaurant without ever considering safety, war, or Ali Abdullah Saleh. We'd sit at long, silver tables with tribesmen and share a bowl of spicy tomato sauce, in which we'd dip pieces of kebab meat sprinkled with salt and cilantro.

But instead I rounded the corner to soq al-bakr, Cow Market, the tiny open square with its dilapidated hospital, roast chicken restaurant, and crouched over, elderly men wearing coke bottle glasses sitting together on silver benches and spending their morning sipping milky tea. The twenty-something man who made fresh squeezed orange and mango juice from his tiny box of a juice stand waved to me, "*Salaam ya Laura,*" he said. "Where were you?"

This was the only place I ever lived where neighbors knew one another—where just by living here, I was sucked into their community as long as I offered a friendly face. I didn't even put forth half the effort Yemenis did at hospitality, I didn't even know the young juice seller's name, yet they still warmly accepted me into their homes. It filled my soul with a richness I didn't think I would ever have in my home country. I didn't even know if it was possible in the West with our insular lives in which we're always focused on what's best for the individual. Despite what looked like turbulent times ahead for this country, I hoped that this part of Yemen would never change.

• • •

On every wall of every building in Sanaa hung the image of one man: Abdurabbu Mansour Hadi. The posters were set to a red, white, and black background, the colors of Yemen's flag. Hadi wore a blue pin-striped suit jacket and large flat blue tie. His receding hairline exposed a large forehead and his lips were turned upward at their ends ever so slightly, as if in a subtle smirk, not the stern face of Ali Abdullah Saleh that had been everywhere before. In some places in the old city, I could still find Saleh posters, residents' hatred for the al-Ahmars drove that loyalty, but otherwise it was all Hadi, all the time.

It was election day in Sanaa. The analysts and wonks from outside the country bemoaned it, complaining about how it even could be called an election with only one man on the ballot. While diplomats in Sanaa rejoiced that this day finally came to pass—and did so nonviolently. Many Yemenis in Sanaa, excited for a breakthrough after a year of despair and war, didn't really care that it was Hadi or bust. To them, this was a step forward, a reason to celebrate.

I saw Mustapha driving a minivan down a main road in front of Tahrir Square in the center of the city. The vehicle was completely plastered with Hadi posters. On its roof perched a loudspeaker that loudly, and crackly, blasted the national anthem.

And my march will always be Arab.

And the beat of my heart will remain Yemeni.

No foreigner shall ever dominate over Yemen.

Mustapha saw me on the sidewalk and gave me a yelp, a wave, and a big smile, still missing his two front teeth. He had found his democracy, even without women in bikinis dancing along the saila.

I walked to Bab al-Yemen, the ancient gateway to old Sanaa, a tall archway of charcoal and red bricks that led to an open square on the inside of the old city. It was crowded today, not with janbiya-baring merchants of sunflower seeds, blankets, and cheap battery-powered electronics from China like it normally was, but with happy voters reveling in the holiday atmosphere. I had never witnessed anything like this in Yemen before because normally during holidays everyone is home in their village. It was like the height of celebrations at Change Square, where Yemenis had fun just because it was a good opportunity to do so, except the whole city was in on this. (All, course, except the staunchest of Saleh supporters of who saw their fortunes disappearing and activists who loathed the GCC Initiative, but they were minorities today.)

There I entered into a large green tent, a polling station. The ballots were piled inside on a plastic folding table. Each was a fourth of an 8 x 10 piece of computer paper. On them was printed the smirking Hadi image of the posters. Beside him was an outline of Yemen, filled in with the colors of the rainbow, with Arabic text underneath that read: TOGETHER WE BUILD A NEW YEMEN.

To vote, one could check the ballot. Or one could circle Hadi's face. I think if you marked anything on the paper it would count as a yes vote. An activist friend wrote "the revolution will continue" on his ballot, but I'm assuming that they probably counted that as a vote for Hadi, too.

After I left the tent, I went over to interview some old men sitting on the steps of Bab al-Yemen's square. They leaned on each other, and on their canes, staring out into the world with expressions set as God's must have been when he decided: "This is good." I asked them why they voted today when only one man was on the ballot.

"No, no!" they called back defiantly. "This was good for Yemen. We voted for the sake of Yemen! Yemenis are ready for change!"

I knew that I should at least let them have this day of celebration despite knowing that the change the protesters called for was far from achieved. Yes, Saleh would no longer be president, but the rest of the regime was looking the same. The civil society the protesters dreamed of was still a world ruled by whomever had the most weapons. The country was a mess, nearly bankrupt, with half the southern part wanting to secede, militants still controlling cities in the South, and other types of militants controlling cities in the north. Ali Mohsin now had more power than ever, and he was a less-than-savory fellow. Yemen was, essentially, what outsiders could classify as a failed state. These so-called elections in Sanaa—they certainly weren't happening countrywide, not by a long shot.

But I needed to let these men before me have this celebration because I needed it too. All year, I watched a city grow deeply divided, yet this election was the only thing almost everyone agreed upon. The opposition saw it as a means to usher Saleh out and the pro-Saleh camp supported it because their beloved president had agreed to it: *Men ajl al-balad.* For the sake of the country. Now, together, let's build a new Yemen.

A middle-aged man poked his head into out interview circle and immediately a look of revelation spread over his face.

"You're the actress!" he yelled, pointing directly at me.

"Yes, but I'm also a journalist. . . ."

It was no use. A rambunctious crowd surrounded me on all sides. Men with turbans wrapped around their heads and young boys in their school uniforms because they had nothing else to wear though there was no school today. They all clapped their hands and sang patriotic songs about the queens that used to rule Yemen thousands of years ago. It was led by a gray-haired man in an expensive turban, white with red flowers with yellow buds. A yellow paisley sash lay over his one shoulder and draped down the front of his body. I stood with my notebook in my hand and laughed at the crowd, because what else could one do in Yemen?

• • •

While in Sanaa, most Yemenis welcomed with open arms the presidential transition, what was happening in Aden, as usual, was quite a different story. I traveled to the city shortly after the one-man election. Adenis saw the GCC Initiative as merely a foreign creation that replaced one member of the regime that "occupied" them with another. They weren't interested in it in the faintest. The hope of the north was only anger here. Adenis were, more than ever before, calling for their own separate state. They felt the government ignored them in the face of a growing al-Qaeda presence in the South, and they were right.

Security in Aden had fallen apart to a much greater extent than Sanaa as well. About five different gangs controlled the city's fractured neighborhoods. One of these gangs was probably left over Saleh balateja, others were loyal to al-Herak. Maybe some of them were even loyal to al-Qaeda, but it was impossible to tell. Adenis weren't tribal, and while that certainly made them seem more sophisticated and western, it was the reason their city deteriorated throughout the government breakdown of 2011. In Sanaa, tribal law came in where state law failed, while Adenis were used to state-enforced rule of law—actually favored it—and, when it was gone, there was no inherent cohesive customary law to keep a semblance of order.

I went to a public school in the center of the city that had been turned into a camp for internally displaced persons who had fled fighting between government soldiers and the Islamic militants in Abyan, the province just east of Aden.

The school's ceilings were leaking water and families were living twenty to a classroom, sleeping on a concrete floor with only a few blankets to share as padding. When I walked through the hallways, a trail of barefoot, fuzzy-haired children in ripped and dirty clothes followed me like I was the pied piper.

"Who likes football?" I asked them.

"Me!" they all yelled, girls and boys, jumping up and down and raising their hands into the air.

"Which team do you cheer for?" I asked.

"Barcelona!" they all cried.

I laughed and the thought crossed my mind that I should go buy them a few soccer balls from a store down the street in Crater, the neighborhood in central Aden. I didn't, though. I was too distracted with work. I still thought it was the most important thing in the world.

I walked out into the school's barren yard. Women dressed in colorful red and purple flowered abayas, not the black of the north, washed clothes in buckets. I approached men sitting outside a shed who, I was told, were new arrivals. I wanted to find someone who had very recently fled the war.

A middle-aged man, Ahmed, sitting on an upside-down water bucket, told me he had just arrived from Jaar the day before, the city in Abyan that had been completely controlled by Ansar al-Sharia, the al-Qaeda-linked militants, for nearly a year. Ahmed was so thin that his cheeks were starting to sink in the opposite direction. He wore a blue button-up shirt and a mawaz of primary colors in zigzag patterns. He told me he was the father of eight children, all living in the school because they had nowhere else to go.

"Ahmed, did Ansar al-Sharia give you food every day?" I asked, eager to find out if Islamic militants in southern Yemen were using such tactics to win over hearts and minds of local inhabitants. I believed such information was important for foreign policy. I would be a good journalist to find out.

I saw Ahmed's eyes grow wide and recognized the expression that overcame his face.

"Ahmed," I said, like a teacher. "Please, could you answer my question?"

"You're the actress," he replied.

My eyes closed for a second and I took a slow breath.

"Ahmed, can you just tell me if al-Qaeda gave you food every day? Please. I'm also a journalist. Please. I write for the *New York Times*."

"How is Ganaf? You're the actress, right?"

I stared straight at him. I told him yes, I am the actress. Ganaf is fine. I saw him in Taiz. Now could you please answer my question? Please make me feel like I am tapping into a foreign policy issue that is way bigger than you and me or any TV show.

Ahmed did, but now that I think about it, I don't think his answer really mattered.

• • •

Back in Sanaa, I had just watched President Ali Abdullah Saleh become former President Ali Abdullah Saleh. And for a brief period in time, it felt like maybe the protesters' efforts hadn't been in vain, and like maybe they had achieved something monumental. It was hard not to get just a little bit excited even when I knew this was a small Band-Aid for a large wound that needed much more surgery to heal.

Hadi had just been inaugurated inside Yemen's parliament building later in the week after Yemenis headed to polling stations for their pre-decided election. The room was packed full of MPs from both the ruling party and the JMP eager to be there for this historic day. Men who had said the absolute worst things about one another over the past year, who were staunch enemies and who I swore would have killed the other if provided the chance, had greeted one another inside parliament with a kiss on each cheek. But this is the way Yemeni conflict worked—quick to anger, quick to forgive, but not forgive in full. I was just starting to understand it. The roots of conflict run deep in this ancient place, and one will never be able to understand the truth until she reaches their starting point.

The diplomats, the guardians of Yemen's transition without whom Hadi would most likely never have been president, were also at parliament this morning, in the front row.

Now I stood in the large, empty space outside the parliament building chatting with an MP from Taiz. Other MPs walked by and said hello. Some stopped to shake my hand. A GPC hawk who had grown rich from Saleh's corruption barely muttered a greeting before shuffling off to the outside gate. I knew so many of them. I had dined with them, chewed qat with them, and been inside their homes. The tight-knit society of Yemen's elite didn't feel invasive now. It felt empowering. I missed that feeling during my short stint in America. A dictator had just been disposed and I felt like I had played a role in it. I recalled when an in-the-know Yemeni official told me that when an article of mine ran it was the first time Saleh had seriously started considering that he needed to leave office. It was easy to let this feeling of power as a reporter grow addictive and make me delusional. This was part of the reason why I had stayed there so long despite the conflict around me.

This was what I had wanted all along. An American can step into Yemeni society and be elevated to a class she would have to work much harder to reach in her home country. I used Yemen to establish a career I still wasn't sure I even wanted, and there was no way I could ever repay the people without whose help I would have floundered. Could a Yemeni just show up in America and do the same? Of course not. This is the nature of how the world is set up. It's unfair, just as the protesters' deaths were unfair.

To my great surprise, one of the al-Ahmar brothers had shown up for the inauguration—Himyar, who was the deputy speaker of parliament. I was surprised since it wasn't so long ago that his family was in an open war with another man who was there that day, a GPC MP, a sheikh who had fought alongside government soldiers during the Hasaba war. Both of these sheikhs traveled with dozens of armed tribesmen, their personal militias, to go to parliament this morning. I knew these guards were standing just outside on the street, not that far from one another. These tribesmen had been the ones battling each other on the street during the war. The idea that they would start a firefight outside parliament this morning crept into my mind and took hold. My ears were tuned to hear gunfire. I knew that a stray bullet could fly over the parliament walls. I knew that people were killed sometimes in the most unlikely of ways. I fully understood. Breathed it. Obsessed over it.

I found Tom and we walked out of parliament together. We talked about where we would grab lunch—should it be roast chicken or meat stew? On the street just outside the main entrance were the tribesmen of the pro-Saleh sheikh. Some of them were standing outside the truck, leaning against the flatbed and watching the scene of Yemeni politicians and foreigners before them. Others sat in the back of the truck, the tips of their assault rifles propped beside them pointed up toward the sky.

My eyes diligently scanned the scene, while Tom's back was toward the truck of tribesmen. I vaguely saw a man in a mawaz saunter over to this group of tribesmen in their thobes, suit jackets, and janbiyas, but paid him little heed, until what happened next. In a flash, I saw one of the guards raise his AK-47 to the sky and the look of hatred that I had come to know so well, the look I saw before one man readied himself to shoot another, spread across his face.

Before I had time to see what happened next, I bolted back through the parliament gate, faster than I had ever run the year before. The soldiers guarding the gate tried to prevent me from entering because they were just shuttering up for the day, but I pushed through them, their hands reaching to stop me and accidentally touching me in all sorts of inappropriate ways.

My quick dash made others seek safety, too. Tom, other journalists, even MPs ran away. "I ran because you ran. I'd never seen someone run so fast in all my life, Laura Kasinof," Tom would tell me later.

I crouched low in a small corner between the front gate and the wall that wrapped around the parliament complex. A small Islahi MP from Taiz took cover with me. He was friendly and asked me what was going on. I told him the tribesmen of Sheikh al-Sagheer were shooting (did I hear gunfire? I couldn't recall. I thought I did) and the little Islahi told me, "Those tribesmen, they never listen."

I peeked around the corner toward the door and saw that the soldiers, in the scene of fleeing Westerners, brought out the bazookas, and pointed them at the street, trying to settle the chaos with bigger weapons.

In the end, all that had happened was that the man in the mawaz, was from Taiz, the more civilized city according to its residents and seemingly so when compared to the uneducated guards of a sheikh. He strolled up to tribesmen, puffed out his chest, and declared: "This is a new civil society. Why did you bring your guns to parliament?" As if society had completely changed with Hadi's inauguration, as if one of the most important goals of the protest movement had actually come to pass.

Only it didn't. And just to prove it, the tribesman had slammed the Taizi in the face with the butt of his rifle.

After the dust settled, we who were hiding slowly emerged, realizing our fears of larger violence were unfounded. The ambassadors and UN envoy were long gone by this point, shuttled away in their armored vehicles. A bystander explained to me what had just occured. "That Taizi should have known better. Where does he think he is, Switzerland?" he said, and laughed heartedly at the thought.

Acknowledgments

There are so many to whom I owe an immeasurable amount of gratitude, and without whom this book would never have come into existence. Of course, this list isn't long enough, because how could it be?

Thank you to my mother, for being the strongest woman I know and for encouraging my harebrained schemes as a child. To Austin, for teaching me that I can be a writer too. To Markus, my agent, and to everyone at my publisher, for believing in this book. To Anna and Emilie, my two partners in crime, whose friendship helped foster a love for adventure and antics. Also, for taking time out of your busy lives to help me edit this. To Shabana, the first person ever to tell me I should be a journalist. To Steve Stanek, for convincing me during a late-night party in Cairo that I too can write for international press. To Sharon Otterman, for pushing and encouraging me further down that road and introducing me to the *New York Times*. To Kyle, for telling me to move to Yemen! And then telling me later that I had better write a book. To Michael Slackman and everyone at the foreign desk at the *New York Times*, for giving me a chance. To my teachers and classmates from the Lighthouse Writers Workshop in Denver, Colorado, for their help and support. To the Rensing Center for providing space to reflect.

Now, moving on to the Yemen crew:

To everyone at CALES, thank you for introducing me to Yemen. To Heather and Abdullah, for much of the same, and for your friendship in those first months in Sanaa that taught me to love Yemen. To Haley, Paul, Robert, Oliver, Portia, Josh, Noah, Iona, Ross, Georgia, Chris, Sam, Addie, and Asil, for your friendship, support, and encouragement, from those calm moments drinking tea along the saila to hitchhiking home at 3 a.m. during the war even when your employer definitely wouldn't allow it. To the activists, for whom a mere "thank you" is not even close to enough. Just to name a few of you: Sulaiman al-Ghouli,

Khaled Toayman, Jalal al-Bakry, Hamza al-Kamali, Nadia Abdullah, Adel al-Surabi, Mohammed al-Jabali, Basem Moghram, Salah Maghles, Salah al-Sharafi, Sadeq al-Maqtari, Boshra al-Maqtari, Ishraq al-Maqtari, Rana Jarhum, Afro, Ahmed Abdo Ali, Abulaziz al-Saqqaf, Sarah Jamal, Farea al-Muslimi, and Hamza al-Shargabi, who helped me particularly with fact checking. To the doctors at the field hospital who would take a moment in between saving lives to help us with reporting, I thank Drs. Mohammed Qubati and Tarek Noman.

There were many people in and around Yemen's government who went out of their ways to help me understand their country better. Without them I would have floundered and to them I am most appreciative.

To Dr. Abdel-Kader and his amazing family in Taiz, as well as Nageeb, my translator in Taiz. To Nadwa al-Dawsari, Saeed al-Batati, Nasser al-Arrabyee, Bilal Gulam Hussein, Abu Ali in Aden, Abdulsallaam, everyone at Seyaj, Radhia al-Mutawakil, Abdulrasheed al-Faqih, Hafez al-Bukari, Jamila Raja, April Alley, Ginny Hill, and Henry Thompson, for their endless support and advice. To Abdullah, the best taxi driver in Sanaa.

Then there are the friends without whom I'm not sure I would have survived 2011. They are, in no particular order, Tom, Jeb, Erik, Marta, Siris, Atiaf, Ben, Samuel, Lindsay, and Abdul-Ghani.

Lastly, no amount of thanks would be enough for Yasser and the entire crew at al-Masdar, who helped me endlessly during the best and worst of times: Abdel-Hakim, Sameer, Mohammed, the two Youssefs, and others.

And to the great watcher of the universe, to God or, as Yemenis call him, Allah, thank you for those small coincidences that bring warmth in the darkest of times.